African-American
Concert Dance

T0385720

African-American Concert Dance

The Harlem Renaissance and Beyond

John O. Perpener III

UNIVERSITY OF ILLINOIS PRESS
Urbana, Chicago, and Springfield

First Illinois paperback, 2005
© 2001 by the Board of Trustees
of the University of Illinois
All rights reserved
Manufactured in the United States of America

This book is printed on acid-free paper.

The Library of Congress cataloged the cloth edition as follows:
Perpener, John O.
African-American concert dance : the Harlem Renaissance
and beyond / John O. Perpener III.
p.   cm.
Includes bibliographical references (p.) and index.
ISBN 0-252-02675-6
1. African American dancers—Biography.
2. African American dance—History.
3. Harlem Renaissance.
I. Title.
GV1785.A1P47   2001
792.8'089'96073—dc21   00-013096

PAPERBACK ISBN 978-0-252-07261-1

For my parents,
Dr. John O. Perpener Jr. and Mrs. Maye E. Perpener,
and for my sister,
Carmena Perpener-Richards

Contents

Preface

THE PRIMARY PURPOSE OF THIS STUDY is to examine the careers of eight black dance artists who contributed significantly to the development of American concert dance during the 1920s, 1930s, and 1940s. These artists are Hemsley Winfield, Edna Guy, Randolph Sawyer, Ollie Burgoyne, Charles Williams, Asadata Dafora, Katherine Dunham, and Pearl Primus. Together they constitute a group of seminal artists who achieved critical and popular recognition as dancers and choreographers during the period 1925 to 1945, which the first seven chapters of this book cover.

I chose 1925 as the beginning year of the study because it marked a point of departure in the careers of several of the earliest artists discussed here. By that year, Hemsley Winfield had become involved in New York theatrical ventures, in Yonkers, Harlem, and Greenwich Village. His efforts would eventually result in the establishment of the first African-American concert dance company in America. Another artist, Edna Guy, had just begun her studies at the Denishawn School of Dance in New York City. At Hampton Institute in Virginia, Charles Williams was refining the physical education and dance demonstrations that would lead to his developing the Hampton Creative Dance Group. In part, Williams was inspired to pursue his interest in dance because of the Denishawn Dancers' visit to the campus in February 1925.

In 1945, two events marked a high point in the development of a black concert dance tradition. Katherine Dunham opened her New York school, the most comprehensive dance training program developed by a black artist up to that time. Her school institutionalized the black dance aesthetics that had been evolving during the preceding two decades. And 1945 was the year that a new and exciting black artist, Pearl Primus, came on the New York dance scene and garnered exceptional praise from critics and audiences alike.

In examining the careers of the individuals mentioned above, I have kept several objectives in mind. The first and most basic of these has been to provide biographical details about the artists as well as information about their artistic development—their earliest dance training, what and where they performed, and exactly what their artistic contributions were. Although this objective may seem simplistic, it is necessitated by the fact that many of the earliest artists discussed here have been given little attention in the documentation of dance history. Ferreting out information about their lives and careers is a very important aspect of placing their work within a broader historical and cultural context.

The seeds for this study were planted in 1973 when I first read Lynne Fauley Emery's *Black Dance in the United States from 1619 to 1970*. I was elated at the publication of a historical survey of black dance in America. Because of my own performance experiences in the concert dance arena, I was particularly interested in the chapters that addressed that topic.

I had long been acquainted with the white pioneers of modern dance, but for the first time I saw published such names as Hemsley Winfield, Edna Guy, and Charles Williams. Emery's book opened my eyes, but I was left with a gnawing curiosity to know more about these artists. During the early phase of my research, my objectives were simple. For example, I felt compelled to compile more information about Hemsley Winfield than had ever been gathered before. As time passed, I became even more committed to the work because I felt that there was little scholarly effort being made to research material concerning the artistic contributions of early black concert dancers.

About a decade after the appearance of Emery's book, I realized that full information in this area was still glaringly absent. New material being published about dancers such as Winfield and Guy remained sparse. When they were mentioned, few new details surfaced. These artists retained a kind of one-dimensionality.

I also discovered that a few early African-American dance artists were in fact fairly well publicized. The most striking example was Katherine Dunham. The fact that she elicited so much attention from the public, the critical establishment, and the popular press during a period of extreme racism in America attests to her phenomenal talent, charisma, and perseverance. But it must also be remembered that she herself created the most substantial documentation of her life and her work. The numerous books and articles she wrote recount her career in more detail than that of any other black concert dancer of the early twentieth century.

Pearl Primus, like Katherine Dunham, was another pioneering African-American concert dancer who is considered to be a significant artist by students and scholars of dance history. But what of the other artists mentioned above? Early on in my research, I began questioning the matter of significance. One of the conclusions I came to satisfied me to a certain extent but seemed unscholarly: significance is determined by the researcher. The historian's powers of persuasion play a part in bringing a particular subject matter into a discipline's revered body of knowledge. If one can convince one's readers that something is important, then it *is* important. There may be many overlooked artists whose contributions are considerable, but until the significance of their work is illuminated through the efforts of a dedicated researcher, they can easily remain unappreciated.

Overall—and again with a few exceptions such as Katherine Dunham and Pearl Primus—gathering information about early African-American concert dancers presented complications that were unique to the task. It became apparent that the careers of most African-American dancers were so poorly documented in dance history literature that questions concerning who was significant and who was not became moot. Prior to the appearance of books such as *The Black Tradition in American Dance* (1989) by Richard Long and *Black Dance* (1990) by Edward Thorpe, there were few studies that delved into this area in any depth. During earlier decades, dance history surveys and collections of essays on individual dancers and choreographers usually dealt with black artists in several standard ways. Sometimes these artists were categorically excluded. Sometimes their inclusion was very brief (as in Walter Terry's *The Dance in America,* in which the chapter "Black Dance" takes up just nine out of two hundred and seventy-two pages). In some works, a single entry on a black artist was included as a token of recognition. Consequently, the research problems associated with this study were compounded.

At the time that I began my intensive research during the mid-1980s, better-known dance research centers such as the Dance Collection at the New York Public Library contained very limited material about some of the artists and no collected information about others. The emphasis here is on the word "collected"—referring to helpful resources such as artists' clipping files. As my research continued and I began to uncover a few fruitful leads, I discovered that I would have to spend more time as a collector than I would if I were writing about a group of white artists of the same period.

Where information about the artists did appear in print, it was often scattered. Leading dance magazines yielded occasional announcements and reviews. More obscure publications such as the *Dancer's Club News* indicated simply when and where some of the artists performed. Programs of performances other than those produced by the artists' themselves—the Dancers' Club Monster Benefit (1932), the First National Dance Congress (1936), and Dance International (1937)—yielded additional information. Biographies and autobiographies of individuals such as Ruth St. Denis, Ted Shawn, Gordon Mumaw, Orson Welles, Ruth Page, and John Houseman also proved to be helpful as I tracked down details about the careers of particular artists. Examining such resources slowly began to reveal that, as a group, early African-American concert dancers were much more connected to mainstream theater and dance activities than the existing literature on American dance history had traditionally indicated.

In addition to the material that was available in dance collections—including the reviews of writers such as John Martin, Edwin Denby, and Walter Terry, which reflected the mainstream critical insight of the time—I found valuable information in collections that were not primarily dance archives. Black magazines and journals such as *Opportunity, The Crisis, The Messenger,* and the *Southern Workman*

yielded important articles about specific performances in which artists appeared and also contributed contextual material on black art and
culture during the early part of the twentieth century. Black newspapers such as the *Amsterdam News* (New York), the New York *Age,*
and the Chicago *Defender* took great pride in keeping track of the
appearances of black artists and entertainers. In many instances, these
sources constituted the only contemporary documentation of some of
these artists' performances. Since these newspapers were published
weekly instead of daily, it was a relatively easy—but still time-con-
suming—task to search their entertainment, music, and theater pages
for relevant material. This method resulted, for example, in my locating
dozens of articles and announcements about the performances of
Hemsley Winfield and his New Negro Art Theatre.

As mentioned before, to unearth substantive details on the lives and
careers of these artists was my initial research objective, but as the
work continued and took on a life of its own, additional questions
begged to be answered. How did black dance artists relate to the white
modern dance artists of the time? How were they a part of the overall
development of theatrical dance in America? Were there common
aesthetic elements and philosophies that connected them to each other? In what ways did the critical accounts of their work reflect perceptions about black artists during the period? This study begins to answer these and other questions and also reveals how much more work
needs to be done to shape a multidimensional picture of African-
American artists. These vibrant artists must not remain shadowy af-
terthoughts in America's cultural history.

Because the following chapters focus largely on just eight artists who
have been omitted from most dance history studies, I would be remiss
in not pointing out that there are many more black concert dancers
whom I mention only in passing or do not discuss at all. My initial
selection process began with the earliest innovators in concert dance
who were mentioned in Emery's book. As my work gained momentum, I became aware of other artists whose names either appeared
recurrently in relation to these primary artists or surfaced in my general research. Clementine Blount, Add Bates, Al Bledger, Francis Atkins, Clarence Yates, Beryl Banfield, Alma Sutton, and Mable Hart are
only a few of these. They often received outstanding mention in re-

views of concerts by the primary artists or in reviews of other theatrical productions, such as Broadway shows. They did not, however, have performance groups of their own or produce solo concerts for themselves. Consequently, it was almost impossible to find articles and reviews that dealt solely with their individual artistry. From the research material I collected for this study, a simple fact became apparent. The most important factor that determined whether an artist's career was substantially documented in the press was his or her ability to form a company, mount concerts relatively consistently, and thereby capture public and critical attention. With the exception of Ollie Burgoyne and Randolph Sawyer, all the artists discussed here were able to accomplish those tasks and assure their own visibility over a number of years.

Information about the artists who were not company founders was often just as fascinating as information about those who were. Maudelle Bass, for example, had a career that included working with Lester Horton in California, appearing in Agnes de Mille's *Black Ritual,* and performing extensively in Mexico. Beryl McBurnie had considerable influence on black dancers in New York during the 1930s, but her primary influence was through her ongoing work in her home country, Trinidad.

Numerous others—Talley Beatty, Lucille Ellis, Carmencita Romera, Archie Savage, Vanoye Aikens, Walter Nicks, and Syvilla Forte (the list could go on and on)—were involved either with Katherine Dunham's early Chicago dance company, her New York company, or both. Many of them went on to establish outstanding careers as teachers, choreographers, and performers.

Then there were the white artists who made concerted efforts to forward the cause of black concert dance. Agnes de Mille created *Black Ritual* (1940) in an attempt to make the American Ballet Theatre's plans for a Negro wing a reality. Eugene Von Grona trained twenty-three black dancers for three years and presented them as the American Negro Ballet, which first performed on November 11, 1937.

At one point in my writing of this book, I had completed a fairly lengthy chapter that attempted to lump many of these artists together. (The title of that chapter, "The Legacy of Katherine Dunham and Other Independent Artists," reflected the forced nature of the under-

taking.) All of these artists fascinated me; I felt that they were important and I did not want to leave them out. Fortunately, I realized that
creating an ever-expanding study had not been my original goal. Just
as important, I realized that many of the artists omitted deserved more
intensive research than I had time to undertake. I did, however, eventually broaden my study beyond the original eight artists in an attempt
to show briefly how their contributions have had an impact on suc-
ceeding generations. The final chapter in my book provides an overview
of these dancers and some of the ongoing problems that African-
American artists encounter while negotiating the labyrinth of America's racial and cultural politics.

Acknowledgments

I THANK THE MANY INDIVIDUALS who helped guide me toward valuable material at the following libraries and collections: Dance Collection, Music Collection, and the Billy Rose Theatre Collection of the New York Public Library for the Performing Arts; New York Public Library Schomburg Center for Research in Black Culture; Hatch-Billops Collection, New York; Gumby Scrapbook Collection, Columbia University Library, New York; Newberry Library, Chicago; Huntington Memorial Library, Hampton University, Hampton, Virginia; Library of Congress Federal Theatre Project Collection, George Mason University, Fairfax, Virginia; Moorland-Spingarn Collection and the Channing-Pollock Theatre Collection, Howard University, Washington, D.C.; Willard and Barbara Morgan Archives, Dobbs Ferry, New York; and Morris Library, Southern Illinois University, Carbondale.

I am also thankful for the funding I received through a Faculty Graduate Study Fellowship from the National Endowment for the Humanities, which enabled me to complete the research upon which this book was based. Additional research funding was also provided by the University Research Board and the Minority Supplementary Research Fund of the University of Illinois, Urbana-Champaign, and by the Newberry Library, Chicago.

For her patient and thorough critiquing of my original dissertation work, I thank Marcia Siegel, who not only advised me well but also—through her earliest published collection of reviews, *At the Vanishing Point*—piqued my interest in dance writing long before I met her.

I am grateful to Joe Nash, who, during conversations over the years, has shared his time, his memories, and his collection of dance material with me. He has always been an inspiration. I would also like to thank Richard Long and Gerald Myers for their careful reading of this material and for their helpful suggestions.

Finally, I thank my mother and father, to whom I owe all that I am, and my sister, who supported my efforts from the beginning of this project. They did not live to see the publication of this book, but their spirits have guided me in every way.

African-American
Concert Dance

1
Early Influences on Black Concert Dance

THE DANCERS DISCUSSED IN THIS BOOK were affected by numerous and complex artistic influences. In placing their careers in a historical context, it is important to define these influences and to examine how they were interwoven. Among them was the surge of creative activity—beginning at the turn of the twentieth century and continuing into the 1930s and 1940s—that propelled the pioneers of mainstream American concert dance toward the establishment of new theatrical concert dance aesthetics. Equally important was the pervasive African-American cultural movement of the 1920s and 1930s that eventually became known as the Harlem Renaissance. This movement was characterized by a unique combination of aesthetic and social concerns. A third major influence was the wide variety of dance material drawn from European-American, African-American, Caribbean, and African sources that African-American artists incorporated into their work.

Another element—historical stereotypes of black performers—was not a direct, positive artistic influence like the others. It did, however, have an impact on critics' writings about black dancers, and it consequently affected the artists' concerns about how they were perceived by the mainstream cultural establishment.

The first two influences are discussed in this chapter. They encompass some of the major themes that shaped the aesthetic thought of pioneering concert dancers—both black and white—during the early part of the twentieth century. A discussion of stereotypes and their effect on criticism is likewise included in this chapter. The artistic influence of dance material from European America, African America, and the Caribbean was revealed in the specific ways that black dancers and choreographers incorporated dance elements from many cultures into their work. Because the impact of this influence varied from one individual to another, it is discussed in the chapters devoted to the specific artists.

Roots of the New American Concert Dance

The burst of creative activity and innovation that, by the 1930s, pervaded concert dance in America can be traced to cultural trends that began in the late nineteenth century and gained momentum in the first decade of the twentieth. Delsartism, the related physical culture movement, and the work of artists such as Isadora Duncan and Ruth St. Denis significantly transformed theatrical dance and the way that it was perceived.

Aspiring black concert dancers and choreographers first became aware of contemporary developments in dance around the mid-1920s and began to assimilate the new dance expressions on the American stage. They soon made distinctive contributions to the development of concert dance in America, and, at the same time, they established their own traditions.

Because blacks were excluded from various segments of American society during the 1920s and 1930s, many doors were closed to those individuals who had the desire and the talent to become involved in contemporary dance. For the most part, dance studios were blatantly exclusive and would not accept blacks as students, and blacks could not participate in the companies of white artists. Eventually, however, certain individuals bridged the division between African-American culture and European-American culture and made inroads into the field of contemporary concert dance.

The ways that black and white artists interfaced will be discussed in detail in the following chapters. There were, for example, Katherine

Dunham's training and performance experiences with Olga Speranzeva, Mark Turbyfill, and Ruth Page. Other examples are Edna Guy's years of study at Denishawn, and Randolph Sawyer's studies and performances with Senia Gluck-Sandor and Felicia Sorel. There are more such connections to be discovered, but the important point here is that links did exist. By the late 1920s and early 1930s, channels were opening through which the nascent modern dance movement was beginning to influence black artists and vice versa. Prior to this, a number of factors were changing the image of theatrical dance in the eyes of American audiences and preparing them for the new dance expressions to come.

During the first two decades of the twentieth century, the most impressive theatrical dance to be seen in America was presented by European ballet companies. American audiences were just beginning to witness non-balletic innovations in the early performances of Ruth St. Denis, who toured as a soloist until 1914, when she and Ted Shawn began to build an expanded company. The explosion of dance activity that would occur in the 1930s and 1940s was still more than a decade away.

The 1916 and 1917 tours of Diaghilev's Ballets Russes gave Americans a brief look at aesthetic breakthroughs within the ballet tradition. Artists such as Adeline Genée, Anna Pavlova, and Mikhail Mordkin had toured America before the Ballets Russes appeared, but Diaghilev's company, with its penchant for scandal and its reputation for notoriety, whetted the American public's appetite for ballet in a special way. As Nesta Macdonald points out in *Diaghilev Observed,* long before the Ballets Russes tours began, "American papers had carried stories about the Diaghilev company, including vivid accounts of the *scandales* attaching to the Nijinsky ballets."[1]

Even though the avant-garde aesthetic of the Ballets Russes departed from the strict formalism and staleness of earlier ballet traditions, it was still an intrinsically European artistic expression. In spite of its somewhat exotic allure, its promise of titillation, and its association with "highbrow" culture—all of which made it appealing to American audiences—Diaghilev's company did not provide artistic expressions that reflected a truly American temperament.

When describing turn-of-the-century European ballet in America,

Nancy Lee Ruyter writes, "There was no sense of social mission coming from Europe, for the Europeans were more concerned with the internal developments of their art than with its relationship to society."[2] To legitimize theatrical dance in America, the art "had to develop positive values for American society."[3]

Before the Ballets Russes tours, other potent forces were working to change Americans' perceptions of the role of physical culture and dance in their society. The most influential of these during the late nineteenth century may be traced to the work of François Delsarte, the French music and drama teacher who developed theories concerning the importance of movement and gesture in dramatic expression. The system of training he developed had roots in science, mysticism, and aesthetics.

An American actor, Steele Mackaye, studied with Delsarte in Paris during the late 1870s and returned to his homeland to lecture and teach methods of expression based on his own expanded version of Delsarte's theories. Two of Mackaye's students, in turn, made important contributions to the American Delsartian movement during the last two decades of the century. William R. Alger, a Unitarian clergyman, taught and lectured, stressing the spiritual and religious overtones of Delsarte's theories. In this way, he contributed to contemporary ideas that would help mitigate Americans' Puritan prejudices concerning the human body as an expressive instrument. His teachings helped physical culture and, consequently, dance acquire an aura of moral propriety.[4]

During the 1880s, Genevieve Stebbins, another of Mackaye's students, brought his teachings and Delsarte's theories a step closer to actual dance performance. Through her teaching, her extensive writing, her own theoretical explorations of movement, and her performances of statue posing (the execution of slowly changing tableaus) and pantomime, she further legitimized the idea that it was healthy, beautiful, and moral to use the human body expressively. Draped in a flowing Greek-inspired tunic, she not only encouraged the acceptance of physicality, she helped make it fashionable.

It was, however, another individual, Henrietta Russell, who took Delsartian aesthetics and physical culture to the height of their popularity during the late 1880s. Russell, who had studied in Paris with François Delsarte's son, Gustave, taught a form of physical exercise that was similar to but less stringent than that of Genevieve Stebbins. Her students were primarily middle- and upper-class society ladies, but toward the end of her thirty-five-year teaching career, she also taught one of the future pioneers of modern dance, Ted Shawn.

Russell and her followers—as well as the followers of Mackaye and Stebbins—spread popularized versions of Delsarte's theories and techniques across the country, where they were taught in private schools and studios and incorporated into a wide variety of classes: expression, oratory, physical culture, dramatics, pantomime, and elocution. In addition, Delsartism soon became an important part of the physical education curriculum of many colleges and universities.

By the 1890s, a considerable number of Americans had, through their active participation in the physical culture movement, been primed for the further development of dance as a performing art. Attracted by the pioneering dance innovations of Isadora Duncan and Ruth St. Denis, this same segment of American society soon comprised a growing audience for America's new dance.

Duncan and St. Denis both began pursuing theatrical careers in the mid-1890s, but Duncan was the first to attract attention as a concert artist. Between 1900 and 1908 she lived and performed in Europe, where her career blossomed. Though she spent most of her life in Europe, only intermittently returning to her homeland to present concerts, she became a figurehead for America's intellectual and artistic avant-garde, for women's liberation, and for the liberation of the human spirit. Because of her notorious lust for personal freedom and expression, her art, by the 1920s, became closely associated with America's rebellion against lingering repressive Victorian morality. Her name became nearly synonymous with the search for an ethos that could reflect new and more honest attitudes toward physicality, sensuality, and sexuality. As Ruyter observes, "At the end of World War I the idea of the artist as potential savior of a deranged America gained ground in some artistic, intellectual, and educational circles. . . . The artist now conceived of himself as outside society, free of its restrictions, in touch with a life and a truth unavailable within society. . . . The high-priestess of this new religion was Isadora Duncan."[5]

During her early exploration of dance, Duncan had rejected classical ballet as being sterile and unnatural. She had also rejected its antithesis—the theatrical dance found in vaudeville shows and popular pantomimes—as being mundane and insignificant. She turned instead to ancient Greece as a source of a more natural, unfettered, and purer form of dance. In this, she followed in the footsteps of American Delsartians such as Genevieve Stebbins.

Though there is some doubt that Duncan had direct contact with American Delsartians, much of her initial work, as Ruyter points out, can be viewed as part of that movement. Like the Delsartians, Duncan believed in the spiritual and moral value of physical culture. She felt that freedom and naturalness were preferable to restriction and artificiality. She claimed that "through the quasi-scientific analysis of movement, new potentialities might be found or old ones rediscovered . . . that physical exercise should be related to the mind, spirit, and emotions."[6]

Duncan pursued her personal visions and opened doors that led to important innovations in dance. She believed that dance could be as movingly expressive as the music to which it was performed. She sought to discover the deep psychological and emotional sources of human movement rather than following empty formal canons. And she saw dance as a continuum of body, mind, and spirit that could express the deepest regions of the human soul. In her later career, she also used dance to express political and social ideologies. She pursued these precepts with a single-mindedness that had not been exhibited by an American dance artist before, and her ideas would soon become the liturgy of America's modern dancers.

The other precursor of the modern dance movement, Ruth St. Denis, was introduced to Delsartian exercises as a young girl. She also studied social dancing, gymnastics, and, later, ballet. During her early performance career she appeared in vaudeville and in the theatrical productions of Augustin Daly and David Belasco. Like Isadora Duncan, she eventually turned to other cultures as a source of creative inspiration. Her first inspiration was Egypt, and by 1906 she had created an Indian ballet, *Radha*, which she performed numerous times in New York. As a dancer, she had a successful career in Europe from 1906 to 1909 and then returned to America to spread her own particular gospel of dance.

Whereas Duncan's magnetism emanated from her rebellious spirit and her promise of freedom for the individual, St. Denis attracted a popular following because of the more conservative nature of her message commingled with exoticism and good theater. St. Denis's dancing represented transcendent spirituality; she was an exotic creature, but the religious overtones of her art made her acceptable (perhaps just barely) within the strictures of middle-class American values. Her theatrical package was attractive to American audiences—message, entertainment, wonderful costumes and scenery, plus a promise of cultural enlightenment. Not the least of her assets was that she was a trouper. In 1909 and 1910 she presented 108 performances in 17 cities, and the following year she presented 99 concerts in 25 cities.[7] She took concert dance to the American heartland.

By the time she joined forces with the young dancer Ted Shawn in 1914 and they began laying the foundation for the Denishawn company and schools, she already had a well-established dance career. But her collaboration with Shawn brought additional positive forces to bear on her popularity. Now there was not only an exquisite female persona on stage, there was also a male counterpart. Shawn cultivated an interest in other subject matter besides the Orient. He turned to Spain, Greece, and America for dance material to expand Denishawn's repertoire. Because of the two dancers' religious and spiritual preoccupations and the outward propriety of their conduct, they surrounded themselves with an aura of morality and brought more respectability to dance as a performing art than had ever been achieved before in America.[8] Together St. Denis and Shawn toured the country for years. They opened a school in California and later one in New York, and they nurtured the three members of their company who would become officially known as modern dancers—Martha Graham, Doris Humphrey, and Charles Weidman.

This triumvirate became the first of a new generation of young dance artists struggling to search for artistic identities. They too were motivated by distrust for and disenchantment with precedents. They joined in the spirited rejection of European balletic models that emphasized the tyranny of a highly codified technique and its concomitant virtuosity. They also found something more immediate to reject—the pseudo-ethnic works of Denishawn. The visions of other cultures as distilled through the theatrical imaginations of St. Denis and Shawn became anathema to the three younger artists, and their desire to extricate themselves from the demands of their mentors led them to leave the Denishawn Company. Martha Graham, the first to defect, in 1923, left to perform with the Greenwich Village Follies, but by 1926 she had gathered a small group of dancers to mount her first independent concert in New York. Over the ensuing years, after a period in which she rid her work of Denishawn influences, she began forging a style and technique of her own that could express her passionate and dramatic theatricality.

Doris Humphrey and Charles Weidman began their careers independent of Denishawn in 1928. They opened a New York studio and worked to establish their individual styles and techniques. Humphrey began laying a theoretical foundation for her work and developing the formal canons that she implemented in her choreography for large ensembles of dancers, while Weidman began devising his own unique combination of pantomime and dance. Much of his choreography became noted for its wry humor, while some of his dances, such as *Lynchtown*, were steeped in social commentary.

By the early 1930s the stage was set for the new dance. Almost five decades of active searching by Delsarte and his followers, by Duncan, St. Denis, and Shawn, and by Graham, Humphrey, and Weidman had pointed the way. A distinctive art form that was individually expressive, unfettered by prior constraints, and unafraid to comment on the emotional, psychological, and political concerns of contemporary America was in its adolescence.

Because black artists have been so poorly represented in the chronicles of dance history, the extent to which they were influenced by seeing the works of their white contemporaries is a subject that has barely been examined. As mentioned before, black dancers were rare in the studios and the companies of modern dancers during the late 1920s and early 1930s. Although they had scant opportunity to join in, they were able to witness the performances of the modern dance pioneers. Through their keen observation of the new trends in dance, black artists were inspired to find their own innovative directions. For example, Edna Guy (as she related in a letter to Ruth St. Denis) watched with rapt attention as Martha Graham performed in the Greenwich Village Follies.[9] In 1925, Charles Williams, who would later establish his own dance company, saw the Denishawn spectacle unfold at Hampton Institute's Ogden Hall in Hampton, Virginia. A few years later, Randolph Sawyer peered at the Denishawn Dancers through the fences at New York's Lewisohn Stadium and dreamed of becoming a dancer himself. The sight and the spirit of the new dance could not be closed off by the studio door.

When examining the influences of white artists, one must ask how black artists accepted those influences. What initial congruences were there between the concerns of black artists and those of white artists? What differences were there? The answers to these questions lie not only in the cultural preoccupations and artistic experimentation taking place in majority America during the 1920s, but also in the cultural and social dynamics that were shaping intellectual and artistic thought in the African-American community during the same period.

For African Americans it was a period of intense self-examination and cultural realignment. At some junctures, their concerns were contiguous with those of white Americans, but at other times they were uniquely grounded in the black experience in America.

The Harlem Renaissance

"The Jazz Age," the "Roaring Twenties," the "Harlem Renaissance": many were the phrases used to describe the period when American society was attempting to break away from the constraints of post-Victorian morality and into the freedom of the modern world. It was a period when old modes of expression were being rejected in a self-conscious search for the new. The vanguard of this cultural revolution called themselves the "Lost Generation," "Bohemians," and "New Negroes." There was, however, a difference between the New Negroes and their white counterparts. Blacks had to determine not only where the *individual* belonged in early twentieth-century American society, but also where a people who historically had been rejected from majority American society fit into contemporary culture.

Like the aspiring black dancers who were aware of the new concert dance taking shape, African Americans in all walks of life recognized the revolutionary spirit of the time. For the post–World War I generation, it was a time of great expectations and new hope. But blacks always embraced new hope with reservation, with a pessimistic wariness born of decades of dashed dreams. No one embodied this mixture of apprehension and optimism more than the black soldiers returning from World War I. They had fought against tyranny in Europe only to return to a country where lynching was still common, to a country that, during the summer of 1919, faced some of the bloodiest race riots it had ever experienced.

After World War I, in the face of the unspeakable violence that African Americans were enduring, the black press heralded the arrival of a New Negro who would fight back rather than tolerate the injustices of racism. A new militancy expressed itself in social and political activism and paved the way for the cultural activism of the Harlem Renaissance. More conservative black leaders, fearing that a confrontational approach would lead to genocide, searched for alternatives, but the self-assertive mood of black America was felt in every segment of society.[10]

Among blacks, the wish to move forward optimistically was frustrated by the realities of American racism. For the artist, the desire to become wholly American through cultural assimilation was countered by the realization that much of the beauty that was blackness had been tempered in the furnaces of a violently segregated society. In earlier days, musical expressions such as spirituals had grown out of the communal experience of a deep metaphysical suffering. The blues were a sensuous moan that welded together pain and pleasure with seamless irony. Jazz became the black music that expressed a desire to be free of cultural restraints. These artistic expressions mirrored the paradox African Americans faced—the paradox of *being* and *not being* American. As art so often does, these expressions grew out of the tensions created by conflicting forces at work within the human soul, and blacks had long been acquainted with such conflicts.

The paradox of wanting to become a part of majority American culture and, at the same time, doubting the wisdom of such an impulse is a theme that runs throughout African-American literature. Claude McKay, one of the Harlem Renaissance's most acerbic poets, said it succinctly in his poem "America":

Although she feeds me bread of bitterness.
And sinks into my throat her tiger's tooth,

Stealing my breath of life, I will confess
I love this cultured hell that tests my youth.[11]

The emotions of the poet's words were rooted in social dynamics that had been at work since the first Africans were introduced into the New World. These dynamics—unique because of the conditions of slavery—determined how black people adapted or were permitted to adapt to their new environment. Slavery precluded one possibility that was open to other newcomers arriving in America: blacks could not begin to be assimilated fully into the nascent social structure of European-American society. Every aspect of the slave system worked against that possibility. Within the narrow parameters of their world, however, the slaves assimilated parts of the surrounding culture. At the same time, they were able to retain some vestiges of their African heritage. Consequently, they engaged in the syncretic process of combining old cultural elements with new ones. Since all aspects of their lives were controlled by the conditions of slavery and the needs of the slave-masters, one of their first creative challenges was to manipulate their environment and their masters in order to achieve a semblance of tolerability in their lives.

For decades, social scientists, like poets, have been trying to assess the ways blacks adapted to their new home and its culture. There were those—such as Richard Bardolph in his 1959 study *The Negro Vanguard*—who contended that the adoption of the cultural patterns of white America was the preeminent method through which African-Americans shaped their lives: "Barred by the color line from the established American order, the Negro began building a makeshift, black replica of white American culture."[12] There were others, such as the anthropologist Melville Herskovits (one of Katherine Dunham's early mentors), who would have disagreed with Bardolph's thesis. In his early studies of the development of black cultures in the New World, Herskovits had placed more emphasis on the importance of African retentions and syncretic processes.

Over the years, passionate disputes have continued over the ways in which adaptive processes affected the development of African-American culture. These arguments have centered on the examination of intricately knotted influences and counter-influences. In the end, however, determining which cultural elements predominated at various points in the development of African-American culture may not be as important as recognizing that the culture is a testament to the profoundly creative ability of a people to survive.

As one looks at the wide variety of ways in which different strata of black society developed during the nineteenth century, theories of adaptation that picture African Americans as a homogeneous group appear more and more inappropriate. After the Civil War, distinctions of class, education, and geographic location strongly influenced the ways in which individual African Americans fit into American society. At one end of the spectrum, there were highly educated blacks who could gain limited access to the mainstream, and at the other there were illiterate sharecroppers who could be considered to be America's peasant population. By the 1920s, African Americans were even more difficult to fit into all-encompassing cultural categories. Strong residual elements of Africa could be found in the music and rituals of southern churches. Yet there were black American artists who worked within European traditions. Among them was Madame Evanti (Lillian Evans-Tibbs), an opera singer who toured Europe and South America in the 1920s and made her New York debut at Town Hall in 1932.

Harlem Renaissance writers made their own efforts to untangle the knotty questions concerning how African Americans fit into American culture. In 1925 Langston Hughes, the leading black poet of his time, wrote a seminal essay concerning the disturbing paradoxes confronting black artists. In "The Negro Artist and the Racial Mountain," he began by examining the negative effects of cultural assimilation:

> One of the most promising of young Negro poets said to me once, "I want to be a poet—not a Negro poet," meaning, I believe, "I want to write like a white poet"; meaning subconsciously, "I would like to be a white poet"; meaning behind that, "I would like to be white." And I was sorry the young man said that, for no great poet has ever been afraid of being himself. And I doubted then that, with his desire to run away spiritually from his race, this boy would ever be a great poet. But this is the mountain standing in the way of any true Negro art in America—this urge within the race toward whiteness, the desire to pour racial individuality into the mold of American standardization, and to be as little Negro and as much American as possible.[13]

Hughes's young poet found himself in a situation that reflected a basic quandary of African-American artists during the 1920s. In a sense, exclusively following European-American cultural models meant rejecting one's self, one's people, and one's culture. Yet qualifying as a serious artist and being given consideration by both the black and white intelligentsia required conversance with European-American canons of art. Hughes, however, hoped for another type of artist: "But then there are the low-down folks. . . . They do not particularly care whether they are like white folks or anybody else. . . . They furnish a wealth of colorful, distinctive material for any artist because they still hold their own individuality in the face of American standardization. And perhaps these common people will give to the world its truly great Negro artist, the one who is not afraid to be himself."[14]

To make his point, Hughes dealt in extremes that were hardly representative of black artists and intellectuals at work during the 1920s. Most individuals did not fit the model of the hypothetical poet, nor were they the progeny of the "common people." The "low-down" folks—lower-class blacks who lived in the rural South or migrated toward northern urban areas in ever-increasing numbers—contributed to serious art primarily by providing the folk culture and the vernacular spirit on which it could be based. The "conscious artists" (a term used by another black poet of the time, James Weldon Johnson) were more likely, like Hughes himself, to be well educated and from a relatively privileged background. They provided the solution to the black artist's quandary. Having knowledge of European-American culture, they became the interpreters of black folk material, used it as a basis for their own artistic innovations, and consequently elevated it to a level of acceptance by America's cultural establishment. As African-American art became a fashionable commodity during the 1920s, it began to gain recognition in the racially integrated artistic and intellectual salons that catered to artists such as Hughes.

The artists who were most representative of the "low-down" folks could not be found in the concert halls, galleries, and publishing houses of "high" culture. The artists who were closer to the folk roots of African-American culture were the thousands of singers, dancers, and musicians who peopled the clubs and cabarets, the vaudeville houses and minstrel shows, and the hundreds of theaters (black and white) across the country where popular entertainment thrived. They were the other artists of the Harlem Renaissance who captured the heady spirit of the time.

In reality, there was no model New Negro, no prototypical man or woman who represented the multifaceted range of individuals who comprised African-American society and artistry. Though the spirit of the New Negro pervaded every level of black America, the term, in its most elite definition, best described a small cadre of extremely well educated men and women whose stellar intellectual credentials and probing minds set them apart from all others. These were men such as William Edward Burghardt Du Bois, Alain Locke, James Weldon Johnson, and Charles S. Johnson. They drew upon history, sociology, political science, and aesthetics to synthesize a guiding philosophy for their people. They wrote and lectured about the black's awakening and the role that culture would play in it.

Du Bois was educated at Fisk University, Harvard, and the University of Berlin. Journalist, sociologist, novelist, civil rights activist, and historian are only some of the titles that describe his capabilities. In 1905, he founded the Niagara Movement, which by 1909 had developed into the National Association for the Advancement of Colored People. His philosophy of social advancement for African Americans included the idea that a small segment of black men and women, the brightest and most talented—what he called the Talented Tenth—would, through their achievements, leadership, and connections with their counterparts in white America, provide the leverage to raise the black masses to a position of equality. In spite of his elitist philosophy, Du Bois was well respected by the African-American masses. As editor of the NAACP's monthly magazine, *The Crisis*, he exerted influence at every level of black society. David Levering Lewis points out that the essays of Du Bois were read by semi-literate sharecroppers, factory workers, and middle-class families alike.[15] Where there was no cohesion of social status or economic reality, Du Bois affected cohesion of thought.

The Talented Tenth included men such as Alain Locke, a brilliant and mercurial scholar who was educated at Harvard, was a Rhodes scholar at Oxford, studied in Berlin and Paris, and later became chairman of the philosophy department at Howard University. The numerous essays he published during the 1920s and the role he played as arbiter in Harlem Renaissance literary circles made him a key figure influencing the aesthetic movement of the period.

James Weldon Johnson, a striking embodiment of wide-ranging intellect and talent, was an educator, a poet, and a lawyer who, by the turn of the century, had also distinguished himself as a lyricist of popular music. He and his brother, J. Rosamond Johnson, published more than two hundred songs, many of which were featured in Broadway's most successful shows. Turning from a lucrative career in show business to the field of diplomacy, he served as U.S. consul to Venezuela from 1906 to 1908 and U.S. consul to Nicaragua from 1909 to 1912. As field secretary for the NAACP, he also distinguished himself as a civil rights activist. He was one of the first among the black intelligentsia to express the idea that the best way for blacks to gain equality in American society would be through their artistic contributions. As Johnson put it, "The final measure of the greatness of all peoples is the amount and the standard of the literature and art they have produced."[16]

But it was another member of the Talented Tenth, Charles Spurgeon Johnson, who synthesized the ideas that produced the motivating philosophy of the Harlem Renaissance. Among Johnson's many achievements, he served as executive director of research and publicity for the Urban League and as editor of that organization's bulletin, *Opportunity*. Later he became the first black president of Fisk University. He took his undergraduate degree at Virginia Union College, but it was as a graduate student at the University of Chicago that he was exposed to the influences that shaped his ideas about black achievement.

Johnson studied with one of the leading sociologists of his time, Robert E. Park. Embracing Park's theory of "sociological positivism," he came to believe that blacks in America would move through ever-ascending levels of progress that, in spite of various setbacks, would lead them irreversibly toward an equal status in American society. Johnson also adopted Park's idea that each racial group had a distinctive essence; for example, Jews were intellectual and Anglo-Saxons were pioneering. The "Negro's essence" was his artistic temperament; consequently, blacks who developed their artistic abilities would be able to interact with other Americans to encourage social acceptance for their entire race.[17] In this way, the nurturing of creative endeavors would foster parity between African Americans and other racial groups.

This sociological construct was an accommodationist tool that fit Johnson's conservative and optimistic nature. Art was an area that had traditionally been a way for African Americans to gain recognition in American society. Creative endeavors produced highly visible results in terms of positive reinforcement for the racial image. For blacks, racism often shut the doors to political and economic advancement, but certain aspects of the arts professions were comparatively more accessible.[18]

As Lewis points out, the idea that creative endeavors could solve social problems was not shared by all: "Nothing could have seemed to most Afro-Americans more extravagantly impractical as a means of improving racial standing than writing poetry or novels, or painting."[19] But the time was ripe for the cultural blossoming of black America. White artists such as Eugene O'Neill had, for some time, been creating black-inspired works that capitalized upon the image of the African American as a kind of primal being who was still in touch with the purity of human nature. This image fit neatly into the Lost Generation's search for a new morality and spiritual regeneration. Since most blacks were far from assimilated into American society, their status as outsiders was considered by some white artists to be an asset rather than a liability. Men such as Du Bois, Locke, and Johnson were perfectly fitted, in turn, to capitalize on the growing interest in black culture. Through their eloquence and their connections with white philanthropists, publishers, and cultural arbiters, they were able to engage in an energetic campaign to promote their race through the sociological positivism of artistic endeavors.

Though the black press began writing of the politicized New Negro movement in 1919, the artistic arm of this movement was officially discovered by the white press in 1925 when the *New York Herald Tribune,* in an article about black literature, announced that the Negro was beginning to find his artistic voice.[20] The Harlem Renaissance was underway. What resulted was almost a decade of artistic outpouring during which a relatively small group of African-American artists produced, novels, plays, short stories, essays, paintings, and sculptures that were usually received with breathless anticipation, though the quality of the work varied. Some of the work was brilliant; some of it was fair; and a percentage of it was mediocre.

For the Harlem Renaissance artist, dance served primarily as a symbol of the times. The image of the dancer, basking in sensuality and free from the shackles of modern society—an image captured in the poetry of Langston Hughes and Claude McKay and in the sculptures of Richmond Barthé—came to represent the connection between contemporary African Americans and their elemental roots.

Perhaps because dance, in its vernacular manifestations, represented what upper-class blacks considered the stereotypical image of their lower-class brothers and sisters, it was not held in high esteem as a theatrical art among the intelligentsia. In the world of cabarets, night-clubs, and house parties, however, dance was the generator that propelled the frenetic escapism and optimism of the time. It physicalized the pervading spirit of abandon of the 1920s. Dance crazes had been sweeping the country since 1914 when Vernon and Irene Castle toured America, fox-trotting to the accompaniment of their black orchestra led by James Reese Europe. As Shawn and St. Denis did in the concert dance arena, the Castles cast a light of propriety on social dance for the American public. In the ensuing decades, new popular dances, inspired by African-American vernacular dances brought to the big cities by southern blacks, appeared with predictable regularity.

When black dancers achieved as much visibility and acclaim as other Harlem Renaissance artists, they did so in Broadway musicals and revues. Black musicals of the 1920s were infused with more kinetic energy and originality than had been seen before, and they became Broadway's hottest productions. As the dance historian Marshall Stearns points out, between 1921 and 1924 nine black shows (beginning with *Shuffle Along* and ending with *Dixie to Broadway*) set new innovative standards for Broadway dancing.[21] During these years—and during another period of intense activity in black musicals, 1928–30—performers such as Josephine Baker, Florence Mills, and Bill "Bojan-gles" Robinson became stellar examples of dance artistry in revues and musicals. Though they did not exemplify the more "serious" and somewhat elitist aspects of the "Negro essence," they were very positive influences of black artistic achievement. They were role models, shining beacons of hope, for the black masses; and they were phenomenally charismatic individuals for black and white audiences alike.

Black dancers who became aware of the innovations in concert dance during the mid-1920s, began performing late in that decade, and gained wider visibility in the early 1930s had much to sort through in plotting their directions. Their perceptions of the work of white dance artists indicated one direction they could take—the pursuit of a freer, more socially significant dance expression. Black artists also began looking for a type of dance that would identify them with modern trends, break with old traditions, and speak to the deep reaches of the human soul. The tradition from which they felt the most pressing need to distance themselves was not, however, European ballet or the pseudo-Orientalism of Denishawn; it was the stereotypical neo-minstrel form of entertainment that was still associated with vaudeville and musical theater. It became clear to the new black performers that they wanted to become more than "Cotton Club–types." As Katherine Dunham later put it, a major goal was "to attain a status in the dance world that will give the Negro dance student the courage really to study, and a reason to do so. And to take *our* dance out of the burlesque to make it a more dignified art."[22]

Like Dunham, all of the earliest black concert dance artists expressed concern about overcoming stereotypes and bringing attention to themselves as serious artists. Charles Williams, for example, wrote about the moral efficacy of what he called the "right" kind of dance and its importance as part of the black cultural heritage. Asadata Dafora constantly spoke of engendering an appreciation for African art and culture among American audiences. These artists' reactions to preconceived notions about black performers was a corollary influence that fueled their creative efforts. As their work gained wider visibility, it came under increased critical scrutiny. In the following chapters, the critical response to their art is closely examined not only because it provides valuable information about performances, but, just as important, because it reveals a number of *idées fixes* held by the critics. A brief look at some of the stereotypes that informed these entrenched ideas is crucial to understanding the black artist's struggle to gain recognition in America's cultural hierarchy.

Stereotypes of Black Performers and the Critical Response

Like the roots of artistic influences, the historical origins of stereotypes were deeply implanted in the soil of American culture. Preconceptions about a group of people—whether they were African American, Jewish, Irish, or Native American—were based on their differences from the Anglo-Saxon *norm* and became accepted as *truth.*

In his essay "Negro Character as Seen by White Authors," Sterling A. Brown, author, poet, and distinguished professor of literature at Howard University from 1929 to 1969, cogently analyzed African-American characters as portrayed in nineteenth- and early twentieth-century American literature. Written in 1949, his discussion is also relevant to studies of dance and drama (which he mentions briefly in his essay), and it reveals themes that are related to the criticism of these art forms.

Brown discusses several Negro stereotypes that white authors established during and after slavery. Whether the writers were pro-slavery, abolitionist, or reconstructionist, their delineations of blacks were used in highly propagandistic writings that supported the author's particular political or sociological point of view. As Brown points out, these characterizations, painted with varying degrees of sophistication, were quite often ridiculous and constituted seven stereotypes: (1) The Contented Slave; (2) The Wretched Freeman; (3) The Comic Negro; (4) The Brute Negro; (5) The Tragic Mulatto; (6) The Local Color Negro; and (7) The Exotic Primitive.[23] All of these, he states, were marked by exaggerations and omissions, stressed the "Negro's divergence from an Anglo-Saxon norm to the flattery of the latter," could be used as justifications for racial proscription, and "were generally accepted as contributions to true racial understanding."[24]

Brown proceeds with a fascinating analysis of the origins of these stereotypes. Though his discussion centers on earlier literary conventions that were used to delineate black characters, he also draws striking parallels between those and later depictions of African Americans during the 1920s. He finds the ideas of the Contented Slave reborn in images of happy-go-lucky, hedonistic Harlem Renaissance dandies, hustlers, and fast women: "The figure who emerges . . . is a Negro synchronized to a savage rhythm, living a life of ecstasy, superinduced by jazz (repetition of the tom-tom, awakening vestigial memories of Africa) and gin, that lifted him over antebellum slavery, and contemporary economic slavery, and placed him in the comforting fastness of the 'motherland.'"[25] The more contemporary types, like their antebellum predecessors, appeared to live in a state of "paradisiacal bondage" that left them bereft of all awareness of the oppressive economic and social realities surrounding them.

Brown's study is relevant here because he makes a strong case for the tenacity of stereotypical images that gained their strength from writers' "sincere unremitting harping upon one argument" until it finally appeared to be plausible.[26] Repetitive arguments voiced in a spirit of what critics considered to be "good-will" and "reason" were characteristic of much of the critical writing about black dancers during the 1930s and 1940s.

Brown discusses three stereotypes that are relevant here—The Comic Negro, The Local Color Negro, and The Exotic Primitive. By the time black concert dancers began performing, these three images had become conventional characterizations of the Negro on the American stage. The Comic Negro–type, for example, had become established in every genre of American popular entertainment. Black characters, pictured as ludicrous buffoons, had, by the turn of the century, become the goat-footed satyrs, the court jesters of the American stage. As the theater historian Allen Woll explains, even when black performers were eventually allowed to portray their own people in minstrel shows and early musical comedies (going against the earlier practice of having black roles exclusively assayed by white performers) they were "forced . . . to perpetuate the genre's derogatory stereotypes" if they wanted to work.[27]

Though some musical shows, notably *The Creole Show* (1890), *The Octoroons* (1895), and *Oriental America* (1896), began to move away from the crasser depictions of blacks, the shadow of the "shuffling darky" lingered in the wings of theaters across the country. More important for this study, at the time African-American dancers began to make concerted efforts to change negative stereotypes, critics were still influenced by a traditional yet specious way of thinking about black performers. These ideas surfaced in ways that ranged from expressions of subliminal bias to pronouncements that were blatantly racist.

The subtle connection between the earlier comic stereotypes and the critical response to early black concert dancers centers around critics' affirmations of the idea that there were some things that black dancers were fit to do and some that they were not. From this point of view, the sight of blacks attempting to perform certain material was almost ludicrous.

Dancers who could be categorized as performing "exotic" material (African- or Caribbean-derived dances) or "local color" material (dances using Negro spirituals, blues, and jazz) were usually accepted. When artists stepped outside these parameters, they were reminded that they were dabbling in areas where they should not venture. The *New York Times* dance critic John Martin reacted with bemused patience to Dunham's attempts to incorporate ballet technique into her early works;[28] and Lois Balcom assumed a position of cultural *hauteur* when she spoke of the absurdity of even thinking of comparing Pearl Primus with Alicia Markova or Martha Graham.[29] Since such a comparison was only a rhetorical device the critic used to underscore the purported impropriety of Primus's endeavors, perhaps the real absurdity was in Balcom's stance.

Even when black dancers attempted to cast "acceptable" dance material in a serious theatrical mode, they were often greeted by derision. With no attempt to suppress his patronizing denigration, John Mason Brown, the theater critic of the *New York Post,* compared Asadata Dafora's efforts to present African dance as serious theatrical art to "children playing in the attic."[30]

The relationship between this type of criticism and earlier stereotypes becomes clearer if we refer again to Sterling Brown's essay. He reminds us that images of blacks attempting to enter what were considered the special domains of whites were a popular comic convention in the literature and on the stage of the nineteenth century. Black characters cast in roles such as businessmen who wore dress suits, doctors, lawyers, or society belles were considered the height of ridiculousness.[31] Later, dance critics' allusions to the inappropriateness of black dancers as concert artists, serious artists, or ballet artists echoed a subtler version of the earlier convention.

It would be unfair to suggest that preconceived racial notions played a major role in all critics' writings. Writers such as Edwin Denby and Margaret Lloyd seemed less susceptible to this type of thinking and more sympathetic toward black dancers who were trying to escape from stereotypical images. Even the critics who most often engaged in racially proscriptive thinking altered their opinions from time to time, sometimes discussing black artists in terms that cast them as cultural interlopers and at other times giving them more credit as artistic innovators in their own right. Examination of these ambivalent viewpoints indicates that some critics may have been searching for an appropriate way to discuss emerging black concert dancers just as the artists themselves were engaged in a journey of self-discovery. On the other hand, a close look at critical writing reveals that questionable ideas recurred so often throughout reviews, they appear to have followed a "party line."

One of the most pervasive of the ideas that dressed older stereotypes in contemporary clothing was what could be called the "alien culture" theory. It provided a tidy rationale for placing black dancers outside the artistic mainstream: African Americans were ill prepared to engage in the serious dance genres of European-American art because the culture itself was foreign to them. I will discuss this idea in more detail in the following chapters, but it should be stressed here that it was a specious construct that—like the ideas of the nineteenth-century authors discussed by Brown—was used to perpetuate a preferred image of black people. Whether conscious or unconscious, the tactical use of this idea had as much to do with sociopolitical motives as it did with the criticism of art.

A society's art and culture are highly valuable resources that rank in importance with economic and political resources. Critics who constantly implied that blacks were cultural interlopers assumed the role of guardians of the status quo of their own culture; they could not let *their* art be defiled without comment.

Although the black intelligentsia of the Harlem Renaissance saw artistic pursuits (as opposed to economic or political pursuits) as a relatively easy way for African Americans to gain entrée into mainstream American society, they seemed to ignore—or at least failed to emphasize—the fact that America's cultural arenas were extremely well guarded. Social positivists such as Charles S. Johnson failed to acknowledge that critics and other cultural arbiters could interfere with African-American artists' efforts to participate in mainstream American culture by repeatedly referring to them as outsiders.

A related idea that placed blacks in a neatly separatist category was based on the image of African-American men and women as the most "natural" beings in American society. This image supplied a number of white artists with a vision of black life that could express the elemental side of human nature. Critical references to black artists as natural performers were a logical extension of this line of thought. Reviews of this type occurred with predictable regularity and emphasized the performers' exotic differences from the Anglo-Saxon norm. In this respect, the idea of blacks as natural performers was closely related to the Exotic Primitive and Local Color Negro stereotypes. It portrayed black dancers as purveyors of atavistic impulses that resulted in a kind of effortless, unconscious expressiveness. Consequently, their work could be referred to as a sociological rather than an artistic phenomenon.

One of the goals of this study is to show how black dancers became involved with contemporary artistic trends in ways that proved the inaccuracy of stereotypes. Through the artistic conventions of Western theater, these artists were attempting to recast dances from the African diaspora in concert versions that could be accepted as serious art. In this process, they also incorporated elements from modern dance and ballet. But as long as critics could speak of black concert dance in terms that negated its artistry and categorized it as unadulterated racial expression, it could be separated from contemporary dance trends.

The history of black concert dancers is a story of their constant struggle for acceptance by the American public and the critical establishment. It reveals the complexity of a situation that was compounded by the artists' unique psychological *agon.* These dancers wanted to take the essence of various black cultures into the American mainstream, but, at the same time, they realized that majority America did not consider the material they used artistically valuable in its own right.

Possibly, the artists themselves had ambivalent feelings about some aspects of their cultural heritage and wondered just how much of the soul of their people they should reveal. They were engaged in a kind of balancing act. If they leaned too much toward the characteristics of black cultures that were most appealing to majority Americans— visceral physical communication, the "exotic" excitement attached to forms that were, for the most part, non-Western—they were often accused of capitalizing on stereotypical images to woo white audiences. They were told that they were becoming too much like the popular entertainers from whom they were trying to distinguish themselves. It was difficult for critics to view the visceral quality and "primitivism" of black artists in the same way that they viewed similar qualities in the works of white modern dancers—as a return to the roots of human impulses to revivify contemporary dance.

Black dancers wanted their art to serve their individual aesthetic agendas; like black writers and intellectuals of the time, they adopted the underlying philosophy of the Harlem Renaissance: art should serve the specific social mission of changing how their people were perceived by the rest of the world.

To achieve their goals, these artists, each in his or her own way, took their impetus from the new dance movement in America and proceeded to redirect its energy, bending it to serve their needs. Concurrently, they reinterpreted material from the folk cultures of the African diaspora and attempted to make a place for it in mainstream American culture. In so doing they created yet another synthesis of African-derived and European-derived cultural elements.

2
Hemsley Winfield

MUCH THAT HAS BEEN WRITTEN about Hemsley Winfield emphasizes the greatness that he might have achieved had he not died at the age of twenty-six. But a deeper investigation of the young artist's life reveals that he accomplished much more than has been assumed. The earliest portion of his career was only peripherally involved with dance, but he was able to make significant contributions to that field because of the breadth of his theatrical background. His experiences as an actor, director, stage technician, dancer, and, eventually, choreographer took him from "little theaters" in Yonkers and Harlem to the avant-garde theaters of Greenwich Village, to Broadway, and finally to the Metropolitan Opera House. Because of his organizational skills and his personal magnetism, he was able to involve dozens of novices and professional performers in his productions and achieve his goal of increasing black participation in theater communities. Consequently, he made a considerable impact upon the black theater and dance scene of the time.

According to the Yonkers, New York, *Herald Statesman,* Winfield would have been twenty-seven years old on April 20, 1934. This places his year of birth at 1907. Born Osborne Hemsley Winfield, he shortened his name during his early years in theater.[1] His father was a successful civil engineer who employed several hundred men in his firm,

Winfield and Franklin General Contractors, Inc., on Sackett Street in Brooklyn, New York.[2] His mother, a nurse by profession, was an aspiring playwright. For theatrical purposes, she too shortened her name, to Jeroline Hemsley.

Little is known about Winfield's childhood except that he graduated from Public School 13 in Yonkers, exhibited early leadership abilities as president of his class, and later attended Yonkers High School.[3] His early years seem to have been pleasant enough in the picturesque town on the banks of the Hudson River. His family lived comfortably in a spacious two-and-a-half-story house that still stands at 24 Wolffe Street. As members of the black middle-class in Yonkers, the Winfields were mentioned regularly in Harlem's *Age*. The paper's column entitled "Interesting Items Gleaned from the Age Correspondents" recounted the social events, church affairs, and cultural activities of the black community. Announcements often noted Hemsley Winfield's participation in the community drama groups that contributed to the local cultural life.

Living and working in Yonkers had its drawbacks. Old-time Yonkers residents recalled that it was common practice for local employers such as the Otis Elevator Company to offer blacks only menial jobs. The white establishment would not permit black doctors and lawyers to practice in the town; and the assignment of the first black Yonkers policeman in 1932 made newspaper headlines in Harlem.[4] One account of Winfield's formative years suggested that he may have given up one of his early attempts at organizing a local little theater group because of racist hostility;[5] but he showed early signs of the obstinate perseverance that served him throughout his career.

Winfield's attempts at organizing black theater groups in Yonkers were not only indicative of middle-class cultural aspirations; they were also part of an important grass-roots cultural movement that took hold in America during the early twentieth century. In putting the American little theater movement in a historical context, Robert E. Gard and Gertrude S. Burley cite several influences that brought it into being. In 1911, the Irish Players toured America "spreading the ideals of naturalness and simplicity" in a type of theater that was accessible to the average person.[6] The idea behind this was that community members could participate not only as audience members at performances, but as actors, writers, directors, and technicians.

Like the influence of the early modern dance movement that changed audiences' tastes for theatrical dance, the influence of the Irish Players helped turn the American public against the stale conventions of the commercial theater. The company's appearances functioned as a catalyst that caused "countless dramatic groups to germinate all over America, as a protest against commercial drama."[7] By 1915, Americans were becoming aware that there could be alternatives to the commercial theater and to theater for the elite. There could be a type of theater that depended on the community for its artistic and material existence.[8] "Little theaters" were established in cities such as Duluth, Cincinnati, Denver, Indianapolis, and Baltimore. In New York, 1915 through 1917 saw the birth of the Neighborhood Playhouse, the Washington Square Players, and the Provincetown Playhouse.

By the early 1920s, the little theater movement had found its way into black communities and was bolstered by the upsurge of interest in African-American culture. Groups of community-based amateurs and semi-professionals created theaters that became training grounds for individuals such as Winfield who would make inroads into mainstream American theater and dance establishments.

Black newspapers and magazines regularly reported news about these theaters around the country. *Opportunity* reported the establishment of The Shadows, a Negro art theater that opened in Chicago in early September 1925. Its stated goal (one often echoed by similar groups) was to create a kind of theater from the life of African Americans that paralleled the Irish Players of Dublin and the Moscow Art Theatre in Russia.[9] In 1929, one of Katherine Dunham's first theatrical ventures was her participation in the Little Theatre of Harper Avenue, also in Chicago. In Boston, there was the Allied Art Centre directed by Maud Cuney-Hare. The Gilpen Players of Cleveland later became known as the Karamu Theatre and established a reputation for professionalism. Philadelphia had its Norman Players, and New Haven had the Dixwell Players.

The ubiquitous civil rights activist and journalist W. E. B. Du Bois established the Krigwa Players—a group that Winfield would also become associated with—in Harlem in 1926. That same year, Du Bois published an article in *The Crisis* that outlined what a black theater should be. His words paralleled the philosophy of the founders of America's little theater movement but expressed those ideas from a black perspective: "The plays of a real Negro theatre must be: 1. *About us.* That is, they must have plots which reveal Negro life as it is. 2. *By us.* That is, they must be written by Negro authors who understand from birth and continual association just what it means to be a Negro today. 3. *For us.* That is, the theatre must cater primarily to Negro audiences and be supported and sustained by their entertainment and approval. 4. *Near us.* The theatre must be in a Negro neighborhood near the mass of ordinary people."[10] Du Bois's second goal was achieved, in part, through the annual prizes *The Crisis* established in an attempt to encourage the development of promising young playwrights. His last goal was achieved by locating the Krigwa Theatre in the basement of the New York Public Library at 135th Street and Lenox Avenue, an intersection that became the cultural hub of Harlem.

Another Harlem little theater group, the National Ethiopian Art Theatre (NEAT), was one of the organizations where Winfield received his earliest training as an actor. Under the direction of Anne Wolter, who had been associated with the American Academy of Dramatic Art, the theater—which included a school for actors—held its official opening on March 17, 1924; its advent "marked a new development in opportunity to be afforded the members of the race who seek training in artistic expression."[11] Wolter considered her school "a movement that is founded on the destroying of race prejudice and the building up of a spirit of comity and good will between all men."[12] The school's goals reflected one of the most pervasive ideas concerning the relationship between contemporary art and racial issues during the time—that artistic pursuits could be used to enhance the acceptance of black people into majority American society. One of its first performances, on June 19, 1924, was a program of dance and choral music. Although Winfield did not appear with the large, all-female group that performed the dance portion of the program, he did appear with the choral group.[13]

Winfield seems to have had a tremendous appetite for different types of theater. At the same time he was working in Harlem and Yonkers, he began to broaden his theatrical experiences by becoming associated with a number of Greenwich Village theaters. The first of these was the Provincetown Playhouse, which had been established in Provincetown, Massachusetts, in 1915 to present the work of new American playwrights. When it moved to New York, in 1917, it was first located at 139 Macdougal Street and then at 133 Macdougal.[14]

During the spring and summer of 1924, the Provincetown alternated two plays by Eugene O'Neill, a revival of *The Emperor Jones* and *All God's Chillun Got Wings*, both starring Paul Robeson. In July, the New York *Age* announced that Winfield had just finished a successful season as a member of the cast of *All God's Chillun*.[15] There is no indication that he had a major role,[16] but his association with the progressive Provincetown Playhouse and with Robeson was an important addition to his growing theatrical experience.

Winfield's desire to gain as much stage experience as possible kept him traveling back and forth between the experimental theaters of Greenwich Village and the black theaters of Harlem. In 1925, he was again performing with the National Ethiopian Art Theatre. Its director, Anne Wolter, managed to secure the use of the Lafayette Theatre for a benefit performance on October 15. Her efforts were aimed at bringing serious theater back to the Lafayette, which was in the heart of Harlem at 132d Street and Seventh Avenue. As early as 1915, the theater had its own stock company of black actors who presented dramatic plays, but by the early 1920s it had become a raucous vaudeville house. The NEAT's performance was relegated to a midnight show that took place after the Lafayette's regular bill of fare.

Three one-act plays were presented. The first two, *Being Forty*, by Eulalie Spence, and *Cooped Up*, by Eloise Bibb Thompson, were written by students of the school. Winfield appeared in the third play, *Bills*, by John M. Francis. It was a comedy that centered on a stuttering lawyer who is mistaken for a bill collector when he visits a young married couple to leave a check for an inheritance. The husband, played by Winfield, and his wife completely befuddle the lawyer and later discover his true mission after he has left.[17] The black critic George S. Schuyler of *The Messenger* had mixed feelings about the performance. Though he did not expect perfection from amateur performers, they were, in spite of their weaknesses, as good as some actors he had seen on Broadway. He also said that Hemsley Winfield did the best he could with a role for which he was not well suited.[18]

At the age of eighteen, Winfield was beginning to gain recognition in the little theater communities in and around New York. There is no indication that he had expressed much interest in dance at this time, but it is likely that he had received some dance training. The NEAT offered dance classes as part of its curriculum, and the importance of these classes was stressed in the school's course outline: "Training in Esthetic Dancing develops grace and poise. It is an indispensable requisite to every stage aspirant."[19] In addition to esthetic dancing—the emotional Duncanesque dancing that many teachers incorporated in their classes—which was taught by Grace Giles, jazz classes were taught by Henry Creamer, the director of the school's dance program.

While Winfield was performing with theater groups in Greenwich Village and Harlem, he continued working with his own little theater group, the Majestic Players, in Yonkers and produced several plays there in August 1925. The importance of the performances was reflected in the stature of the Harlem luminaries who were present—people such as Eric Walrond, the poet and drama critic for *Opportunity*, and May Jackson, daughter of Harlem's millionaire heiress, A'Lelia Walker.[20]

In 1926, Winfield made an important step from little theater productions to Broadway when he appeared in *Lulu Belle*, which opened at the Belasco Theatre in February. Written by Edward Sheldon and Charles MacArthur, the David Belasco production told the story of a Harlem prostitute, Lulu Belle, who convinces one man to desert his wife and children and then leaves him for a prizefighter. She ends up in Europe with a degenerate French count and is finally murdered. According to the theater historian Bruce Kellner, "The play had a considerable vogue with white audiences newly fascinated by tales of Harlem lowlife."[21]

Lulu Belle was a breakthrough for black actors on Broadway. Although the lead female role was played by a white actress, Lenore Ulric, in dark makeup, the cast was racially integrated. As the reviewer for *The Crisis* pointed out, "Ninety-seven persons in the cast of one hundred and fourteen are really colored and not ridiculous imitations."[22] Writing in *Opportunity*, Hubert H. Harrison observed that (with the exception of earlier plays by Ridgely Torrence and Eugene O'Neill) Negro characters were usually abominably impersonated by white actors. Harrison further commented that "the dominant atmosphere of the play was furnished by the overwhelming mass of Negro actors on the stage."[23]

The realism of its cast was enhanced by stage sets, costumes, and action that convincingly detailed the tenement life of San Juan Hill, the downtown area that predated Harlem as New York's major black community. Impressed with the realism of the setting (an element that was characteristic of David Belasco's productions), Brooks Atkinson of the *New York Times* described one of the street scenes: "The first act . . . supplies every detail of raucous neighborhood life[,] . . . with tenement houses represented exactly from door to fire-escape. . . . Every episode of street life is likewise represented by a huge mob of colored actors—crap shooting, Salvation Army serenaders, hair-pulling, and a wedding party reproduced[,] from the taunts of the jealous neighbors on the fire-escape to the Ford automobile rolling the principals and relatives down the street toward the church."[24]

As part of the "mob" of black stereotypes, Winfield played the minor role of a neighborhood character named Joe. Though the play was not a musical in the strictest sense, it alternated dramatic scenes with scintillating interludes of jazz music and dance sequences.[25]

Lulu Belle introduced the young actor to other black performers such as Edna Thomas, the brilliant actress who later starred in the WPA Federal Theatre production of the "voodoo" *Macbeth* (1936). During the run of the show, he also became acquainted with Ollie Burgoyne, who in a few years would become the leading performer in Winfield's first dance company. She would also be singled out later for her outstanding role in *Run Little Chillun'* (1933).

The following year, after finishing his appearance in *Lulu Belle,* Winfield returned to his little theater work. But it was not long before he was rehearsing for his next major production, *Earth,* which opened in March 1927 at the New Playwrights Theatre. The play, written by Em Jo Basshe, was another in a long line of 1920s dramas that white playwrights wrote about black characters. Although these plays caused some consternation among African-American intellectuals, the theater historian Doris Abramson points out that they also helped destroy minstrel stereotypes and helped make it possible for black performers to be taken seriously in the theater.[26]

Basshe was a Russian immigrant who had worked in Harlem as early as 1921. Later he pursued his interest in black folk material by traveling for six months in Virginia, Georgia, Kentucky, and Florida. The result of his experiences was a play set in 1880 that recounted the story of an impoverished sharecropping community where the people wavered between Christian and "voodoo" religions. Winfield portrayed one of the defenders of the Christian religion, Barnabas.[27] Theophilus Lewis, the theater critic for *The Messenger,* coolly referred to Winfield's work as being "creditable"; and he found the production in general to be the "best so-called Negro play since 'The Emperor Jones.'"[28]

Working on the production of *Earth* brought Winfield in contact with another individual who would play an important role as a mentor in his career. Inez Clough, who had the female lead in the play and was praised by critics, later joined Winfield in several productions he either performed in or directed. The fact that Clough, an experienced and highly regarded actress, would become involved with such a young director attested to his charismatic leadership abilities and the serious artistic intent that others perceived in him.

Clough, who was more than thirty years older than Winfield, began her career in 1896 in the first all-black show to appear on Broadway, *Oriental America.* After touring Europe with that show, she remained in England, where she performed for ten years, and then returned to America, appearing in musicals, vaudeville shows, and black stock companies. One of her greatest triumphs as a serious actress was in a series of plays presented under the title *Three Plays for a Negro Theatre* on April 5, 1917, at the Garden Theatre in Madison Square Garden. The plays, *The Rider of Dreams, Granny Maumee,* and *Simon the Cyrenian,* were written by the white playwright Ridgely Torrence, and the evening was noteworthy because it was one of the earliest attempts to present black actors instead of white actors in plays dealing with the black experience. For her performances, Inez Clough was cited by the critic George Jean Nathan as one of the ten most distinguished performers on the New York stage that year.[29]

Another professional relationship Winfield established while performing in *Earth* was with Hall Johnson, who provided the choral music for the play. Johnson, who later collaborated with Winfield on a pageant presented at the Roxy Theatre in 1932, had arrived in New York in 1914. His first job was as a violin player in James Reese Europe's Orchestra in performances with Vernon and Irene Castle. He also played in the orchestra of *Shuffle Along* (1922), organized his own successful choral group in 1925, and wrote the highly acclaimed folk-play *Run Little Chillun'* in 1933.

Winfield had an admirable ability to seek out and establish associations with innovative people on the New York theater scene. Kathleen Kirkwood was one of these individuals. A former magazine editor, Kirkwood had established the Triangle Theatre in 1923 at Seventh Avenue and Perry Street in Greenwich Village. As part of the little theater movement, it quickly gained a reputation for promoting young playwrights and performers. It also became one of the bohemian literary and artistic salons that attracted people such as Ethel Barrymore, Ned Wayburn, F. Scott Fitzgerald, and Theodore Dreiser.[30]

The *New York Times* announced in April 1927 that a play Winfield had written would be presented on a program of one-act plays to be presented at the Triangle. All that is known about his contribution to the evening is that it was entitled *On.*[31] A month later he appeared in Kirkwood's revue *1927, Bare Facts.* The writer who announced the production in the *Amsterdam News* informed the public of Winfield's first expressed intentions of choreographing: "Mr. Winfield will have a unique opportunity to display a new form of dance composition."[32] There was no further indication of what his dances were like except what their titles suggested. *The South* was a plantation scene choreographed to Negro spirituals; in another dance, *The East,* he performed as the Master of the Slaves; and *Foots* was choreographed for himself and another male dancer.[33]

Winfield was happy with his involvement in the artistic life of New York and the surrounding area. One of the highlights of his year was the glowing mention he and his Sekondi Players (the name he had begun using for his group in early 1927) received from Theophilus Lewis:

> The guiding spirit of the Sekondi Players is Heemsley [sic] Winfield, and right now I know of less than half a dozen figures of more value to our theatre and drama. . . . His experience in modern stagecraft combined with his knowledge of how to apply it to the special requirements of the little theatre marks him as the present outstanding leader in his field. No one group should have a monopoly of his services. All the little theatre movements in the metropolis should call him in to help out with their problems of staging.[34]

During 1928 and 1929, Winfield directed several productions of Oscar Wilde's *Salome,* which brought him further visibility and encouraged him to begin making his career transition from actor to dancer, from director to choreographer. He may have thought of producing the play because of an earlier production Kathleen Kirkwood had presented in March 1927 at the Triangle.[35] Winfield had a minor role in that production. There had also been an earlier all-black *Salome* directed by Raymond O'Neill at the Frazee Theatre in 1923.

Another all-black version of the Oscar Wilde play seemed to be a logical step since *Salome* had enjoyed tremendous popular success in numerous incarnations since the turn of the century. The dancing seductress Salome—as a personification of late Romantic ideas about the fusion of life, sexuality, and death—was one of the most performed roles of its time. Actresses and dancers such as Ida Rubenstein, Loie Fuller, and Maud Allan had performed the role of Salome, but Winfield had the distinction of being one of the first men to attempt it.

When the New York *Age* announced a performance of the play at the Alhambra Theatre, 126th Street and Seventh Avenue, on March 9, 1928, Winfield's name was not listed as a cast member.[36] This suggests that initially Winfield did not perform in the play but only directed it. His actual appearance as Salome was not mentioned until more than a year later (in July 1929) when the *Amsterdam News* assured everyone that his performance of the role would be "well worth seeing and interesting."[37]

The July 1929 performance of *Salome* was originally to have opened on the fifteenth at the Provincetown Playhouse where the New Negro Art Theatre (Winfield's current name for his group) was in residence for the summer. But when those plans fell through, the Cherry Lane Theatre was substituted, and the play opened a week later.[38]

The reviewers of Winfield's performance seemed to write with incredulous smiles on their faces, and their remarks focused primarily on his female impersonation. The correspondent for the Chicago *Defender* reported that Winfield was dressed in little more than a beaded curtain but gave an energetic performance.[39] Another (unidentified) writer said that the "freakishness of a colored female impersonator" portraying Salome was worth a trip to the Village in spite of the bad acting.[40] Reviewers also compared his performances to those of white female impersonators who were performing during the time—Albert Caroll of the Grand Street Follies, Karyl Norman, and Julian Eltinge. Elaborate shows featuring female impersonation also had a place in the black community. Carl Van Vechten, the critic, author, and "negro-phile" who was practically an official tour guide for Harlem's night life, frequently served as a judge at integrated transvestite balls held at the Savoy Ballroom and the Rockland Palace Casino during the late 1920s.[41]

Winfield's initial appearances as Salome may have occurred out of necessity. According to Randolph Sawyer, a former dancer in Winfield's company, the young actor assumed the role because one of his actresses, Enid Raphael, did not show up for a performance.[42] Since Winfield eventually could have found a permanent replacement for her, it appears that he continued to perform the role by choice. Perhaps he became fascinated with creating one of the ultimate illusions of theatrical characterization, the metamorphosis from one gender to another. Perhaps he began to enjoy his "star turn." One of the most probable reasons he continued the role is that he began to enjoy performing the solo dances that were required.

Not much is known about Winfield's actual dancing, but Vere E. Johns, an actor and writer, who along with Inez Clough eventually joined the cast of *Salome*, remembered journeying downtown to the Cherry Lane Theatre to meet Winfield for the first time. Johns was "graciously received by a fine looking affable young man whose every movement proclaimed that he was a dancer."[43] Johns continued, "He was determined to overcome the handicap of color and push his art to its furthest limits."[44]

Richard Bruce Nugent, another performer who sometimes danced with Winfield, also had memories of *Salome:* "He, for instance, did a show . . . in which he played the role of Salome. And, well, it sounds like a laugh, but it wasn't a laugh, because he was Salome. There was nothing camp about it. He just was Salome. He was absolutely dedicated to what he was doing. This was a very avant-garde thing to do. I mean, to be a female impersonator and still avoid the stigma that might easily be attached to that."[45]

During the time that he presented various productions of *Salome*, Winfield continued to try to out-pace himself by being involved in one theatrical production after another. On April 18, 1928, he appeared again with the Provincetown Players, this time in a play by E. E. Cummings entitled *Him*, which was called "one of the most unusual and abstract plays of its time."[46] Winfield appeared recurrently through-

out the play as several characters who represented black archetypes—
Porter, Male Black Figure, Ethiopian, and King of Borneo.[47] In November of the same year, his New Negro Art Theatre presented Ridgley
Torrence's *The Rider of Dreams* at the Lincoln Theatre in Harlem. The
play had been presented before by his company, but in this performance
one critic found it to be beyond the reach of its young actors.[48] The
reviewer from *Opportunity*, Eulalie Spence, who had worked with
Winfield during his earlier NEAT days, briefly commented that his
enunciation was less than perfect.[49]

With the exception of *Salome*, by far the most important productions
Winfield took part in during this period of his career was the Broadway show *Harlem*. Co-written by a black author, Wallace Thurman,
and a white author, William Jourdan Rapp, it was another "black-belt-
slice-of-life" that writers compared to *Lulu Belle* and *Porgy*.

According to Doris Abramson, Thurman was responsible for the
story, the dialogue, and the details, while Rapp shaped the play; then,
both penciled in notes.[50] It was Thurman's first attempt as a playwright,
but he had already established himself as a leading figure among Harlem Renaissance writers. He was a novelist and a journalist who had
the unique distinction of being employed by both black and white
magazines and journals.

Harlem told the story of a family trying to survive after moving to
New York from the South. The characters included a long-suffering
matriarch (played by Inez Clough), a father who gave rent parties at
the family's apartment in order to pay the landlord, and a strumpet
daughter named Cordelia. The characters included a number of Harlem types—numbers runners, "sweet-backs," and "hot-stuff" men.
Winfield played one of these colorful characters (Jimmy) in a cast of
sixty that was noteworthy for the time because it was all-black, with
the exception of one character.

Abramson points out that what was new about *Harlem* was its attempt to let its sensational melodrama develop through a delineation
of the *real problems* of Harlem: poor living conditions, racial prejudices
among men of color, racketeering, the problems of transplanted south-
erners, and unemployment.[51] She writes, "Wallace Thurman was one
of the New Negroes who, suffering the indignities of being a Negro in
America, wanted to record Negro life honestly, but who usually settled
for capitalizing on its exotic-erotic elements in order to succeed."[52]

Harlem received mixed reviews. One thing that people agreed on, however, was that the incidental dances were the highlight of the show. The reviewer from the *New York Times* spoke of "sizzling dancing."[53] Alson Smith of the *Morning World* reported performers "writhing lustily through their barbaric dances"; he went on to corroborate the specious theory that blacks were natural performers by adding, "There is always the sense of an authentic picture which intermittently flares into life with a vivid magic of its own. . . . Part of this is due to a Negro cast which has, for the most part, the vivid actuality which belongs to their unique racial talent for make-believe."[54]

Many of the reviews were so similar that they appeared to have been sent out from some central bureau for reviewing black stage productions. Richard Lockridge of the *New York Sun* wrote his variation on a theme when he described the rent party scenes:

> In those scenes the stage is crowded and in them, most completely, the members of the cast seem to forget that they are acting and to give themselves over to rhythms—the slow, sensual, deeply felt rhythms which the negro has brought to the white man and which the white man, however he may try, is always a little too self-conscious to accept. The boys and girls who dance on the stage of the Apollo are unself-conscious and barbaric. They are also amazingly direct. . . . The play is, in a sense, a motion picture thrown upon the background of negroes dancing. They dance lustily, swayingly, shamelessly and reveal the simplicity and deep earthiness of their race's hold on life. . . . Men and women who dance like that have the strength for violence.[55]

Harlem, which opened at the Apollo Theatre at Broadway and Forty-second Street on February 20, 1929, gave downtown theater-goers a chance to visit that dangerous, black enclave without going to the trouble of actually traveling uptown. But what was it that had writers vying for words to describe the heat of the dancing? It was the Slow Drag, a couple dance in which a man and a woman pressed their bodies tightly together in a smooth bump and grind as they kept the rhythm of the music. As Marshall Stearns put it, "The Slow Drag hit Times Square, and Broadway was staggered by a glimpse of the authentic roots of Negro dance. Unlike most musical-comedy dancing, the Slow Drag was social dancing—Negro folk variety—and beyond registering alarm, nobody knew what to make of it."[56]

Even the playwright Wallace Thurman joined in the fray by publishing an article in *The Dance Magazine*. After a discussion that traced black vernacular dances from southern migrant workers into the cabarets of black urban communities and finally onto the Broadway stage, he stated: "What one wishes to know now is whether or not the Negro will continue to make salient contributions to the modern American dance."[57] He concluded by saying that there would always be new and innovative dance material moving up through America's complex strata of class and race.

During its run, *Harlem* was plagued by controversies. Many members of the black community were incensed because the play painted a picture of the underside of black urban life. Censors visited performances of the New York and Chicago productions and threatened to close the show if the language and dancing were not toned down. An internecine battle broke out between the cast and the show's management.

Winfield played an important role in the final controversy that closed the show. In an article in the *Amsterdam News*, he explained the events that led up to the debacle. He had energetically recruited cast members for the show. Five performers had come from his own New Negro Art Theatre, and he also brought in seven other cast members. In addition to performing, he was the stage manager of the show, and initially he had been a fervent supporter of the project, its producer, Edward A. Blatt, and its director, Chester Erskins.[58]

According to Winfield, Erskins became habitually abusive to the cast. But the real source of animosity was a promise by the management to increase the cast members' eighteen-dollar weekly salary if the show was successful. When this promise was not kept, the cast refused to appear in the rent party scene one night. The boycott incensed the management, and Winfield was fired from his position as stage manager for supporting the players. After one final outburst from Erskins, the show closed on May 11, 1929.[59]

Not one to let adversity get him down, Winfield continued to search for other performance opportunities for his company. It seemed that the controversy surrounding *Harlem* gave him even more energy than usual and made him more determined than ever to produce and direct his own shows.

The next production he mounted was a collaboration with his mother. In mid-August 1929, the New Negro Art Theatre began rehearsals for *Wade in De Water*, again at the Cherry Lane Theatre. Jeroline Hemsley explained that the play, which belonged to the same southern folk genre as Em Jo Basshe's *Earth*, was inspired by her years in Virginia where she attended St. Paul's School in Lawrenceville. At that time, and later when she remained in Virginia to teach, she encountered people who became prototypes for the characters in her play. She wove their stories together in an attempt to "bring to life some of the . . . great Negro women of the past who were unconsciously makers of history for a race."[60]

The play was not warmly received by the reviewer from the *New York Times*, but it was pointed out that the incidental music and dance were one of the play's strong points. The writer was most positive about the performances of Inez Clough and Hemsley Winfield, noting that they were "to be considered apart from the rest of the cast by virtue of professional experience."[61]

The Chicago *Defender* reprinted part of a review from the *Morning Telegraph* that had similar praise for Winfield and Inez Clough: "'Miss Clough and Mr. Winfield are the only actors in the group. Positive, sincere and intelligent, they continually dominate the stage. Particularly fine is Mr Winfield's voice, mellow and controlled, with a peculiar timbre in frenzied moments that is sure to send shivers down the spine of the most austere theatergoer.'"[62]

Shortly after *Wade in De Water*, Winfield announced that his company would be housed in the Greenwich Village Theatre at Seventh Avenue and Sheridan Square, where they would present a season of eight plays.[63] By February 1930, however, they were again in residence in Harlem, this time at the auditorium of the Urban League Building at 202 West 136th Street. There, they inaugurated a series of Sunday performances; the first of these, *The Gathering of the Muses*, was a program of drama, comedy, music, poetry, and dance.[64]

Winfield was by now gaining a national reputation. Perhaps because of his press coverage in the Chicago *Defender*, he was invited by the National Negro Pageant Association of Chicago—an organization that sponsored African-American historical pageants around the country—to direct a performance at Carnegie Hall in New York. The production was entitled *De Promis' Lan'*, and its script was written by Jeroline Hemsley. It had only one performance, on May 27, 1930.

De Promis' Lan' qualified as a pageant in the sense that it had a large cast (more than two hundred fifty performers) and it was composed of numerous historical scenes that were loosely connected in theme and subject matter. On the other hand, it differed from typical early twentieth-century pageants because it was performed in a concert hall instead of a large outdoor space such as Lewisohn Stadium, where similar productions often occurred in New York.

The importance of the American pageantry movement was that it was a means of getting nonprofessionals involved in dance, expressive movement, and other aspects of theater. Pageants served as an introduction to dance and drama for large numbers of novice performers, stimulated interest in the performing arts, and helped create audiences. In these respects, the pageantry movement resembled the little theater movement.

There had been a number of all-black pageants during the early twentieth century. The tireless W. E. B. Du Bois had written *The Star of Ethiopia,* which was first performed in New York in 1913. It was later performed in Washington, D.C., in 1915, in Philadelphia in 1916, and finally at the Hollywood Bowl in Los Angeles in 1925.[65] There had also been an earlier black pageant at Carnegie Hall. *The Open Door* had been performed on November 22, 1921, as a benefit for Atlanta University.[66]

De Promis' Lan' took place in fourteen scenes. After the overture, there were scenes such as *Along the River Congo* (with Ollie Burgoyne dancing the lead role, personifying the river), *A Louisiana Slave Market,* and *Folk Lore.* Other dance sections included *In Quest of Beauty—interpreted by the Brown Nymphs* and *Life and Death—an emotional study in dance form.* The evening, which was a very lengthy one, concluded with two one-act plays in which Inez Clough had the lead, *The Rider of Dreams* and *Mammy Triumphant.*[67] The production brought Winfield a step closer to making his final transition from drama into the field of concert dance. He choreographed most of the scenes, and one of them, *Life and Death,* later became a staple in his concert repertoire.

As Winfield became more involved in choreography between 1925 and 1930, there were a number of events that might have influenced his move in the direction of a dance career. Martha Graham made her first Broadway concert dance appearance in April 1926 during the time when Winfield was appearing on Broadway in *Lulu Belle*. In spite of the dominance of female artists in American and German modern dance, Winfield may have been encouraged by seeing the small contingent of male dancers that began appearing on the scene by the late 1920s. The German concert dancer Harald Kreutzberg performed in America in 1929 and 1930; Ted Shawn's first solo performance was at Carnegie Hall in 1929; and Charles Weidman was also performing in New York at the end of the decade. These artists were undertaking new ventures, receiving increased attention from the press, and gaining wider audiences. Because of Winfield's healthy appetite for all types of theatrical experiences and his energetic involvement in the New York theater scene, it is safe to assume that he saw some of the groundbreaking dance events that were occurring around him.

Information about the teachers he had studied with up to this point in his career is sketchy. It is clear that he had some association with Ruth St. Denis, who would be one of the patrons of his first major dance concert, in 1931. This association came about through Edna Guy (a student of St. Denis), who shared that concert with him. Guy later mentioned that Winfield had studied with Mikhail Mordkin, who had been a member of the Bolshoi Ballet in Russia and later opened a studio in New York in 1924.[68] Helen Tamiris is also mentioned as having been associated with Winfield during the early days of his career. This is a strong possibility since Tamiris was a European-American modern dance pioneer who perhaps was the most racially liberal of her contemporaries. She is known to have taught dance classes in Harlem, and she was noted for her social activism and for her early interest in black subject matter as a source for dance. Her cycle *Negro Spirituals*, which she began in 1927, was among her best known works. When reviewing a 1933 program that Tamiris shared with the Bahamian Negro Dancers at Lewisohn Stadium, John Martin said of her: "She has often expressed her conviction of kinship with the Negro dance— the 'dance toward freedom.'"[69]

Despite the lack of information about Winfield's dance training and artistic influences during the late 1920s and early 1930s, it is clear that many of his theatrical experiences included involvement in dance; his appearances in *Salome* had led him further in that direction. He had

developed valuable skills that could be applied to dance theater, and
he had broadened his exploration of the choreographic process while
working on *De Promis' Lan'*. As he became more committed to his
new artistic direction, it became apparent that he would follow in the
footsteps of the major modern dancers of the time by casting himself
as the central focus of a company of dancers.

A typescript in the Schomburg Center for Research in Black Culture
contains Winfield's description of *Life and Death*, the dance he choreographed for *De Promis' Lan'*, which remained in his repertoire for
several years. As the personification of Life, standing center stage,
Winfield struggles for survival while dancers personifying Death (a
group of fifteen males at the Carnegie Hall performance) crawl toward
him and finally surround him. Life breaks free, is pursued from one
corner of the stage to another, and is agonizingly lifted into the air.
Again at center stage, the Death figures form a semicircle around Life,
begin to close in, and clamber over one another like amphibians struggling up a slippery bank and sliding back down. Life flees once more,
but finally, "Death surrounds Life, claws in mass movement, until
passion, will and strength are all gone. Life is no more. Death rises to
triumph."[70]

A photograph of *Life and Death* shows Winfield lying on the floor
surrounded by his group of male dancers. One of the dancers nearest
Winfield grips his hand so that their arms form one long, sinewy line.
The other dancers incline intently toward the center, their arms
stretching tautly toward the defeated protagonist.

The photograph is a visual metaphor for the relationship between
Winfield the charismatic dancer-choreographer and his devotees. As
in the works of other modern dancers of the time, the structure of his
choreography reflected in microcosm the organizational and social
structure of his fledgling dance company. In this relationship, the director-choreographer was the organizer, the teacher, and the one who
proceeded, with missionary zeal, to convince the dancers of the importance of their work.

There is little information that documents Winfield's activities
during the ten-month period between his Carnegie Hall appearance and
his next performance. Considering that this was a time when he was
making his final transition from drama to concert dance, it is possi-

ble that he put aside his hectic performance schedule and engaged in a reflective period of studying, rehearsing, and redefining his aesthetic goals.

When the New Negro Art Theatre presented its first full concert of dance, it had undergone another name change. On March 6, 1931, the company, which was still predominately male, appeared as the Bronze Ballet Plastique in a benefit performance for the Colored Citizen's Unemployment and Relief Committee in Yonkers at the Saunders Trade School. Perhaps Winfield felt that the dance contingent of his theatrical organization deserved a distinctive name, but, from all indications, this was the only time the group used that name. Among the dances on the program were *Jungle Wedding, Life and Death, St. James Infirmary,* and *Negro.* The concert was also Winfield's first collaboration with Edna Guy, whose contribution to the program consisted of two solos, *Madrassi Nautch* and *A Temple Offering.*[71]

In several respects, the Yonkers performance was a dress rehearsal for an event that would occur nearly two months later—a concert entitled the "First Negro Dance Recital in America." On the evening of April 29, 1931, this program was presented in what was popularly known as "The Theatre in the Clouds" at Lexington Avenue and Forty-second Street. The theater occupied the fiftieth and fifty-first floors of the Chanin Building, developer Irwin S. Chanin's Art Deco monument to modernity and efficiency. Though the Chanin Theatre's orchestra and mezzanine seated only two hundred, it was well equipped for concerts. The small auditorium was packed to capacity that April evening, and as one of the dancers, Randolph Sawyer, remembered, it seemed that "everybody in society was trying to get into the event."[72]

The program was another collaboration between Winfield and Edna Guy in which she functioned as co-director. Eighteen dancers participated in the performance, and with a few exceptions—such as the augmentation of the female members of the company with Ollie Burgoyne—the company was the same as had appeared earlier in the Yonkers performance.

The program consisted of thirteen dances. Two of the dances, *Ritual* and *Temple Offering,* were group works featuring Edna Guy. She also performed three solos, *A Figure from Angkor Wat, Get on Board Little Chillun',* and *Weeping Mary.* There was a duet for Winfield and Guy,

Song without Words, and Winfield also performed a solo, *Bronze Study.* His other choreographic contributions to the program consisted of two dances he performed with his group and four dances that were apparently performed by the group alone.[73]

John Martin called the concert "the outstanding novelty of the dance season" and commented that the Negro, though admirably suited, had not previously approached the concert dance field. He continued by saying that the program was an unmistakably worthy effort in which the performers "maintained an imperturbable poise."[74] Martin further noted that Edna Guy's performance of *Figure from Angkor Wat* was a "commendable effort" whereas Winfield's solo proved to be merely the exhibition of an exemplary physique. Martin went on to discriminate between these works and those that he felt were more appropriate for black artists: "It is not in these dances which echo and imitate the manner of the dancers of another race that the Negro dancers are at their best, but in those in which their forthrightness and simplicity have full play. Miss Guy's group of 'spirituals' and the primitive ritual dances by the group can be counted in this category."[75]

Martin's mention of the "forthrightness" and "simplicity" of the dancers was one more allusion to the idea of blacks as natural performers. His comments also reflected his bias concerning the inappropriateness of black dancers performing European-American dance techniques and styles, or, as he put it in a later article, the art of an "alien culture."

In addition to overlooking the fact (as will be discussed in the next chapter) that Guy had studied at Denishawn for six years by this time, Martin ignored the complexity of the African-American cultural experience in America. Among America's minorities, blacks were not first-generation arrivals; their ancestors had arrived in America more than three hundred years before. As mentioned earlier, they had begun to engage in a form of cultural syncretism that melded vestiges of their African heritage with European culture. Between blacks and whites, a complex web of borrowings and appropriations resulted in artistic amalgams—such as vernacular dance and music forms—that became a major part of American popular culture and also influenced serious art forms.

Several things seemed to escape the attention of proponents of the "alien culture" theory. First, the reverse process—whites successfully and lucratively capitalizing on elements of black culture, which, according to this line of thought, should have been considered alien to them—had been occurring for decades with little complaint from critics. The practice of having entirely white casts in dark makeup presenting dramas of "Negro life" was an example of this double standard.

Second, blacks had always been discriminated against socially and economically, but their access to and assimilation of mainstream cultural elements could not be so easily controlled. By the twentieth century, they were able to gain additional insight into European-American culture through the mass media. Radio, print media, and movies were accessible to most Americans in urban areas regardless of their race. As we have seen, in the little theater and pageantry movement blacks participated directly in national cultural trends. Other contemporary trends such as the physical culture movement were also not lost upon blacks. The musician and educator Maud Cuney-Hare, for example, included Dalcroze eurythmics (the movement system originated by the Swiss composer and teacher Emile Jaques-Dalcroze) as part of the curriculum of her little theater group in Boston as early as 1927.[76]

Only a year later, in another article, did John Martin admit that Winfield and Guy were not only attempting to join the new movement in American modern dance, but they were also achieving dance innovations in their own right. Another reviewer of the "First Negro Dance Recital in America," Charles D. Isaacson of *The Dance Magazine,* was full of praise and caught the excitement of auspicious beginnings in his enthusiastic tone. He predicted that within the next five years the most important development in dancing would come from the Negro; and that the New Negro Art Theatre's dances should be looked upon as important choreographic creations that would soon "rival the productions of the Russian Ballet."[77]

A month later the Chanin program was repeated in the more spacious Mansfield Theatre on West Forty-seventh Street. Shortly afterward, Winfield and Guy performed together for the last time, in a Broadway revue entitled *Fast and Furious.* This show, which lasted less than a week, was a collection of vignettes contributed by J. Rosamond Johnson, Porter Grainger, and Zora Neale Hurston. Critics found little that was noteworthy about the production. Among the dances was one from Winfield's repertoire, *Dance of Moods,* and Edna Guy performed *Madrassi Nautch.*

Winfield's 1932 season opened with several performances at Roerich Hall on Riverside Drive. These concerts took place on January 19 and 30 and February 6 and again indicated his affinity for working with large numbers of dancers. The program listed an "auxiliary dance group" numbering thirty-six in addition to the nineteen regular company members.[78]

The next place the company performed that year was a far cry from the tiny stage of the Chanin Theatre. They appeared in *Let Freedom Ring* with the Hall Johnson Chorale at the 6,000-seat Roxy Theatre. The performance, which took place during the third week of February, was another spectacle that traced the history of African Americans from slavery to the present. One critic called the program "a large and vital stage show, an intellectual, visual and artistic high spot in the Roxy's list of presentations."[79]

It was also on the occasion of the Roxy performance that Martin wrote an incisive essay about Winfield and his company and about black dance in general. Though more thoughtful than his earlier review of the Chanin performance, the piece still revealed some confusion about the direction African-American concert dancers should take. After he pointed out that returning to the primitive was a fundamental motivation in the development of modern dance, he went on to say that African primitivism was only "a few brief steps behind the Negro of today."[80] By referring to the African heritage of black dancers—though his time frame was inaccurate—Martin began to contextualize their choreography by acknowledging a cultural continuum that influenced their art.

In his article, he mentioned another important source for contemporary black dance, the African-American experience from slavery to the present. This source, in tandem with the African heritage, provided a rich storehouse of material on which to build a dance that would be wholly the product of racial culture. But, he continued, since this artistic undertaking had to be carried on in the midst of an alien civilization, there were two temptations that black artists could succumb to—either copying the white man's art or giving the white man what he choose to believe was Negro art. In Martin's opinion, Winfield had, fortunately, avoided both of these temptations and easy devices.[81] Though Martin did not indicate what Winfield had accomplished by avoiding these two pitfalls, he did mention several things that were exemplary in his work. He found Winfield's group to be professional and disciplined in their approach to their art in that they followed a strict schedule of rehearsals, classes, and regular performances.[82]

Martin's final appraisal was an interesting mixture of positive and negative comments that ended on a note of encouragement. After pointing out the crudity of the work, he went on: "The form of many of the compositions is confused and overelaborate; the composer's point is frequently not made because of so much accent upon unessential matters. . . . It is here . . . that he has most work to do if he is to hold his audiences. The many effective moments in his compositions to date give reliable evidence that he will eventually work his way out to a satisfactory conclusion."[83]

Keeping a close eye on Winfield's professional progress, the *Amsterdam News* announced the forthcoming ballet *Gambodi,* which was to be performed as the prologue for an adventure motion picture, *Explorers of the World.* The performance was to take place at the Westchester County Center on Saturday, April 23.[84] The *Dancers' Club News* announced in May that the same dance and film presentation would tour the New England states for twelve weeks.[85]

Winfield's growing interest in using the music of contemporary African-American composers was reflected in his next concert in Harlem when, on September 22, the Friends Amusement Guild presented his company at the Harlem Academy, 108 West 127th Street. The choreography included *Four Spirituals, Festival,* and a dance choreographed to the Duke Ellington piece "Mood Indigo." The other contemporary composers represented on the program were Lawrence Freeman, an African American, and David Guion, a European American. Freeman had written a number of operas and several cantatas, symphonic poems, and ballets. For Winfield's company, he composed new music for *The Slave Ballet,* a work for orchestra and choral ensemble. Guion was known for his concert arrangements of Negro and cowboy songs, and he had composed an African ballet, *Shingandi.* His contribution to the Harlem Academy program was the music for a dance entitled *Creation of Man.*[86]

Because of his growing reputation in the New York dance community, Winfield was invited to participate in a huge performance by local artists on December 11, 1932. Sponsored by the Dancers' Club, a service organization that provided various kinds of support for struggling artists, the Monster Benefit took place at Mecca Temple (now called City Center). The primary reason the event attracted so much attention was because of the number and variety of artists it involved. On the day of the performance, Martin explained in the *Times* that the eclectic nature of the upcoming concert was reflected in the fact that Ruth St. Denis, Ned Wayburn, and Michel Fokine were jointly directing the program. The balance of the article was spent listing the forty-five artists who were "positively guaranteed to appear."[87] By comparing Martin's list of performers with the one printed in the program, it appears that prominent no-shows were Martha Graham, Helen Tamiris, and Doris Humphrey. Among those who did appear were Ruth St. Denis, Charles Weidman, Bill "Bojangles" Robinson, Felicia Sorel, and Fred Astaire. Winfield had the distinction of performing the opening dance, *Dance of Moods,* and of having the only company that appeared twice on the program.[88] Martin was extremely pleased with the overall performance. He found the dancing to be of surprisingly high quality in spite of the fact that every conceivable type of dance was represented. He found no reason to discuss the comparative merits of the various performers and singled out for individual mention only Gertrude Hoffman's "masterly burlesque" of the German modern dancer Mary Wigman.[89]

After the Dancers' Club benefit, Winfield had planned to end his 1932 season with the initiation of a unique series of concerts. The Midnight Theater of the Negro Dance was to begin on Christmas Day at 229 Lenox Avenue and continue every Sunday night until further notice. These plans were postponed, however, after negotiations began for Winfield and his company to appear in the Metropolitan Opera production of *The Emperor Jones.*[90] Although Winfield had performed in major theaters and had begun to be recognized as an important force in the dance community, the Met engagement was the most prestigious performance opportunity he and his company had been offered so far. Martin later noted that the appearance of Winfield's group at the Met was the first time an entire dance company had been engaged by the opera since the Russian ballet stars Anna Pavlova and Mikhail Mordkin had performed there during their first two American seasons.[91]

The *Emperor Jones* project was conceived by Louis Gruenberg, a Russian emigré who had been brought to America at the age of two. By the time he was nineteen, he had begun traveling back and forth between Europe and America, during which time he studied in Berlin, was piano soloist with the Berlin Philharmonic Orchestra, and performed in Europe and America. The outbreak of World War I forced Gruenberg to remain in America, where he eventually retired as a pianist and devoted himself to composition. Early in his career, he began to focus his creative energies on incorporating what he considered "native American" elements into his music; his primary borrowings were from jazz and Negro spirituals. His compositions included *The Daniel Jazz*, for tenor and eight instruments; *The Creation*, scored for baritone and eight instruments and incorporating sermons written by James Weldon Johnson; and the piano pieces *Jazzberries*, *Jazz Masks*, and *Six Jazz Epigrams*.[92]

In using African-American musical elements in his works, Gruenberg belonged to a growing list of European and American composers who had done the same. Anton Dvořák, in his *New World Symphony* (1894), had used themes from Negro spirituals to great effect. Darius Milhaud used jazz elements in his 1925 ballet *La Création du Monde*. Aaron Copland used the rhythmic patterns and harmonic sequences of jazz in his *Piano Concerto*; George Gershwin's *Rhapsody in Blue* was an example of the same type of usage that received praise during the 1920s.[93]

Gruenberg had received Eugene O'Neill's permission to adapt the drama for the operatic stage approximately two years prior to the January 7, 1933, premiere at the Met. The original play, which had its first performance at the Provincetown Playhouse twelve years earlier, told the story of Brutus Jones, a black man who escaped from an American prison and found his way to an island in the West Indies. He cunningly appeals to the superstitions of the natives, exploits them, and appoints himself emperor. They rebel, however, and begin to pursue Jones through the jungle, where—because of his fear and panic—he is tormented by a series of hallucinatory visions: "the formless fears";

his imprisonment; the murder he has committed; and his atavistic memories of a slave ship and an auction block. During his attempted escape, Jones discards the garish trappings of his emperor's uniform until he has stripped to a loin-cloth. He discovers that he has traveled in a circle during his attempt to escape, and his pursuers capture and kill him. O'Neill's expressionistic telling of the story elucidated the conflict between man's attempts to reshape his world to fit his perceptions of what it should be and the reality of the atavistic forces within him that ultimately determine his destiny. Brutus Jones's "civilization" finally succumbs to the "primitive" within.

Originally, arrangements had been made for the opera to open in Berlin, but those plans were abandoned because of concern about the rise of Adolf Hitler's National Socialist Party in Germany. An alternative was proposed by one of the opera's most energetic supporters, Olin Downes, music critic for the *New York Times*. He convinced Giulio Gatti-Casazza, general manager of the Metropolitan Opera, to premiere the work in New York during the 1932–33 season.

To create a libretto from the original drama, Gruenberg received permission from O'Neill to make a number of changes. Some lines were deleted while others were repeated for emphasis. In an article that appeared three months before the opera's premiere, Downes discussed other changes. A Negro soldier's chorus would be added to comment on the stage action. A spiritual, "Standin' in the Need of Prayer," would be sung by Jones at a critical moment near the end of the opera. Finally, instead of being murdered by his pursuers, Jones would commit suicide.[94]

After *The Emperor Jones* premiered, critical opinion was divided about the changes, as well as about the merit of the opera as a whole. Downes led the affirmative camp. He felt that the chorus was an important addition that became the embodiment of the forces bent on destroying Jones. He commented that this was a "musical transmutation of the essence of the play."[95] He also felt that the addition of the Negro spiritual—at a point where Jones had become repentant—worked effectively to establish sympathy for a character who had few redeeming features. Furthermore, Jones's singing of the spiritual provided the only true "moment of lyrical expansion" in the opera.[96] On the other hand, Paul Rosenfeld of the *New Republic* found the "interludial outcries," "the blood-curdling shrieks and bellowings of the chorus" to be merely noisy. He found little of merit in the opera that was not inherent in the original play.[97] Rosenfeld was referring to Gruenberg's use of expressionistic music techniques that incorporated dissonance, complex rhythmic patterns, and *sprechtstimme,* or song-speech, in the place of arias. These elements were used to help convey the ever-growing terror of Brutus Jones.

The critic who gave the opera its most positive review was, again, Olin Downes. He called it "the finest American opera yet produced anywhere."[98] This was faint praise considering the fact that very few American operas had been produced at the Met since its founding in 1883. Most critics commended Lawrence Tibbett, the singer who portrayed Jones. *Time* magazine was impressed with his realistic interpretation of a Negro; and he was complimented for his rendition of the spiritual, which sent chills down the audience's spines.[99]

Winfield's role as the hallucinatory witch doctor received as much critical attention as Tibbett's performance. Appearing at the most important point in the opera, when Jones has exhausted himself and is ready to cease his attempt to escape, the witch doctor danced the final incantation that sealed Jones's doom. As originally planned, Winfield and the chorus were to make their entrance by clambering onto the stage from the orchestra pit, but because there was no room, the plans had to be changed. Instead, Winfield entered alone, squeezing awkwardly onto the stage through the prompter's box. According to Downes, the witch doctor's entrance created a nightmarish effect as he appeared like a horrible snake rising from the ground.[100] To enhance his menacing appearance, Winfield was covered from head to foot with swirling patterns of light-colored body paint. Through his dancing, Winfield became the personification of Jones's fears and the leader of his pursuers. After he cast his hypnotic spell, he was joined by the chorus as it closed in on its victim. At a climactic moment, Jones ended his life with the last of his six silver bullets, which he had convinced the natives were the only effective instruments of his destruction.

Mary Watkins of the *New York Herald Tribune* was one of the dance critics who reviewed *The Emperor Jones,* and Winfield's performance seemed to mesmerize her. For her, the thrilling dance event that was included in the opera was a welcome relief from the uninspired dance

performances that usually accompanied Metropolitan Opera productions. She found the dancing appropriately shocking, raw, and violent:

> Mr. Winfield was, as a matter of fact, after Mr. Tibbett, the hero of the
> occasion. Such vocalization as he contributed, extemporary or not, was
> fittingly and effectively enunciated, and his sinister and frantic caperings
> as the Witch Doctor made even the most sluggish, opera-infected blood
> run cold. . . . The scene as the curtain fell was a vortex of horrid gaiety, a
> bloody revel for which Death beat the intoxicating rhythms. . . . Congrat-
> ulation to whomever was inspired to seek out Mr. Winfield and make his
> achievement possible, either through sage direction or carte blanche.[101]

After *The Emperor Jones* was performed for the last time, on February 11, 1933, Winfield turned his attention to other projects. In the
spring of that year, he began planning a revival of his mother's play,
Wade in De Water, with a cast that included his own company and
well-known black actors such as Laura Bowman and Lawrence
Chenault.[102] In July of that same year, he presented an outdoor concert at the Lido Terrace on West 146th Street. The concert again featured the music of black composers such as Duke Ellington, Alston
Burleigh, and William Grant Still. And in October, he took part in a
program organized by the Workers' Dance League at the 135th Street
YWCA.

The Workers' Dance League was an organization of leftist dance
groups: the New Dance Group, the New Duncan Dancers, the Rebel
Dancers, the Red Dancers, and the Theatre Union Dance Group. "What
Shall the Negro Dance About?" was the first in a series of forums sponsored by the league. Winfield and his company performed *Red Lacquer
and Jade*, a suite of seven dances, and two members of the Workers'
Dance League (including the black dancer Add Bates) performed the
choreographer Edith Segal's *Black and White Solidarity Dance*, which
dealt with the theme of class solidarity among workers. Bates, who had
been working with Segal's Red Dancers for several months, later distinguished himself in several productions sponsored by the Federal
Theatre and Dance Programs, including Charles Weidman's *Candide*
and an all-black production of *Androcles and the Lion* with stage
movement choreographed by Helen Tamiris.

The performance section of "What Shall the Negro Dance About?"
was followed by an open forum. Bates—a member of the Communist

Party—called for a more militant direction for black artists. Another (unidentified) member of the audience spoke with revolutionary zeal: "We have come to a newer type of dance . . . a dance that has social significance. Since we recognize the Negro as an exploited race, our dance should express the strivings of the new Negro. It should express our struggle for social, economic and political equality and our part in the struggle against war."[103] Winfield's comments were brief and comparatively low-key. He said that there were fundamental human feelings to be expressed in movement regardless of race. But he also acknowledged the significance of the African heritage and African-American folk traditions in dance. He concluded by simply saying, "It's hard for me to say what the Negro should dance about. What has anyone to dance about?"[104]

His questioning attitude seemed to be an appropriate one for him to have assumed at this point in his career. The variety of approaches he had used to bring black performers into the mainstream of American theater and dance reflected the self-searching quandary of Harlem Renaissance artists who struggled to find their identity in a world that was complex with racial issues. In his attempt to solve the problems of black performers, Winfield decided to cover as many bases as possible. Much of his tremendous appetite for different theatrical experiences came from his youthful enthusiasm and optimism. But it also came from his insatiable desire to experience New York's cultural scene to the fullest so that he could better understand the role that he and other black artists could play in it.

There is little record that Winfield spoke about the strategy of using art to improve the status of black people in American society. But he seemed to know instinctively that his presence and the presence of his company members would have an impact that would eventually result in increased respect for black performers and for his people. Every aspect of his career contributed to that end.

He did not (as Langston Hughes's hypothetical poet might have done) try to escape his racial identity by going to Greenwich Village and becoming totally absorbed by the avant-garde movement. Instead, he made artistic sorties—looking, participating, digesting—and then returned to Harlem or Yonkers to share what he had learned and incorporate what he could use into black art.

Having achieved what he did during a time when racial prejudice was a severe impediment to all efforts of African Americans to improve their lot in American society, Winfield certainly had many reasons to ask the question, What shall the Negro dance about? His participation in the Dance League's forum might have indicated the beginning of a phase of his career in which he would find new answers to this question. The regularity with which critics had mentioned his leadership, discipline, dedication, and blossoming artistry pointed toward a special promise, the promise of continued development of his individual aesthetic, even greater artistic output, and the codification of a dance technique that took into account the cultural roots of black artists. As it turned out, however, these tasks would be left to others, and his pioneering efforts would be cut short.

According to his mother, Winfield became exhausted and suffered a "breakdown" in October 1933 because of overwork, concern over how he would sustain his company after the Met success, and worry over family problems.[105] Because of further medical complications that led to pneumonia, he was hospitalized three months later at New York Hospital on East Sixty-eighth Street. While there, he named one of his dancers, Leonard Barros, to be his replacement in *The Emperor Jones*, which was scheduled for a repeat performance at the Met during the first week of January 1934. From his hospital bed, he sent directions to his rehearsing company.[106]

Winfield died on January 15, 1934. His body was returned to Yonkers where his funeral was held at his parent's home. Three weeks later, more than 150 friends and relatives attended a memorial service at the last studio he had used at 232 West 135th Street. A portrait of Winfield by the noted Harlem Renaissance sculptor Augusta Savage was unveiled by Richard Sylvester, general manager of the Dancers' Club. Sylvester remarked, "Mr. Winfield was the pioneer in Negro concert dancing. In that field he attained for his race an eminence comparable to that of Paul Robeson in the musical field. He achieved amazing results in such a short time."[107]

The New Negro Art Theatre completed its second run of *The Emperor Jones* at the Metropolitan Opera with Leonard Barros performing Winfield's role, and the opera was performed in Hartford, Connecticut, on January 30. It was announced that the company would continue with Barros directing the dance component and Albert Patrick directing the drama component,[108] but apparently the company dissolved very quickly without the charismatic leadership of its founder. The New York press carried no further mention of its activities. It would be several years before another African-American dance company would receive the recognition that had been garnered by Winfield and his company.

3

Edna Guy, Randolph Sawyer, and Ollie Burgoyne

ONE OF THE MOST IMPORTANT WAYS in which Hemsley Winfield's work had an impact on the African-American artistic community was through the performance experiences his company provided for large numbers of aspiring black dancers and actors. Most of these individuals were novices who did not pursue performing careers after the New Negro Art Theatre was discontinued. A few, however, had trained and performed before appearing with Winfield and continued to do so after his death. The most important of these were Edna Guy, Randolph Sawyer, and Ollie Burgoyne. Edna Guy's distinction among these dancers was that she had been a featured performer in Winfield's earliest dance concerts and had also co-directed his seminal New York concert, the "First Negro Dance Recital in America."

Edna Guy

Guy was born in 1907 in Summit, New Jersey, and attended public schools there. Little is known about her mother and father except that they were supportive parents who, in spite of their poor economic situation, encouraged their daughter's early interest in dance and tried to find money to contribute to her training as best they could. As an only child, she was an introverted dreamer who escaped from loneliness by reading, writing poetry, and, as a teen-ager, writing letters to her idol, Ruth St. Denis. Her many letters to St. Denis date from 1923 to 1940.[1]

The young girl first met St. Denis in October 1922 after sending her a note during the intermission of a concert.[2] When the dancer appeared at the stage door wearing an Egyptian costume and smiling beatifically, she seemed to Guy to be a heavenly apparition.[3] St. Denis wrote of this first meeting in her autobiography, *An Unfinished Life.* She was touched by the poetic note that was signed "Edna Guy, Colored Girl." She remembered that the young girl expressed her intense desire to dance; and she said that the relationship they established that day eventually led to Guy's studying and living at Denishawn and touring with the Denishawn company as a wardrobe mistress and personal assistant. In St. Denis's words: "From that day until now I have been her white mama."[4] The mother-daughter relationship alluded to by St. Denis became very important in Guy's life after her mother died in 1926.

Soon after they met, Guy visited St. Denis at the Denishawn School, which was headquartered in a brownstone on West Twenty-eighth Street in Manhattan. After asking for advice about how she should approach her dance training, Guy agreed that she should not begin studying at Denishawn until her basic dance technique was stronger. In the meantime, she would remain with her current teacher (referred to only as Miss Linnel in her letters), who taught her private classes in New York on weekends.[5] Guy continued to enjoy Linnel's classes but realized that she was missing the challenge and stimulation of studying among other students; consequently, she began looking for another studio that would permit her to attend.

Her search was disappointing. First she tried a studio directed by the Broadway dance director Anthony Nelle on West Fifty-eighth Street. He sounded encouraging at their initial meeting, and there seemed to be a strong possibility that she would be accepted as a student. But during a second visit, he apologetically told her that she could not enroll because the other students would be upset.[6] She had a similar experience when she wrote to investigate the possibility of attending Portia Mansfield's school in Steamboat Springs, Colorado, during the summer of 1924. Though Mansfield was impressed with the teen-ager's sensitive and articulate letter, she too expressed concern about the prejudices of her students and their parents.[7]

Guy looked into other schools in New York, but she apparently continued studying with Miss Linnel until arrangements were made to begin classes at Denishawn. In a letter dated August 31, 1924, Guy mentioned making plans to begin attending Denishawn in October. According to the Denishawn brochure for that year, the seven-month winter course began on October 22 and consisted of two hours of class and one hour of practice five days a week.[8] The full course cost seven hundred dollars.[9] The price was steep for Guy's parents, but St. Denis arranged for the payments to be made in installments.[10]

Dressed in the long black bathing suit that was the Denishawn class uniform, Guy began attending classes. Based on Ted Shawn's belief that ballet was an essential part of a dancer's training, the classes at Denishawn were structured around a free adaptation of ballet technique.[11] Students began with a half-hour of stretches and exercises at the barre, then moved on to center-floor exercises. This section of the class usually ended with a non-balletic exercise called "Arms and Body," a loose swinging of arms that increased in range until it involved the torso in large swooping and circling movements. Movement combinations across the floor included steps such as *jeté, pas de chat,* and *pas de bourrée,* which differed somewhat from the academic ballet steps of the same names; the class concluded with the students learning sections of dances using stylized movement from countries such as Spain, Tunisia, and Greece.[12]

Guy's primary teacher at Denishawn was Katherine Edson, who taught technique classes as well as classes in dramatic gesture based upon the teachings of François Delsarte. Guy also received private classes from Paul Mathis and repertory classes from Hazel Krans, who taught her dances such as *Temple Bells* and the *Dancing Girl of Delhi.*[13] Studying at Denishawn was a dream come true, which Guy summed up in her own words: "The future holds too much brightness for me—I smile, I learn, I dance, and wait—and I'm happy."[14]

During her first year at Denishawn, Guy worked hard. She received special attention from her teachers, who took a particular liking to her and pressured her to try to achieve her maximum potential. Her evenings consisted of more dance practice and attending classes at Hunter College, where she studied typing and shorthand.[15] During her second year at the school, the Denishawn Dancers toured the Orient, from September 1925 to November 1926. Guy continued her daily studies and anxiously followed the news of the company's progress as recounted in the American press and in the letters she received from St. Denis.

After St. Denis and Shawn returned, they immediately embarked upon several tours of the United States. The first of these lasted from December 1926 to April 1927. Their next tour—the first one during which Guy traveled with the company as St. Denis's personal assistant—lasted from September 1927 to May 1928. Organized by George Wintz, the tour was a particularly distasteful undertaking for St. Denis because the Denishawn Dancers performed as part of a Ziegfeld Follies road company. Though the tour was very lucrative, it conflicted with St. Denis's ideas concerning her artistic mission of bringing serious art to the American public. To keep her audiences interested, she found herself relying more and more on cheap theatrics; and she was dispirited when Wintz removed one of her dances, "White Jade," from the program because "it did not have enough pep for a Follies program and it puzzled her audiences."[16]

Although it was the first time Guy had come into constant contact with her mentor, it was also the beginning of a period of particularly strained relationships between the two. The crux of Guy's dissatisfaction was her feeling that the woman she worshiped so completely seemed to become more distant and uncaring as the tour progressed. Guy was now twenty years old, but her obsessive, almost childlike attachment to St. Denis had grown since the death of her mother. The letters and poems she wrote were always full of worshipful imagery in which she depicted herself as a servant and St. Denis as a mistress/goddess. In one poem she spoke of St. Denis as being "utterly beautiful," and she spoke of bowing down to her in "devotion and humbleness."[17]

Guy's adulation of St. Denis was not unusual for a young woman of her time. During her long career, St. Denis had become a role model for many young women, a cult figure of sorts, a standard of spiritual beauty and sublime womanhood. But the intensely personal nature of St. Denis and Guy's particular relationship brought more complex dynamics into play. The younger woman had developed psychological and emotional bonds that in some ways had been encouraged by the older. This was typical of St. Denis's relationships with the women that were close to her. St. Denis's biographer, Suzanne Shelton, quotes her concerning these matters: "Something in me attracts and holds them in a strong selfless devotion. . . . They believe in me and serve my ideals with enthusiasm and endless patience. I in turn am egotistically unresponsive, sometimes to the point of cruelty on the merely human side, while being deeply grateful in the spiritual."[18]

Guy's race added another dimension to the complexity of the situation. Not only was she a servant in a spiritual sense, but she was a servant to St. Denis in the real sense of being an employee who served her personal needs. During the Ziegfeld tour, Guy had to endure the racial prejudice she encountered as the company traveled through the South. She continued to write her thoughts and feelings to St. Denis even when they were traveling together. In one of these letters she hinted that St. Denis was in some way responsible for the painful slights she felt because of racism. At a moment when she seemed particularly distraught, Guy mentioned that she had been warned that St. Denis would turn out to be "like all other white people." In a bitter conclusion, she said that she would continue to be the "perfect servant."[19]

Many things had changed since St. Denis became fascinated with the intelligent and sensitive girl who had come backstage to meet her five years before. At a period in her life when her career was beginning to wane, her marriage was approaching its final stage of deterioration, and her artistic integrity had been compromised, St. Denis had little emotional energy to squander on Guy.

Taking a short break from the Ziegfeld tour, St. Denis and Shawn returned to New York in December 1927. They were elated to find the project they had begun after their tour of the Orient was now completed—a new home for Denishawn at 67 Stevenson Street in Van Cortlandt Park in the Bronx. Guy's letters do not indicate exactly when she moved into the spacious Moorish-style mansion, but she was living there when she penned the following words on Christmas night of 1928: "Someone to serve—when I am with you—the attendant to the great Goddess—with service and love and love always."[20]

Guy continued to accompany St. Denis on her tours during the latter part of 1929 and early 1930. Because of the extreme anxiety and depression the young woman was suffering from during this period, she began to express fears about her mental stability and asked St. Denis to assist her in finding help.[21] Guy's emotional problems and the pressures of St. Denis's unraveling professional and domestic life deepened the rift between the two. According to one of Guy's letters, the situation apparently came to a head when Guy and Pearl Wheeler (Denishawn's talented costume designer, whose designs contributed significantly to the company's popular success) had a heated argument in July 1930.[22] As Jane Sherman points out, Wheeler was also St. Denis's friend and confidant, "the guardian dragon of the dressing room door."[23] It is easy to see how competition for St. Denis's attention might have led to conflict between her two devoted assistants, with Guy coming out the loser. Shortly after their altercation, St. Denis asked Guy to leave Denishawn. Speaking of this period Guy said, "Sometimes like a sudden summer rain, through my consciousness comes the feeling that you are gently but forcefully pushing me out of your life."[24]

Another reality that must have disheartened Guy was the fact that she had never become a member of the company. For all the idealistic desires she expressed about dance in her letters to St. Denis, she never mentioned any hope of joining the Denishawn Dancers. She probably realized—particularly after traveling with them—that such a hope was unrealistic. On the other hand, it is likely that St. Denis's wide-ranging touring experiences, which kept her fingers on the pulse of American audiences, made her realize that the late 1920s was not the time to present a racially integrated company.

Guy's separation from Denishawn seems to have been the impetus she needed to begin exploring the possibilities of a career of her own. She had performed only in student recitals during the six-year period of her closest association with St. Denis. One such performance was a program presented by Denishawn students for Franklin D. Roosevelt, who was governor of New York at the time.[25]

After leaving Denishawn, Guy struggled to survive by doing odd jobs as a maid, a cook, and an artist's model. As she tried to weather the early years of the Great Depression, her life became increasingly difficult; and she was forced to live with various friends or stay in boardinghouses in New York City. At some point during this period, she met Hemsley Winfield. It may have been during one of her unsuccessful auditions for shows and revues where, according to her, she was always rejected because she was not the right type—the type she described as "the light-skinned girls with the 'flashing eyes' who always get the parts."[26] As a young black woman trying to establish a serious career in dance, there seemed to be no place for her in New York theaters of the time. Her fortuitous meeting with Winfield was the event that enabled her to begin to make a place for herself.

As mentioned earlier, Guy was performing as a featured artist with the New Negro Art Theatre by March 1931. The dances she performed on her first program with Winfield (the March 6 performance at the Saunders Trade School in Yonkers) were primarily in the style of Ruth St. Denis. Among these, the *Madrassi Nautch* Guy choreographed was a variation on one of the most popular types of dances in the Denishawn repertoire, a type that St. Denis had been performing in one form or another since 1908. In describing one of St. Denis's nautch dances (*The Green Nautch* of 1919), Jane Sherman, a former Denishawn dancer, said it was "impertinent, vain, and outrageously flirty."[27] The dance included fluidly rippling arms, coquettish little runs, spiraling turns, wickedly raised eyebrows, and a *danse du ventre;* it was enhanced by the swirl of yards and yards of colorful fabric and tinkling jewelry at the ankles and wrists.[28] Considering Guy's adulation of St. Denis, no doubt she recreated this sensuous and exotic image as closely as possible.

Guy's contribution to the second concert she co-directed with Winfield in April 1931 (the "First Negro Dance Recital in America") included a St. Denis–style dance, *A Figure from Angkor Wat.* It is not clear whether the choreography was by Guy or St. Denis. Quite possibly, St. Denis restaged one of her solos, *Bas-relief Figure from Angkor-Wat,* for Guy. The original St. Denis solo, choreographed in 1929, had later been expanded to include other dancers and had been premiered at Lewisohn Stadium in August 1930. The larger version of the dance painted a picture of a day in the life of a Cambodian king. Its central section was the solo for St. Denis as the Naga Queen, symbol of the principle of wisdom.[29] When Guy performed *A Figure from Angkor Wat,* John Martin, as stated earlier, was not very impressed.

At the Chanin Theatre concert, Guy also presented works that were not in the St. Denis style, most notably her "dance spirituals." She later spoke of these dances, which interpreted the deeply religious emotions of African-American slaves, as first being inspired when she heard Paul Robeson sing.[30] Although she considered herself the initiator of this dance genre,[31] the accuracy of her claim is questionable because Helen Tamiris had used spirituals in the suite of dances she began choreographing in 1927. Moreover, it is highly probable that Charles Williams or some of his co-workers at Hampton Institute had begun experimenting with the choreographic use of spirituals before Tamiris.

In spite of their earlier rift in 1930, Guy and St. Denis continued their involvement in each other's lives. St. Denis was one of the patrons for the Chanin concert and, as mentioned above, she either contributed the choreography for or consulted with Guy about one of the dances.

After St. Denis performed with Shawn for the last time in 1931, she entered a three-year period that she described as "increasingly barren, with a strange gray aridity and no real sense of substance."[32] At some point during this time, she and Guy reconciled their differences and reestablished some of their former closeness. St. Denis remembered that during this particularly bitter period in her life, there were a few friends she could count on. Guy remained one of them: "I would throw myself wearily on my bed[,] my little Edna Guy would softly bring the Bible and, crouching down by my side, find some lovely page from the Psalms, and the beautiful lines, half-chanted, half-spoken, would gradually lull me to sleep. It was then I called her my little black prophetess as she called me her white prophetess."[33]

Another example of their continuing involvement was a program Guy organized in May 1931, shortly after the Chanin concert. The evening's presentation, which took place in the auditorium of Harlem's 138th Street YWCA, consisted of Guy's choreography, which she performed along with a group of dancers she had been training. Afterward, St. Denis presented a lecture entitled "Dance as an Art," during which she complimented Guy for the talent she exhibited in the field of dance and for the performance she had presented that afternoon.[34]

Several months after she appeared on the joint program with St. Denis, Guy became associated with the Dance Centre, a studio-theater located at 105 West Fifty-sixth Street, which was directed by Senia Gluck-Sandor. Gluck-Sandor had trained at the Neighborhood Playhouse, and he had also performed with the Metropolitan Opera Ballet and toured with Adolph Bolm. His wife and co-director, Felicia Sorel, had studied with Michel Fokine and Mary Wigman. Their company became noted for its evening-length dances that mixed ballet and modern idioms, and they also had the distinction of establishing one of the first racially integrated companies in New York. Along with Guy, Gluck-Sandor and Sorel welcomed another black dancer who was an ex-member of Winfield's company, Randolph Sawyer.

In August 1931, *The Dance Magazine* announced that Edna Guy would have "an important role" in yet another reincarnation of *Salome,* to be presented at the Dance Centre.[35] The performance took place in October, and when it was reviewed one critic described it as "the most interesting dance endeavor of years." He found the production to be a refreshingly unpretentious combination of dance and theater, and he had the highest praise for Salome, as portrayed by Sorel, and the rest of the cast—Harry Losee, Charles Laskey, and Dorothy Lee. Unfortunately, the only mention he made of Guy and Sawyer was that they added pictorially to the ensemble.[36] Apparently, both artists' roles were minor since they did not receive further comment.

In April 1932 the New York *Age* announced that Guy was preparing her first fully mounted independent concert.[37] For this performance, at Roerich Hall on May 7, she presented five solos. Among these was *African Plastique,* her first attempt to use African themes as a source for her choreography. Other solos that had not been seen in her earlier collaborations with Winfield were *Luleta's Dance* and *After Gaugin* [sic]. In addition, she presented two group pieces performed by eight dancers, *Gimme Yo' Han'* and *Juba.*[38]

By this time, Guy was attempting to maintain a company of her own, but her lack of performances during 1933 indicates that she was not very successful. In 1934, however, she did present a concert at Studio 61, Carnegie Hall, on April 24. In a review of the performance in the *Dance Observer,* the critic Ralph Taylor began by saying, "Contrary to expectations, Miss Guy has none of the loose-jointed flippancy usually associated with the negro dancer." He then went on to make remarks that were similar to John Martin's appraisal of her and Winfield in their Chanin concert. According to Taylor, her more serious numbers, such as *In the Night* and *Chudda Plastique,* were beyond her capacity and too studied; but in the danced spirituals "her charming blend of lightness of movement and naivete of posture gave the songs an authentic outline."[39]

Randolph Sawyer also participated in the concert as guest artist. He was complimented on possessing "a powerful and beautifully modeled physique"; but, in spite of showing definite potential as a dancer, his solos, *Blues* and *Dance African,* were considered "rudimentary in theme and treatment."[40] Guy's concert appearances continued to be few, but she participated in two events that involved her in the wider New York dance community. The first of these—the First National Dance Congress and Festival—was organized by the Dancers' Association, the New Dance League, and the Dance Guild. It attracted fourteen hundred people to performances and lectures in New York between May 19 and May 25, 1936. In addition to Guy, the black participants were Alison Burroughs, Leonore Cox (who presented a lecture, "On a Few Aspects of Negro Dancing," during the congress), and a group of Bahamian dancers. On May 24, Guy performed two of her spirituals in a concert that she shared with Mura Dehn and Roger Pryor Dodge.[41]

John Martin found very little positive to say about the congress. Since it was hastily organized, he said, there was no representative participation from outside of New York; therefore, calling it "national" was a misnomer. He felt that there were glaring absences from the programs because of artists who were either unable or unwilling to perform.[42] (He believed this even though the programs included artists such as Charles Weidman, Anna Sokolow, Helen Tamiris, Gluck-Sandor, Felicia Sorel, José Limón, Letitia Ide, Jane Dudley, and Hanya Holm.) Martin continued, "It became clearly evident that this was not a dance congress at all, but an unofficial political rally making use of the dance merely as a springboard. . . . Certainly the young left-wingers, who kept the congress in their own hands, must accept responsibility for its ineffectualness."[43]

Among the few positive aspects of the congress he mentioned were some "hopeful" resolutions that were passed during the final session. These included one concerning black dancers: "Whereas the Negro People in America have been subject to segregation and suppression which has limited their development in the field of creative dance, be it resolved that the Dance Congress encourage and sponsor the work of the Negro People in the creative fields."[44] This vote of confidence encouraged Guy and Burroughs to begin making plans for another important dance event that would occur the following year. Together they organized the *Negro Dance Evening*, which took place on March 7, 1937, in the Theresa L. Kaufmann Auditorium of the Ninety-second Street YM-YWHA. Like the dance congress before it, it was composed of a variety of artists, but this time they were all black. It was the first joint undertaking of its kind and caliber in America, and it was a credit to the vision and organizational skills of Guy and Burroughs.

Alison Burroughs was the daughter of Charles Burroughs, who directed and performed in pageants during the early 1920s (including W. E. B. Du Bois's *Star of Ethiopia*) and was also associated with the little theater movement in Boston and Harlem. By 1931, she was following her father's interest in the arts. As reported in *The Crisis*, she traveled to Geneva, Switzerland, where she studied at one of Emile Jaques-Dalcroze's schools of eurythmics.[45] Little else is known about her dance career except that she taught at the New Dance League School at one point and had also performed with the choreographer and social activist Edith Segal as early as 1929.

Burroughs and Guy's 1937 *Negro Dance Evening* was organized to create an overview of the aesthetic range of black dance from different cultures of the African diaspora. Among the artists presented was the African dancer Asadata Dafora. He appeared with two of his company members, Abdul Assen and Alma Sutton, in six dances that comprised the first part of the program. Katherine Dunham and six of her dancers traveled from Chicago to perform Caribbean dances in the second section of the program, "West Indies." "United States," the third section of the program, opened with *Shout*, performed by Guy and Burroughs along with Clarence Yates, Archie Savage, and Leonard Barros, the latter of whom had danced with Winfield's company. The fourth and final section of the program, "Modern Trends," opened with a solo each for Guy, Burroughs, and Dunham—dancing, respectively, *After Gaugin, Composition,* and *Moorish Dance*—and closed with *Negro Songs of Protest*, which was co-choreographed by Guy and Burroughs.[46]

J. A. Kaye of *Dance* magazine called the program "spectacular entertainment" that was "fascinating both for its dance and ethnographic content."[47] His highest praise was reserved for Asadata Dafora, whose choreography he held superior to that of the other artists on the program: "Of all interpreters of the Negro dance, Asadata Dafora Horton is undoubtedly the best." Alison Burroughs's solo was called "sincerely designed and sincerely performed." Kaye concluded by saying that Katherine Dunham's dances, in spite of their exotic subject matter, lacked character and tended to be dull.[48]

Overall, the concert was an extremely successful effort. There had been other attempts to create programs of this sort (for example, the historical pageants of Winfield). But this was the first time the participating artists had specialized knowledge about each type of dance they performed—Asadata Dafora in the dances of his native Africa, Katherine Dunham in Caribbean dance, and Dunham, Guy, and Burroughs in modern dance. For Guy, the organization of this event was one of her major contributions to the development of black concert dance. In *Black Dance,* Lynne Fauley Emery emphasizes this fact by saying, "'The Negro Dance Evening' brought together the established and the rising generations, the people who opened the door and those who stepped across the threshold."[49]

Guy's most successful endeavors seem to have been large projects in which she participated with other artists. Her next important project of this type was Dance International, an even longer and more elaborate affair than the First National Dance Congress. This dance exposition, which lasted from November 21, 1937, to January 2, 1938, took place at Rockefeller Center and included performances by approximately forty groups of dancers from around the world. There were also exhibits of dance-related books, paintings, sculptures, photographs, and costumes on view daily.

During the final week of the festival, Edna Guy and her group of dancers appeared in concerts at the Rainbow Room (one of several locations where performances were given) on December 28 and 30. They shared both programs with a remarkable variety of artists including Bill Robinson, Esther Junger, dancers from the Philippines, groups representing both North and South American Indians, Mexican dancers, and American square dancers.[50]

Following Dance International, there are fewer accounts of Guy's activities. She opened a school in New York in 1938, but (judging from the lack of information about it) it was apparently short-lived and unsuccessful. She also presented a few concerts that same year, one of which she shared with Frances Atkins and Randolph Sawyer at the Lincoln School for Nurses on May 1;[51] and one of her last performances was at the 135th Street YMCA Little Theatre on May 21, 1939.[52]

By 1941 she had married Walter McCully and moved to the village of Enfield, New Hampshire, where she and her husband renovated an old farmhouse that they ran as a guest lodging. By this time, she had given up her dance career. No doubt the disappointments of trying to survive as an artist during the Depression had dampened her lifelong desire to pursue a career in dance. Whatever yearning she may have had to recapture her dream was destroyed because of health problems. During the mid-1940s, she suffered a series of heart attacks and was told that she could no longer engage in strenuous activities.

By the 1960s, she was living in Hudson, New York, and teaching in the recreation department of the New York State Training School for Girls. At one point, she wrote to John Martin to ask his assistance in getting dance supplies for her students. In one of his columns, he responded by asking for donations after reminding his readers of who she was—"Edna Guy McCully (who used to dance as Edna Guy with Ruth St. Denis and Hemsley Winfield and was something of a pioneer in the Negro concert dance)."[53] She died in 1982 in Fort Worth, Texas, where she had lived for eight years.

Though Edna Guy was able to sustain a dance career for a longer period than was Hemsley Winfield, her contributions to the development of blacks in concert dance were not as extensive as his. Perhaps her retiring personality and her emotional problems kept her from maintaining the momentum needed to keep herself in the public spotlight, produce more concerts, and gain wider public and critical attention. Through her training at the Denishawn School, her travels with the Denishawn Dancers, and the concerts she was able to produce, she did, however, serve as a role model for younger black performers. She proved that a black woman working exclusively in the field of concert dance could gain a certain amount of recognition during a time when that was unheard of. In these respects she was a first. In a 1938 article in the Dance Herald, she reminded readers of this fact by stating that the Negro dancers who were currently attempting to pursue concert careers could study at many New York dance studios because of three pioneering individuals—Hemsley Winfield, Edna Guy, and Katherine Dunham.[54]

Guy's role in directing and organizing the *Negro Dance Evening* and her involvement in organizations such as the American Dance Association (where she served on the conference committee in 1939) indicated that one of her most valuable contributions to the development of black concert dance was her role as a facilitator.

Randolph Sawyer

The male member of Winfield's company who had the most successful performing career was Randolph Sawyer. Besides appearing in joint concerts with Edna Guy and being a featured artist at Gluck-Sandor's Dance Centre, he danced with Asadata Dafora's company and performed with Katherine Dunham in several projects she undertook during her early days in New York; he also appeared in Broadway musicals.

When he was a teenager, Sawyer became interested in dance after he saw Ruth St. Denis and Ted Shawn perform at Lewisohn Stadium.[55] He pored over newspaper and magazine articles about dancers and was fascinated by photographs of the artists. Eventually, a friend of Sawyer's, who was aware of his interest in dance, introduced him to Gluck-Sandor and Felicia Sorel. He had no prior training when he auditioned for them; but, as he remembered the situation, he performed an "interpretive dance" that he based on his impressions of St. Denis and Ted Shawn's performances. Although Sawyer was a neophyte, Gluck-Sandor and Sorel were impressed with his talent and asked him to join them in a Keith Circuit vaudeville tour they were planning. Sawyer's mother would not let him leave home at the time because she wanted him to finish school. Shortly afterward, he contacted Hemsley Winfield, whom he had heard about, and was immediately taken into his company. He later performed in several concerts with the New Negro Art Theatre, including the Chanin Theatre performance.

In 1931, Gluck-Sandor again invited Sawyer to perform with his company, this time in its season-opening production of *Petrouchka*. Sawyer remembered the Dance Centre as having a "beautiful company" where he felt very much at home. Gluck-Sandor extended him a special vote of confidence by telling the other dancers that anyone who had objections to a black man being in the company would have to leave.

Petrouchka opened in August with Sawyer dancing the role of the Blackamoor. John Martin was very positive about the production and pleased that he could see an enjoyable dance performance that was not "cosmic" and over-refined "in matters pertaining to esthetics and philosophy."[56] But his appraisal of Sawyer's performance was confusing:

> Again, though Randolph Sawyer dances the Blackamoor well, there is a suspicion that the role is less suitably filled by a Negro than it would be by some one pretending to be a Negro. In the Blackamoor's solo in the third scene, the choreography for the first time appears forced, for the simple reason that it is not racially differentiated from that of *Petrouschka* [sic] and the others. This necessity might not arise if Mr. Sawyer's talents did not equip him to do a type of dance quite out of the range of his colleagues.[57]

Did Martin's final sentence mean that the choreography danced by Sawyer was more difficult than that of his colleagues? If so, what did that have to do with racial differentiation? And what did any of it have to do with the role's supposedly being more suitably filled by someone pretending to be a Negro? It seems that Martin had again fallen prey to his habit of becoming bogged down in racial issues to the point where clarity escaped him.

Sawyer considered the Blackamoor his most important role as a concert dancer. He remembered that the audience was filled with celebrities such as Otto Kahn and the ballerina Rosina Galli, who later prevailed upon her husband, Giulio Gatti-Casazza, to audition members of the Dance Centre for a chamber dance series sponsored by the Met. Word of Gluck-Sandor's production of *Petrouchka* also reached the ballet's composer, Igor Stravinsky, who expressed pleasure that the Blackamoor's role was being danced by a black man.

Sawyer searched for other means of supporting himself as a dancer, and, during the spring of 1933, he performed briefly in a burlesque show produced by Harold Minsky. When the show opened for a week's run in Baltimore, he was required to paint his body green in a pseudo-Arabian number so the audience would not know that a black man was performing with white women. In 1933, Sawyer also returned to the New Negro Art Theatre and appeared in *The Emperor Jones* at the Metropolitan Opera. He danced in only one performance, however, because Gluck-Sandor did not like the idea of his performing with companies outside of the Dance Centre.

Performing the role of an African warrior, Sawyer made his first appearance with Asadata Dafora in the tremendously successful run of *Kykunkor* at the Unity Theatre in May 1934. That same year, he collaborated with another dancer, Clarence Yates, in an attempt to provide training for African Americans who were interested in dance. He and Yates conducted weekly classes in Harlem for a group of twenty-four men and women. The project continued until 1936 when the group of dancers was accepted into the Federal Theatre production of *Macbeth* (choreographed jointly by Yates and Asadata Dafora) at the Lafayette Theatre. But for some unexplained reason Sawyer was not cast in the production. Sawyer had always seemed to be welcome in companies he had performed with before.

During the 1937–38 season of the Dance Centre—which, after a four-year hiatus, was reestablished at a new location, 117 West Fifty-fourth Street—Sawyer returned to portray the role of the Sorcerer in the company's production of *El Amor Brujo.* The cast included José Limón in the lead male role and Jerome Robbins (performing under the name Robin Gerald) in a supporting role.

The opening of Asadata Dafora's dance-opera *Zunguru* at the Davenport Theatre in August 1938 marked Sawyer's second appearance with that choreographer. When John Martin reviewed the performance, Sawyer was mentioned among the members of the company who excelled in "first-rate" solo work that won the particular favor of the audience.[58]

Sawyer's brief appearances with Katherine Dunham included performances at the Labor Stage during her tenure as choreographer of the revue *Pins and Needles* in 1939. He performed with her again in 1940 when she choreographed the dances for a dramatization of Vachel Lindsay's narrative poem *The Congo,* presented by the Greater New York Fund at Madison Square Garden. Although he enjoyed working with Dunham, his relationship with her was never a very amiable one because he was not interested in joining her company permanently.

The first musical Sawyer performed in was a short-lived show, *La Belle Hélène*, which opened at the Westport Country Playhouse in Westport, Connecticut, on July 7, 1941. This all-black musical was based on an Offenbach operetta that told the story of Helen of Troy, and Sawyer played Ajax, king of Salamis. He was also a member of the chorus, which included several black performers who had established careers in dance. Among these were Mable Hart, who had performed in Agnes de Mille's *Black Ritual* (1940), and Al Bledger, who had performed with Eugene Von Grona's American Negro Ballet Company in 1937.

La Belle Hélène, which lasted only one week, never opened on Broadway. The reviewer of its first performance had little to say about the show except that the audience cheerfully indicated it was better than the usual summer fare, and it was attended by luminaries such as Edna Ferber and Katharine Hepburn.[59] By this point in his career, Sawyer had displayed a special talent for acquiring the technical and stylistic skills required for performing in different types of companies and productions. He continued refining his skills in African dance, and during the early 1940s he again became associated with Asadata Dafora's company. In March 1940 he performed in a reworked version of the dance-opera *Zunguru* at the Cherry Lane Theatre, and in August 1942 he appeared with that company at the Jacob's Pillow Dance Festival in *Spear Dance, Batu,* and *Challenge Dance.*

The following year, Sawyer danced in his most important role, in an all-black adaptation of Bizet's opera *Carmen.* The Broadway musical, *Carmen Jones*, was produced by Billy Rose; its libretto was written by Oscar Hammerstein and it was choreographed by Eugene Loring. The show opened to enthusiastic reviews on December 2, 1943, at the Broadway Theatre. Hammerstein was commended for the way in which he adapted the tragic story of love and violence. The *Times* drama critic, Lewis Nichols, wrote that "Mr. Hammerstein has taken the plot of an opera, has matched it scene by scene, but has neither bowed down before it with diffidence nor used it as the basis for a literary prank. It is quite a libretto he has turned out."[60]

The setting was transposed from Spain to the southern United States where the characters worked in a parachute factory instead of a cigarette factory. Don José became Joe; Micaela became Cindy Lou; and

Escamillo, the toreador, became a boxer named Husky Miller. The Toreador song, consequently, no longer referred to bullfighting but to a boxing match and became "Stan' Up an' Fight." Within this context, Loring created a boxing ballet that was performed by Randolph Sawyer and Melvin Howard. Sawyer found Loring to be a "very meticulous" choreographer who created difficult (often non-balletic) dances that he drilled relentlessly until he got what he wanted. In his appraisal, Lewis Nichols simply spoke of the choreography as being tongue-in-cheek, cheerful, and fast.[61]

Carmen Jones had a long run of 502 performances from December 1943 to February 1945 and later toured nationally. After this show (with the exception of a few acting roles and jobs as a movie extra) Sawyer's performing career ended. It had been a comparatively short one, but he, like Winfield, was one of the first to prove that black male dancers could find a place on the American stage as something other than popular entertainers. In doing this, he was often singled out for his strikingly masculine beauty and his dynamic performances. His participation in Gluck-Sandor's company further distinguished him as one of the earliest black dancers to participate in an integrated dance company on a regular basis. In addition, his performances with Winfield, Dunham, Dafora, at the Dance Centre, and on the Broadway stage indicate that he was one of the most versatile black dance artists of the 1930s and early 1940s.

Ollie Burgoyne

The third person who had an important stage career before and after she performed with the New Negro Art Theatre was Ollie Burgoyne (sometimes also referred to as Olga or Olive). Unlike Guy and Sawyer, she had a remarkably long career, spanning approximately fifty years. Born in Chicago in 1885, she began dancing at the age of six when she embarked upon a tour of Europe with a group of singing and dancing girls.[62] In 1903, she appeared with the talented actor-comedian-dancer Ernest Hogan in the vaudeville production *Uncle Elph's Christmas.*[63]

Between 1910 and 1928, she continued her international tours with various shows, and her travels took her to Germany, Denmark, Sweden, Hungary, France, Switzerland, Egypt, and Turkey. In U.S. vaudeville circuits, she was often billed as an "Algerian girl." Her specialty was exotic dances—the Brazilian dance, the snake dance, and the Spanish dance. As the theater historian Henry T. Sampson notes, "Her arms, hand motions, and the swing of her graceful body in doing these dances caused the theatrical critics to rate her the peer of any dancer in the world."[64]

Among the many experiences that made Burgoyne's personal and professional life unique were those she had while living in Russia during the early 1900s. During one of her European tours, she somehow became stranded with a company of dancers in Leipzig, Germany. From there she found her way to St. Petersburg. By her own account, black girls were a novelty in Russia so she had no trouble finding places to perform, such as the Christoph Gardens and the Aquarium in St. Petersburg, and Tsarskoe Selo, the summer palace of Czar Nicholas II. After dancing for the czar, she received an imperial document of commendation for her performance.[65]

She found her life to be gay and full of youthful excitement, but she also worked hard, saved money, and put her entrepreneurial skills into action by buying a lingerie shop in St. Petersburg and eventually employing twenty-seven workers.[66]

An interesting photograph shows the front of her shop with black mannequins placed in the show windows.[67] Unfortunately, her successful career in Russia came to an end. While she was out of the country on vacation in Marienbad, World War I began, and she was advised by the American consul not to return to Russia. She heeded the advice and, consequently, abandoned her shop and all her possessions.[68]

Upon her return to the United States, she continued her career as an actress and a dancer. She appeared in numerous black musical shows.[69] These included *They're Off* (1919), a show in which Burgoyne appeared with her cousin, Ida Forsyne, the famous eccentric dancer who had also toured Russia and studied folk dances there. Other shows included *Over the Top* (1919) and *Keep It Up* (1922). *Ollie Burgoyne and Her Darktown Strutters* (1925), which Burgoyne produced and was featured in as a "classic" dancer, also included Forsyne as a "Russian" dancer.[70]

During the 1920s and 1930s Burgoyne appeared in many Broadway dramas in which she was the only African American. In these, she was often cast as the maid. The shows included *Lady Lies* (1928), *Solitaire* (1929), *Recessional* (1929), and *Blessed Event* (1932). During the same period, she was cast in various roles in all-black dramas such as *Lulu Belle* (1929), *Make Me Know It* (1929), and *Constant Sinner* (1931).

Burgoyne's first appearance with the Winfield company was as a soloist in 1930. As mentioned earlier, she danced the part of the River Congo in the pageant *De Promis' Lan'*. Her many concert performances with the company included the Chanin Theatre concert, the Roerich Hall performances, and the Monster Benefit at Mecca Temple. Her most memorable Broadway performance was in *Run Little Chillun'*. Hall Johnson wrote the libretto and composed and arranged the music for the folk-play that opened at the Lyric Theatre on March 1, 1933. His choir, supplementing the cast of approximately 175 performers, provided resplendent choral music for the play, which recounted the story of a rural southern community caught up in the conflict between two different religious groups, the Baptists and the moon-worshiping New Day Pilgrims. The Christian group's leader, Reverend Jones, had a son, Jim, who was tempted by Sulamai to forsake his wife and his religion. After being introduced to the rituals of the New Day Pilgrims, Jim finally returned to his own religion. In a climactic final scene, the pregnant Sulamai confronts her lover in his church, is rejected by him, and is struck by lightning.

Though critics thought little of the plot, they highly praised the play, especially for its music. Some of its songs were called "superb" while others were spoken of as being "more than good."[71] The dances were also singled out for praise. Doris Humphrey choreographed several of the sequences and arranged others. There was a solemn female processional for the opening ritual of the New Day Pilgrims. As the rhythm of the drums became more exciting, there was a solo for Mother Kanda (daughter of Tongola, the spiritual leader of the New Day Pilgrims), danced by Ollie Burgoyne. Finally, there was a passionate, orgiastic climax for a group of men and women who leapt out of the woods, whirling to the accompaniment of booming drums and chanting human voices.

Humphrey later discussed her approach to the work she did for the production in an article written for the *American Dancer*. She described how a ritualistic mating dance had found its way from Africa to the

Bahamas and into the choreography of *Run Little Chillun'* by way of a group of Bahamian dancers who were members of the cast. Her primary tasks were to adapt and edit the dance so that it did not "over-top" the drama; devise an entrance that was appropriate for the stage space; and teach the dancers how to use theatrical projection while performing ritual material that was being transposed for the stage.[72]

John Martin described Humphrey's staging and choreography as "thoroughly workmanlike"; he described the entrance she staged for the ritual as "a triumph of simplicity over choreographic invention," and he complimented the more inexperienced dancers for capturing the spirit and reverence of ritual dignity.[73] He also took the occasion to repeat his opinions concerning the role of black dancers on the concert stage. African-American dancers were best when performing ethnic material, and they had not found themselves when they attempted to perform "more sophisticated dancing." They were little more than imitative when they departed from folk ways (here he mentioned the names of dancers active around the time—Hemsley Winfield, Edna Guy, and Randolph Sawyer), and previously no white choreographers had supplied black dancers with worthwhile material.[74]

This brought him to his final point: "Miss Humphrey has apparently recognized the fact that Negroes cannot be expected to do dances designed for another race, and consequently she has moved with great caution in creating for them. The result is considerably more successful than usual, and bears added testimony to the breadth of Miss Humphrey's capabilities and the excellence of her theatrical judgment."[75]

Among the choreographers of her time, Humphrey was admired for the intense attention she gave to exploring the logic of movement and developing formal structure in dance. In this respect, her work in *Run Little Chillun'* contributed to the overall success of the production. In addition, she had acquired notable experience in the theater working with people who were not professionally trained dancers. She had choreographed incidental dances for the Philadelphia Theatre Association's production of *Lysistrata* in 1930 and for productions of *Carmen* and *Aida* at the Cleveland Stadium in 1932. Consequently, the cautious approach Martin purports she took in *Run Little Chillun'* was due perhaps to the fact that she understood the limitations of her cast as *theatrical performers* and not because she considered them incapable of doing the dances of another race.

It is not known to what extent Humphrey worked with Burgoyne on her solo. But there probably was some meaningful exchange between the two since Burgoyne was the most experienced dancer in the cast. One observer described Burgoyne's dance sequence in the second scene of the play, when she enters and sits unnoticed until she emerges as a luminescent, sensuous presence:

> Suddenly she is erect, standing out from the black figures, silhouetted against the light moon and torches. Slowly, sinuously, she steps forth. Her hands arrest the eye, hands remarkable for their length and slim suppleness. She weaves them in no intricate design, but they are knowing hands, undulating over her body, suggesting lingering caresses, the pantomime of a priestess invoking the gods of life and love to inspire her people. With erect torso she sways from side to side hypnotically, with a monotonous rhythm which increases to a sharp staccato, while the chanting and deep booming of drums rises strangely, weirdly. . . . One could imagine it symbolized all the joys of life, love—yearnings, fulfillment, comforts of encircling arms. Kanda reaches a state of rapturous abandon.[76]

The author's words capture the striking beauty for which Burgoyne was noted and suggest the years (she would have been about forty-seven at the time of the performance) of worldly experiences she had enjoyed on and off the stage. After *Run Little Chillun'*, Burgoyne appeared as one of the witch-women in the Federal Theatre production of *Macbeth* (1936). Her last documented performance was in Clare Boothe's comedy *Kiss the Boys Goodbye* (1938). After this point her professional activities become a mystery.

During her long career Burgoyne had distinguished herself as a truly multitalented woman with immense energy and an adventuresome spirit. Of the artists discussed in this study, she is the only one who actually participated in most of the theatrical genres that preceded the advent of black concert dance. Having performed in many types of productions—from minstrel shows, musicals, revues, and vaudeville shows in the late nineteenth and early twentieth centuries, through black and white musicals and dramas of the 1920s and 1930s, to performances in Winfield's company—Burgoyne traveled a career path that illustrated in microcosm black performers' transitions from one dance and theater genre to another.

4

Charles Williams

AN EXPERIMENT IN BLACK CONCERT DANCE during the
1930s took place far from the busy world of New York little theaters,
concert halls, and Broadway houses, in a setting that was unhurried,
provincial, almost pristine. Near the town of Hampton, Virginia, at the
end of a peninsula in the Chesapeake Bay, Hampton Institute became
the home of the Hampton Creative Dance Group, a company that
helped bring further national attention to African Americans in concert dance. The company's contributions to this development were
influenced by its director, Charles Williams, as well as by the American modern dance movement and African and Caribbean culture. The
history of the institutional setting where this dance experiment took
place also had an impact on the development of the aesthetic that
guided the company.

The story of Hampton Institute began shortly after the end of the
Civil War in 1865 when black and white Americans began searching
for solutions to the tremendous educational, economic, and social problems of four million former slaves. Members of white organizations
such as the American Missionary Association (AMA), a group that had
begun assisting black freedmen before the war, ardently debated questions concerning how the ex-slave population could best be enfran-
chised in American society.

In the area of education, the AMA decided that the first step should be to train blacks as teachers so that they, in turn, could educate other members of their race. To accomplish this, a number of schools were established in black population centers. In 1867 and 1868, eight such schools were founded in Macon, Savannah, and Atlanta, Georgia; in Charleston, South Carolina; Louisville, Kentucky; Nashville, Tennessee; Talledega, Alabama; and Hampton, Virginia.[1] The first administrators and teachers at these schools were white, and they pursued their work with sincere—though sometimes misguided—zeal. At Hampton, for example, the school's future was shaped by a former officer in the Union army whose involvement with blacks included serving as a colonel with the 9th Colored Regiment during the Civil War. Samuel Chapman Armstrong based his administration of the school on ideas that seemed practical within his narrow philosophical construct but were specious from other points of view.

He believed in a vigorous educational system that would focus on eradicating the black man's weaknesses as he saw them: lack of foresight, honor, morality, judgment, and direction. These shortcomings were viewed by Armstrong and others as innate disabilities rather than the result of social conditions that had developed because of two hundred years of enslavement. According to him, the hope for the race was blacks' enthusiasm for improving their lot, their docility, and their perseverance.[2] Ironically, his racist philosophy underlay a successful experiment in nineteenth-century African-American education.

Deciding that it was not important to attempt to produce accomplished scholars, Armstrong concentrated instead upon building character and instilling "habits of labor" in his students so that they would develop "moral force." His graduates would then concentrate on teaching practical courses to their fellow freedmen. With these ends in mind, he eventually established a curriculum in which firsthand involvement in agricultural and mechanical subjects shared equal importance with academic programs.[3] Other schools had experimented with similar types of curricula and found them untenable for the most part, but Armstrong, with his strong administrative skills and his even stronger will, clung to the concept because of its "moral" efficacy and made it work. Hampton's earliest students found themselves spending part of each school day engaged in various types of manual labor.[4]

His imprint was left on every aspect of the school's life. Though art and culture held little importance within his scheme of things, he knew the important role that one cultural element, African-American music, could play in attracting philanthropic donations to the school. To this end, he established the Hampton Singers, a group that toured northern cities and contributed to the growth of the school by "singing up" a number of buildings on Hampton's campus. By the time of Armstrong's death in 1893, Hampton was widely noted for its music ensembles.

During the early twentieth century, a fascinating outgrowth of these musical fund-raising ventures developed. On March 13, 1908, Hampton students presented a folklore concert at New York's Mendelssohn Hall. They were assisted by Harry T. Burleigh, a talented black musician noted for composing and arranging African-American folk music. His musical background included studies at the National Conservatory of Music in New York in 1892. At that time Anton Dvořák was the director of the conservatory, and Burleigh often assisted him by singing Negro songs for the composer during the period when he was creating his folkloric *Symphony from the New World*.[5]

The concert in which Burleigh and the Hampton students collaborated presented labor songs, dance songs such as "Juba," Negro dialect songs, Negro folk stories, and American Indian songs. The latter were performed by Native American students, the first of whom had been brought to Hampton in 1878 as a further experiment in educating minority Americans. The program also included a section entitled "Illustrated Songs," in which the music was accompanied by pantomimic movement.[6] Overall, the concert tended to be more than just a presentation of music since it also featured elements of drama and dance.

By 1913, Hampton's folklore programs of African-American and Native American life had moved close to becoming pageants as they included expanded dramatic scenarios and more dance. A program presented at Carnegie Hall that year opened with "John Smith's Visit to Kiquotan," a vignette composed of speeches, songs, and dances telling the story of how the first English settlers of the Hampton area were received by Native Americans. The program also included "The First Slaves Find a Home," in which African songs and dances were used to recount the initial introduction of slaves into the Hampton community.[7]

A variation on this format was undoubtedly one of the most unusual series of productions in which Hampton students ever participated. During the summer of 1914, a number of Hampton men sailed from Hampton Roads, Virginia, to Bar Harbor, Maine, in an eighty-five-foot schooner. They were the cast, chorus, and crew of *Hampton Afloat and Afield,* a pageant that was performed for more than three months at stopping points along the eastern seaboard. The tour covered ten states in a campaign to raise money for the school's scholarship fund. Among the dances performed in the pageant were a Cherokee ball dance and an Apache war dance. Other dances occurred in scenes depicting the labor of black field hands and in a vignette that captured the religious fervor of a church camp-meeting.[8]

Hampton's pageants, folklore concerts, and music groups—ranging from a full chorus to a male quartet (the Armstrong Quartet, which also toured extensively)—created a colorfully variegated performance environment for students during the first two decades of the twentieth century. One student, Charles Holston Williams, who enrolled at the school in 1905, would later contribute to these performance activities by establishing a nationally recognized dance company.

Williams was born in Lexington, Kentucky, on January 25, 1886. By 1904, he was attending high school at Berea College. The following year the state general assembly passed the Day Law, which stated that blacks and whites could no longer attend schools together, so Williams transferred to Hampton Institute where he finished high school at its academy and stayed on to begin his college work.[9]

During his college days, Williams was an outstanding athlete, excelling in football, basketball, and baseball. His athletic activities were almost ended in 1910 when he fell from a scaffold while painting a house. He injured his knees and was told he would never walk again.[10] His unwavering persistence (an individual trait that enabled him to complete several visionary projects during his lifetime) pulled him through, and that same year, he became director of physical training at Hampton.

One of his first organizational successes grew out of his concern about the lack of rules and regulations at intercollegiate athletic events. On February 2, 1912, he called a meeting of athletic directors from four other black schools—Shaw, Lincoln, Virginia Union, and Howard—and under his leadership, the group founded the Central Intercollegiate

Athletic Association, which influenced the organization of sports at black colleges for years to come.[11]

Williams's initial interest in dance was rooted in his background in physical education and recreation. In 1917, in an article he published in Hampton's monthly journal, the *Southern Workman*, he first expressed his ideas concerning the importance of physical pursuits in the lives of young black people. He wrote that rural and urban community leaders needed to find ways to put "normal play" back into the lives of their youth and to instill the younger generation with the moral lessons to be learned from organized games and other recreational activities.[12]

He discussed athletic and social games, track and field meets, and other rhythmic movement activities as tools for self-improvement and development. Dance, for Williams, served an important purpose among these. Not only did it develop physical, social, and artistic skills, but it could be used to connect black people with their heritage, "giving them a greater appreciation for past ceremonies and customs, and also developing race pride."[13]

Though Williams was at this point primarily concerned with the recreational use of artistic forms such as dance and drama, his ideas presaged those of Harlem Renaissance aestheticians who, a few years later, would speak of the importance of the African past in shaping contemporary African-American art and the function that art could serve in developing pride within the race as well as garnering approval from without.

In other ways, his thinking was related to the American physical culture movement, which stretched from the last decades of the nineteenth century into the early twentieth century. When Williams spoke of "pride in a good physique" and the influence of good posture and recreation upon the development of mental growth, initiative, alertness, and foresight,[14] his words echoed the ideas that had been brought to America by the disciples of François Delsarte, whose principles stressed the moral and spiritual efficacy of movement activities. Williams also agreed with the popular idea that black people found a special joy in music, dance, and other rhythmic activities, but the overriding moral tone of his message led him to discriminate between good and bad types of dance. On the negative side there were "cheaper vaudeville shows," "the lowest type of theatre," and "evils in the modern dance and the public dance halls." (In using the term "modern dance" he was referring to social dance rather than concert dance.) On the positive side, there was theater that acted as a socializing agency, arrested moral attention, and cultivated interests in things of social concern. "Good" theater, the "right" type of dance, and supervised recreational activities resulted in "clean, strong, American citizens."[15]

In the same year that he published his first article, 1917, Williams also initiated an annual series of physical education demonstrations in which Hampton students and faculty members performed drills, gymnastics, and dances for the public. In 1922, the fifth of these events was reported in the *Southern Workman.* Male and female students performed L'Zoronta, a characteristic Spanish dance, and the Tarantella, an Italian folk dance. The program also featured two solos by faculty member Emily Pipal—*Oriental Moon Dance* and *Russian Rhapsody.*[16] Judging from the content of the program, Williams had not yet incorporated his ideas about the heritage of black people into the performances he organized. He would take this step a few years later. There was, however, another important influence in dance that made its presence felt at Hampton during the mid-1920s.

Ruth St. Denis and Ted Shawn had toured together on and off since 1914, but by the mid-twenties their company was at the height of its popularity and had an unprecedented impact on American audiences. This was largely due to three annual tours organized by Daniel Mayer, one of America's leading impresarios and bookers. Embarking upon these tours, Shawn and St. Denis criss-crossed America from October 1922 until April 1925.

When the Denishawn Company performed at Hampton's Ogden Hall on February 21, 1925, the college community saw what the leading purveyors of mainstream concert dance were bringing to American audiences: a colorful array of dances that fell into the categories of exotica, music visualization, and Americana. These were performed by Shawn, St. Denis, and a company of twelve dancers that included two important members of the next generation of American modern dance, Doris Humphrey and Charles Weidman.

"Social Sidelights on the Denishawn Tour—1924–1925" in the *Denishawn Magazine* reported the company's enjoyable stay on the campus, which included a presentation of Negro spirituals performed by Hampton students.[17] By far, the most important impact of the company's visit to Hampton was the establishment of a mutually supportive relationship between Charles Williams and Ted Shawn. During the 1930s, their friendship resulted in three performances at Hampton by Shawn and his men's company (in 1933, 1934, and 1938), and Shawn also contributed one of his dances to the repertoire of the Hampton Creative Dance Group in 1934.

In 1928 Williams continued his exploration of the relationship between art, recreation, and the folklore of black Americans in a book entitled *Cotton Needs Pickin'*. The book documented a number of the folk dances of southern blacks. Written descriptions, accompanying lines of music, and photographs recorded the steps and rhythmic movements of country dances or plantation "break downs," animal dances, and dances thought to be the rural origins of the Charleston.[18]

John Martin wrote an article about Williams's book several months after its publication. His lengthy commentary was one of his earliest discussions of the cultural confluences in African-American dance. He noted that many of the dance steps described bore similarity to American and English folk dances while others were "purely negro." This, he continued, exemplified the culturally "strange situation" in which black Americans found themselves. Their African past was shadowy (a point about which Martin proved to be ambivalent during the next decade), and they took their ideas from a foreign race, assimilated them, and created markedly altered but derivative artistic forms.[19]

In the same year in which he published *Cotton Needs Pickin'*, Williams had also begun to make his own contributions to the African-American and American cultural continuums in dance. Unfortunately, there are only sketchy clues concerning his early dance training and how it may have influenced his efforts to become a choreographer and a company director. His only training at Hampton Institute would have been from other physical education teachers. Even if dance classes were available in the nearby towns of Hampton or Newport News, it is doubtful that he would have been able to enroll in them. He would likely have faced the same bleak prospects as other aspiring black concert dancers searching for classes during the 1920s.

It is more clear where Williams studied dance during the 1930s, though the details of his studies are incomplete. His student records at the Harvard University Summer School of Physical Training, where he completed his master's degree in 1930, show that he took dance classes there, but the types of classes were not indicated on his transcript.[20] In 1937 and 1938 he visited the Bennington Summer School of Dance where he observed classes and attended performances.[21] The meticulous financial records he kept show that in 1938 he also spent part of the summer studying with Doris Humphrey and Hanya Holm in New York.[22]

As he was studying, researching, and developing his approach to dance, Williams drew upon a variety of sources and experiences. In addition to investigating folk dance and modern dance, he learned more about the theatrical possibilities inherent in African dance when he traveled to Chicago for the 1933 Century of Progress Exposition. Although in the doldrums of the Depression, the city celebrated its one-hundredth anniversary with a brilliant display of scientific marvels and a colorfully eclectic array of geographic exhibits such as the Walled City of China, the Streets of Paris, and Darkest Africa.

Writing of his impressions of the fair in the *Southern Workman*, Williams described the African village that arrested the attention of passers-by. The curious were drawn into a program of acting and dancing that was beyond their expectations. There were performers from Nigeria, French Equatorial Africa, Algeria, the Belgian Congo, the French Congo, and "Kamaroon"; a "lecturer" presented geographical and cultural facts about the countries represented and added his own Midway hype to the presentation.[23] Williams, however, was most impressed with the authentic costumes of the Nigerians, who were led by Prince Adeboyo Alawumi, and he particularly liked the sinewy athleticism of their sword dance. This group also performed more sensational feats such as fire eating and fire walking.[24]

One of the Nigerians, Abdul Assen, was the audience's favorite as the hissing, praying, ecstatic witch doctor. On witnessing Assen's mesmerizing acting and dancing, James O'Donnell Bennett of the *Chicago Daily Tribune* called his performance one of the finest he had ever seen.[25] This was the same Abdul Assen who, the following year, would receive profuse praise from New York critics when he appeared as the witch doctor in Asadata Dafora's *Kykunkor*.

The Royal Ashanti Ceremonial Dancers and Drummers of Ghana also left a vivid impression in Williams's mind. He felt that their dances met the requirements of the true dance. "They tell a story of war, thanksgiving, death or love, and are connected in some way with the life of the people." "Most important of all," he continued, "there was an absence of the sensuous in the dances. This was a pleasing discovery, because the accepted opinion with reference to African dances is just the opposite."[26] Perhaps the dancing lacked "sensuousness" because it was authentically African and not the pseudo-African dancing featured in plays, musicals, and films of the time, which stressed "wild abandon." Most American audiences were not familiar with authentic African dance; consequently, they were not aware that it could have more pristine and reserved nuances. Furthermore, Williams's attention would quite naturally be caught by the features of the dances that supported his ideas about the impropriety of certain types of dance and the propriety of others, ideas that eventually influenced the performance style of his company.

At the Chicago exposition, he had ample opportunity to shake a finger at what he considered the evil aspects of dance. Among the "many daring ladies of the dance to attract swarms of popeyed visitors" was Sally Rand (Helen Gould Beck), the sensation of the fair, whose fan-dances and bubble tossing set the Streets of Paris afire.[27] Her performances were perfect examples of the type of theatrical dance Williams would strive to conquer with his visions of a dance art that was morally and racially uplifting.

Whatever negative distractions he may have found at the exposition, Williams returned to Hampton inspired by his glimpses of African culture. He had a heightened desire to make connections between the performances he had observed and his own ideas about the importance of dance and folklore as a means of enlightening black people about their rich cultural heritage. He began implementing these ideas at his next student program.

The occasion was the celebration of Hampton's sixty-sixth anniversary, on April 26 and 27, 1934. A large number of guests visited the campus for this event, including students from distant schools such as Harvard, Vassar, and Cornell.[28] On the first day of activities—after Hampton students and visiting students had met to discuss "problems

of mutual interest to students of both races"—a program of "interpretive dances" was presented. The visitors saw seven groups of dances,
which included the first two African dances to become part of the
Hampton Creative Dance Group's repertoire. *The Feast of Ramadan*
portrayed the night-long celebration that ends the Muslim fasting
period, and *Ya Ma Wisee* was a dance of thanksgiving.[29] These dances
not only indicated how Williams had been influenced by what he had
seen at the Chicago exposition, but they also forecast a practice that
would become characteristic of his company—having the African dances
in the repertoire performed almost exclusively by male students. The
probable reason for the predominately male casting was that male students from Africa, who were attending Hampton at the time, assisted
Williams with the choreography. The African students may have felt
more comfortable working with other men. Frank O. Roberts (Tonia
Masequoi) from Liberia was Williams's most outstanding assistant in
this capacity. He became a featured soloist with the Hampton company and later distinguished himself by performing at Dance International in 1937 and at the New York World's Fair in 1939, where he
appeared with a company of his own on a program with Asadata Dafora.

Male dancers were also featured prominently throughout the Hampton group's repertoire. Cast lists from the mid-1930s show that men
played an increasingly important role in performances, and they usually comprised the majority of the company members. Their prominence is corroborated by souvenir programs, which show considerably
more photographs of male dancers than of female dancers.

Williams's presentation for the 1934 anniversary program included
another dance that showed his affinity for working with male students.
Men of Valor, with its high-energy athleticism and movement motifs
drawn from sports activities such as boxing, sprinting, and shot-put-
ting, proved to be a tremendous success. Though Williams's background as an athlete served as the major source of inspiration for this
particular dance, his interest in this direction had also been reinforced
by the appearance of Ted Shawn's newly formed male dance company, which had first appeared at Hampton in December of the previous year.

There were similarities between Williams's and Shawn's dance careers. Williams drew many of his dancers from physical education

students and athletes. In 1933, Shawn spent a semester at Springfield College in Massachusetts (where Williams had, coincidentally, studied in 1924) teaching dance to five hundred male students who were preparing to become physical education teachers. His best students and former Denishawn dancers such as Barton Mumaw formed the nucleus of the all-male company, which began touring that same year. A virile, muscular masculinity became one of the features of Williams's company. It was *the* important feature of Shawn's company, which one critic, Walter Terry, later described as being "supermasculine."[30] Shawn had what amounted to an obsession with the beauty of the male body. In pursuing his goal of legitimizing the role of males in dance, he translated the Greek ideal of the beautifully proportioned warrior-athlete into an American ideal. Williams, whose interest in male beauty was apparent though not obsessive, took the African ideal of the warrior-athlete and turned it into an African-American ideal.

There were other similarities. Both men were interested in black folk material as subject matter for dance. Shawn's first African-American–inspired piece was *Juba*, choreographed in 1921 to a score that—in another interesting coincidence—had been arranged by the director of Hampton's music department, Nathaniel Dett, although Shawn did not actually meet Dett until the Denishawn company performed at the school in 1925. *Juba*, a trio for women, featuring Martha Graham, Betty May, and Dorothea Bowen, was included in the repertoire of a touring company Shawn organized during a period of estrangement from Ruth St. Denis.

In 1933 Shawn continued his exploration of black themes when he choreographed *Negro Spirituals* for his men's company. *Fetish*, a witch doctor's solo choreographed and performed by company member Barton Mumaw, also became part of that company's repertoire. Shawn's interest in black culture went beyond merely using its elements as subject matter for his dances. As his biographer, Walter Terry, pointed ed out, he included black artists in his Jacob's Pillow Dance Festival for all of the thirty years he was director.[31]

To draw parallels between Charles Williams and Ted Shawn is not to suggest that the major portions of their careers were parallel, although they both opened doors in the field of concert dance. Shawn's sixty-year devotion to dance was total, while Williams's deepest involvement in dance spanned a shorter period, from 1935 to 1949, and he devoted a large portion of his time and energy to non-dance activities such as athletics, university teaching and administration, and community recreation programs. Dance director–choreographer was only one of the many hats he wore.

The mutual interests of the two men and their meetings when Shawn and his company visited the campus during the 1930s promoted a bond of friendship and respect that was beneficial to both of them. Shawn appreciatively pointed out that the five-hundred-dollar fee he received at Hampton was his company's highest guarantee during a period when many of his performance receipts were extremely small.[32] His visits to Hampton were high points in what was often a dismal touring schedule. "We felt we were in heaven," he said as he described the charming guest house where they were lodged, the packed auditorium, and the tremendous ovations—particularly for dances such as *John Brown Sees the Glory*, which was not always well received in the South.[33] Shawn also received considerable satisfaction from knowing that he had made a significant contribution to the growing interest in dance at the college. During his second visit, in April 1934, plans were made for Williams to visit Jacob's Pillow the following summer so that he could begin to pattern his choreography for the Hampton men more closely after Shawn's own.[34]

In return, Williams and the members of his company benefited from the encouragement of one of America's leading dance artists. They had the opportunity to observe Shawn's rehearsal-performance process, study with him, and learn a dance from his repertoire, which they added to their own. *Cutting the Sugar Cane* was first performed by Hampton dancers on March 2, 1935, approximately a year after Shawn's second visit to the campus.[35] It was an ideal addition to Williams's growing repertoire of folk-inspired dances.

When Shawn had traveled to Cuba in 1928, he was struck by the rhythmic vitality of black field hands. His impressions of the men cutting sugar cane with their gleaming machetes while chanting and shouting in cadence led him to create a pantomimic dance that captured a day in the lives of four Cuban workers—the beauty and breadth of their movement, and the pain and joy of their lives. Shawn and Williams realized that a dance with an Afro-Cuban theme would be a fitting addition to the African-American and African dances that the students were already performing.

The dance was the closing number of a program in which Williams returned to his familiar format of presenting students first in demonstrations of calisthenics, drills, and other exercises and then closing with dances. The format itself was almost a metaphor for his transition from physical education demonstrations to concert dance. Through this approach he was also shrewdly introducing the college community to an art form that was questionable in the eyes of its more conservative members. According to Williams, there were, in fact, faculty members who had voiced opposition to his initial efforts to introduce dance into the physical education curriculum. No doubt it was viewed as frivolous (if not treasonous) in a school that had a history of stressing "practical education."

Shawn's dance was presented again two weeks after its Hampton debut, this time as part of a fully mounted dance concert that was the first off-campus performance of the Hampton Creative Dance Group. *Cutting the Sugar Cane* was offered as one part of a group of dances called "Labor Rhythms," which included *Dis Ole Hammer—Water Boy*, a dance choreographed by Williams. The performance took place at the Mosque Theatre in Richmond, Virginia, on March 23, 1935, as part of a brief tour to test the feasibility of establishing a dance company as a permanent addition to Hampton's other performance groups.[36]

Perhaps the torrential rains that fell that evening were responsible for the small audience. The low attendance certainly was not due to poor publicity. One of Williams's many practical skills was his knack for public relations. Before the performance, he sent press releases to local papers and wrote letters to public school principals extolling the educational and cultural significance of the event. He also emphasized the fact that the dance company was the first group of blacks to perform at the huge theater, which was the cultural center of the former capital of the Confederacy.

The program, consisting of eight groups of dances, opened with *Cycle of Depression*, a dance about the effect of the economic upheaval in America and the struggle to overcome it. The second section of the program, "Dances of the People," consisted of African-American, Russian, Polish, and Italian folk dances.[37] The European dances particularly struck one reviewer as impressive proof that the students could interpret "alien" dances.[38]

Another reviewer wrote that the section of six African dances contributed the most excitement to the program, and the students' "fervor and frenzy" in these made up for their "lack of enthusiasm" in some of the others.[39] This comment was especially interesting because some of the students—who, like some faculty members, had expressed skepticism about dance being introduced into the physical education curriculum—had been particularly hostile concerning the African dances.[40] Williams's ability to change his students' minds indicated that he was a man of firm persuasion.

The concert concluded with "Labor Rhythms" and "Negro Spirituals." Overall, it was a pioneering effort that brought black concert dance to a community that would not have been exposed to it otherwise at the time. The undertaking also marked the beginning of support from the college administration, community leaders, and Hampton alumni groups for Williams's visionary ideas. This support would enable his company to tour extensively into the next decade.

For the Mosque Theatre concert, Williams was assisted by another Hampton faculty member, Bernice M. Smothers. None of the reviews or program notes offer any revealing information about her except to mention her choreographic contributions. These included the three dances that comprised the section "Negro Spirituals." She choreographed most of the women's group dances while the men's dances were choreographed by Williams.

Through the years, Williams continued to have female faculty members assist him. The best known of his co-directors was Charlotte Moten, who worked with the company from 1936 to 1942. She was the daughter of Robert Rassa Moten, president of Alabama's Tuskeegee Institute, which was founded by Booker T. Washington, a Hampton graduate. Like Hampton, Tuskeegee was a pioneering institution in black education. Charlotte Moten came from a privileged background and an environment steeped in educational tradition. She attended Boston University's Sargent College of Physical Education, where she received her B.S. degree, and she also attended the Bennington Summer School of Dance, America's leading summer dance festival during the 1930s.[41] By the time she became Williams's assistant in 1936, his company had become officially recognized as a welcome addition to the other performance groups at the college and was about to embark on its most extensive series of tours.

During this same period, Williams became more and more involved with national dance activities, both through his traveling and observing what was current in the dance world and through his participation in important events. In March 1937, he attended the *Negro Dance Evening* at the Ninety-second Street YM-YWHA in New York and saw the leading black concert dancers of the period—Katherine Dunham, Edna Guy, and Asadata Dafora.[42] In May, he participated in the newly formed American Dance Association's first annual convention, where he spoke at a forum, "Dance in the Changing World," held at the New School for Social Research. In June, he was invited by John Martin to present a lecture demonstration, which also took place at the New School. That summer also marked his first visit to Bennington.[43]

Williams began to use every contact he had to procure performance opportunities for his company. Shortly after he had seen the *Negro Dance Evening*, for example, he contacted William Kolodney, educational director of the YM-YWHA, and began negotiating for a date of his own.[44]

The preceding year, 1936, had not been particularly eventful for the dance company. There had been only three local performances and one at Howard University in Washington, D.C., but in 1937 the company embarked on one of its most extensive touring seasons. There was a southern tour in April that took the company to major black colleges—Florida A&M in Tallahassee, Tuskegee Institute in Alabama, and North Carolina A&T. There were also performances for enthusiastic high school audiences and for community organizations, groups that were especially important in Williams's concept of dance education. In spite of the racial prejudice of the time, Williams was surprisingly successful at getting bookings for his company at non-black institutions, primarily high schools, colleges, and universities. This indicates that his influence in the larger educational community was growing along with his company's reputation.

The following winter the company gathered momentum and performed at Bryn Mawr College in Pennsylvania, high schools in New Jersey, the YM-YWHA's Theresa L. Kaufmann Auditorium in New

York, and the Lafayette Theatre in Harlem. The latter two performances met with a fair amount of critical acclaim; most important,
though, the New York performances and the press coverage they received brought the company to the attention of a wider, more sophisticated dance audience.

In a brief review of the YM-YWHA performance, Albertina Vitak of
the *American Dancer* made the standard comments that were used
for emerging black concert dancers. She found the company natural,
rhythmic, and enjoying what they were doing "without trace of striv-
ing to appear artistic." For her, the most exceptional performance of
the concert was Frank O. Roberts's fervent *Pagan's Prayer*, in which
the Liberian student danced the invocations of a tribal chief asking the
gods to intercede on behalf of his people's welfare. Vitak was also
impressed by Roberts's other solo, *Mamah Parah*, calling it "amazingly
effective."[45] In this dance, Roberts displayed the spectacular technique
of West African stilt dancing and stunned the audience with his virtuosity.

In a lengthier review of the YM-YWHA concert, Walter Terry observed that the Negro was new to the field of concert dance and was
still searching for a dance form that was theatrical and inherently racial at the same time. The Hampton dancers, he felt, had not yet
achieved this synthesis. The African dances were exciting, colorful,
and theatrically stimulating, but since "they were borrowed from an
almost forgotten past [they] could not be considered as truly creative
work" for the contemporary Negro.[46]

It seemed that individual critics were adept at constructing their own
version of the African-American performer's relationship to his past.
Terry's was the "forgotten" past; Martin's had been the past that was
a "few brief steps behind" at one point and "shadowy" at another.
Nobody seemed to know which. All that was agreed upon was that
black dancers who were attempting to enter the concert field were
stranded somewhere between Africa's rituals, Harlem's "highjinks,"
and the leaden seriousness of modern dance. But they were searching
for a way out.[47]

The dance spirituals—a form that was being explored by both black
and white concert dancers—offered one option, one way of creating a
serious theatrical expression of African-American culture through

dance. Terry, however, found the company's performance of these to be disappointing and irritating in its "stern stylization, plodding movement and . . . complete lack of emotional projection." "It seems," he said, "incredible that the spirituals of Tamiris and Ted Shawn should be more effective than those of the Negroes themselves."[48]

It is not necessary to spend time conjecturing whether or not the spirituals of Tamiris and Shawn were more effective than those of the Hampton company. Even if they were, there were several reasons— none of them "incredible"—why this might have been the case. Williams's company was barely three years old, and it seems—as was often observed by critics—that his dancers' performances were sometimes stilted. This may have been due to their relative lack of performing experience and their lack of training in matters of theatrical projection. The dance spirituals were, after all, modern dance interpretations of folk music. Their effectiveness relied on the use of theatrical dance techniques and not on the vitality of indigenous folk-dance forms. There would be little reason to assume that Hampton's spirituals would be more effective than those of other modern dancers unless one adhered to the idea that there were certain things that blacks were supposed to do naturally.

It was apparently this sense of naturalness that made Terry more pleased with dances such as *Juba* and *Cake Walk*—dances based on folk-dance forms. But he saved his highest praise for the Shawn-inspired dances of the "Labor Rhythms" section of the program. He felt that the dramatic, heroic movements were well suited to the bodies of the Hampton men. Time and experience, he predicted, would produce a dance form that not only fitted the dancers' physiques but also their tempers and ideas; then the Negro dance would become "an articulate form of contemporary theatrical expression." His final advice to Williams was that he should begin to experiment with freer, more improvisational movement and include a greater use of pantomime in his work.[49] Similar advice was given by Martha Hill, director of the dance department at New York University and the Bennington Summer School of Dance. After seeing the YM-YWHA performance at Williams's invitation, she wrote him and pointed out that the company was in a transitional stage: "I think most people have first a very spontaneous desire and ability to express something freely, then they go through this period of disciplining it into a form which may act as a very definite limitation until they have worked out the other side of it."[50]

In theory, her assessment of the situation was reasonable, but there may have been other reasons why the company's approach to their material seemed ambivalent, why they sometimes seemed to dance with fervid abandon and at other times were more restrained in their performances. One of the primary reasons for a kind of stylistic schism in the company was that Williams was influenced by conflicting ideas. On the one hand, he believed in the role of dance as a tool in the moral development of black youth, and his ideas were deeply grounded in Hampton's conservative educational tradition. On the other hand, he was aware of the liberating force of art as expressed in the philosophy of the modern dance movement of the time.

As noted earlier, Hampton's conservative tradition of education—based on the philosophy of its founder, Samuel Armstrong—was immutably tied to a strict program of moral indoctrination. According to Armstrong, "Hampton Institute was to be a 'little world' in which all the proper attitudes of morality, diligence, thrift and responsibility were to be assiduously cultivated."[51] By the 1930s many things had changed at Hampton, but the conservative thinking that led some students and faculty members to question Williams's dance experiments was still pervasive. His task of creating a dance company within the confines of this environment was not an easy one. He formulated the rationale for his company by liberally interpreting the words of Samuel Armstrong, who had said that "not only was it the hope to create an institution which should train 'pedagogues,' but [one] which would send out, as well, *those whose culture shall be upon the whole circle of living.*"[52]

In mentioning cultural endeavors, Armstrong was referring to the primary one that fit into his practical scheme of things—the performances of Hampton's music groups and their fund-raising potential. Even by the time Williams began touring with his dance company, the demand for performances by Hampton's music ensembles was so great that many of his sponsors would not host a dance concert unless the Armstrong Quartet (the male vocal ensemble) also appeared on the program.

When Williams initially pressed his case for the establishment of a

dance company at Hampton, he drew a parallel between the music
traditions and the dance traditions in black culture:

> Hampton Institute has heard many descendants of those who came from
> that African background raise their voices and sing, as only American
> Negroes can sing, the deathless Spirituals which their race has created and
> added to the culture of the United States—of the world. Listening to these,
> and conscious of the aptitude of the Colored People for making their own
> dance measures and rhythms, Hampton believes that in the field of dance,
> the Negro can make another significant contribution to the aesthetic life
> of America.[53]

The parallel he drew, like his physical education demonstrations, was
a pragmatic means of forwarding his pioneering efforts in dance, which
were experimental, innovative, and controversial within the context
of his community. Within the broader context of American concert
dance, however, his company was not viewed as being particularly
innovative. Even though it was warmly received, the limitations of its
performances were repeatedly pointed out. The restraint that was often mentioned in conjunction with the group's performances was due
to the obligation Williams felt to present his dancers with a propriety
that illumined them as being wholesome, upstanding, young black
Americans who were morally beyond reproach.

A related factor that motivated the company's performances was the
idea that the power of art should be harnessed for the "social uplift"
of black Americans. There was something that Williams had to prove
to his audiences (both black and white, at home and abroad): "At every performance the audiences have been deeply interested and greatly impressed, especially by the fact that serious effort is being made
to present Negro and African dance material in a dignified artistic
form."[54]

When compared to other black dance artists performing during the
1930s, the Hampton dancers sometimes seem distinctly reserved. The
few extant photographs and descriptions of Hemsley Winfield's company, in dances such as *Life and Death* and in *The Emperor Jones*,
delineate performances that were unsettling, almost anarchic in their
intensity. Even though critics of Katherine Dunham seemed more
intent on titillating the readers of their reviews than she did on titillating her audiences, part of the attraction of her theater was certain-

ly its scintillating, colorful glamour, much of which emanated from her own stage persona. Asadata Dafora drummed and danced New Yorkers to the edge of their seats, while his soloist Abdul Assen teetered back and forth on the liminal brink between true possession and great theatrical performance.

On the other hand, photographs of Williams's company reveal an idealized African community, one that would not tolerate disorderly outbreaks of spiritual possession. In *Wandi War Dance,* for example, the Hampton men, in spite of their impressive muscularity, seem mysteriously uninvolved in what they are doing. With their spears poised to challenge and shields raised for defense, they seem to be frozen in time, as if they were a beautifully realistic museum exhibit. Even though most of the group's photographs were obviously posed to create static tableaus rather than to capture the dancers in motion, their particular stasis reflects an image of a tightly controlled world from which the more chaotic tendencies of art have been banished.

Fortunately, there are other photographs of the company. In a dance such as *Middle Passage,* choreographed by Charlotte Moten, the camera captures a more tortured, less orderly world where the depiction of the suffering of slaves in transit from Africa to America edges out restraint. Eight women in a diagonal grouping stand with their legs wide apart, their hands tightly clasped across their chests, their elbows jutting sharply out to the sides. They seem to be unbalanced by a force (perhaps the rolling of a ship) that bends them so severely to the side that their elbows are almost perpendicular to the floor. Their faces—in profile—are turned upward, and they stare blankly past three barechested men who tower above them with raised arms and clenched fists.

Where there are pictorial records that capture an inescapably powerful group image such as the one described above, or the kinetic excitement of deeply cantilevered back bends amidst swirling skirts, as in photographs of *Finding a Way Out,* one senses a different company trying to cast off all the missionary baggage that encumbered them. One can sense the performers dancing back and forth between the visions of General Armstrong on one side and the image of the "New Negro" as a modern dancer on the other—with Williams standing diplomatically in between, orchestrating the whole with consummate pragmatic skill.

The later 1930s found the Hampton Creative Dance Group continuing their eastern and southern tours with little change in their repertoire other than the addition of a suite of Haitian dances. The company's schedule for 1938 and 1939 included New York concerts at Columbia University's Horace Mann Auditorium and at the Heckscher Theatre. Other performances took them to Baltimore, Hartford, and Boston.

The review that appeared in the *Boston Evening Transcript* after the company's March 20, 1939, performance presented another interesting but specious approach to explaining the relationship between African-American dancers and their source material. The critic (identified only as W. R.) wrote that this relationship was one of "cousins twice removed." Since white modern dancers had found their sources in primal, improvisational, and natural movement, then Williams's group, which had gained access to these sources solely "through the interpolations of Graham, Holm, Tamiris, and the Bennington School," was another example of black dancers finding themselves in a peculiar situation.[55]

It is true that modern dance choreographers of the 1920s and 1930s were dedicated to finding primary human movement instincts, tapping into basic emotions, and exploring aesthetic realms that had little to do with the artificial beauty of ballet. The exposure of Williams and his students to modern dance trends certainly had significant effects on their dance training, their performance style, and their artistic objectives. But the primal impulses of modern dance pioneers were a *part* of the Western theatrical dance tradition even though they were a *reaction* to that same tradition. Some early modern dance was considered "primitive" because its earthiness and percussiveness contrasted so completely with aspects of the tradition to which it was related—classical ballet. It had very little resemblance to the dance of traditional cultures. The dance traditions of Africa and the Caribbean, for example, were so deeply rooted in religion, ritual, and the daily lives of the people that they not only reflected the sources of human movement motivation, they were inseparable from them.

What African-American performers gained from early modern dance was far different from the elements that were related to their African or Caribbean heritages. Contrary to the Boston critic's opinion, it may have been more accurate to say that modern dance was the "cousin twice removed" from elemental human movement. What African-American dancers gained from modern dance was entrée into the new development in Western theatrical dance and the spirit of innovation that movement embraced.

Another review of the 1939 Boston appearance of the Hampton company indicated that the dancers had experienced commendable artistic growth as performers. Walter Terry, who had first seen the company two years previously and was now writing for the *Boston Herald*, called them "promising and often brilliant." Predictably, he complimented them on their "enviable command of all the intricacies of rhythm" and their fresh naturalness. He singled out the men of the company as being "masters of the dance"—another indication of the special aura that surrounded Hampton's male dancers.[56]

Terry also felt that the company's repertoire reflected choreographic growth. He considered Williams's labor dance, *Dis Ole Hammer*, one of the finest contributions to the program, "a magnificent fusion of song and rhythm, strength and beauty of movement and a spirit of play in work."[57] The critic from the *Boston Evening Transcript* had, likewise, been impressed by Williams's choreography and described the "fantastically delicate treatment" of his *Cake-walk* as minuet-like.[58] Although the company had always been well received by its audiences and generally well spoken of by critics, this was the first time Williams's choreography was singled out as being outstanding. These acknowledgments of his artistic development were particularly remarkable considering that he was a man who had begun his major choreographic work for the theatrical stage at the age of forty-eight.

After another southern tour in 1940, the company entered a four-year period during which it performed very little. America was inexorably drawn into World War II, and many of the young men who would have been attending school and dancing at Hampton found themselves defending their country instead. After the war, the company regained some of its momentum and in 1946 resumed touring in the eastern, southern, and midwestern United States, but it lapsed into another period of fewer performances for the balance of the 1940s. This was perhaps due to Williams's waning interest in the company and the pressures he felt from his many university, community, and business responsibilities. Whatever the reasons, the Hampton Creative Dance

Group apparently could not maintain its highly visible and successful performance ventures without the strength of his leadership.

When Williams retired from Hampton in 1951, he had served as an outstanding athletic director who coached many winning teams, as the chair of the health and physical education department, and on the governing boards of many national health and physical education organizations. He was the author of two books and numerous articles, and his business acumen resulted in the development of the New Bayshore Corporation, which provided much-needed resort and recreational facilities for thousands of black people in the Hampton area.

His contributions to the development of black concert dance were similar in many respects to those of other black artists who were attempting to establish companies during the 1930s. This was especially true in regard to his synthesizing dance material from different cultures. Through his resourceful direction, he established a company and built a concert repertoire that enabled him to accomplish what he had begun writing of as early as 1917: to make his people aware of their diverse cultural heritage and to share that awareness with others. He accomplished this before other black artists such as Asadata Dafora and Katherine Dunham had begun touring nationally with their companies.

Charles Williams differed from other black dance innovators of the time in that his artistic achievements took place primarily within a scholastic environment. By studying at two important institutions that trained physical education teachers during the early twentieth century, Springfield College and the Harvard Summer School of Physical Education, Williams was able to incorporate contemporary innovations in physical education into his program at Hampton. These included introducing dance-related subject matter such as aesthetic calisthenics, gymnastic dancing, folk and national dances, and eventually modern dance. In this respect, his pioneering efforts were an important part of the overall impact that physical culture and dance had on American university education; consequently, his contributions were similar to those of other early dance educators who were associated with the Bennington School of Dance. He was the first African American to make inroads in these areas, and he was very likely the first American of any color to establish and maintain a national touring company composed of college students.

Hemsley Winfield and Francis Atkins in *Jungle Wedding*, 1931.
(Courtesy of the Joe Nash Collection)

Hemsley Winfield's New
Negro Art Theatre Dance Group in
Life and Death. Winfield is on the
floor, center. (Courtesy of the Joe
Nash Collection)

EDWARD A. BLATT presents

"HARLEM"

THE THRILLING PLAY OF NEW YORK'S BLACK BELT

By William Jourdan Rapp and Wallace Thurman   Staged by Chester Erskin

Harlem! . . . The City that Never Sleeps! . . . A
Strange, Exotic Island in the Heart of New York! . . .
Rent Parties! . . . Sweetbacks! . . . Hincty Wenches!
Number runners! . . . Chippies! . . . Jazz Love! . . .
Primitive Passion! . . . Voodeo! . . . Hot-stuff
Men! . . . Uproarious Comedy! . . . Powerful Drama!

MAJESTIC THEATRE
CHICAGO
Commencing Sunday Night, APRIL 28th

Playbill for *Harlem*, 1929. (Billy Rose
Theatre Collection; New York Public
Library for the Performing Arts; Astor,
Lenox and Tilden Foundations)

Run Little Chillun', 1933. Ollie Burgoyne is in the top row,
second from right. (Billy Rose Theatre Collection; New York
Public Library for the Performing Arts; Astor, Lenox and
Tilden Foundations)

Ollie Burgoyne as Mother Kanda in *Run Little Chillun'*, photo by Stella F. Simon (Photographs and Prints Division, Schomburg Center for Research in Black Culture, New York Public Library for the Performing Arts; Astor, Lenox and Tilden Foundations)

HAMPTON AFLOAT AND AFIELD

❡ For a hundred days in ten states a score of colored boys and Indians from Hampton will hold pageants through the summer of 1914.

❡ Upon the little, eighty-five-foot schooner "Hampton" the chorus will make the long voyage from Hampton Roads, Virginia, to Bar Harbor, Maine.

❡ To be crew, cast, and chorus; to act, to sing, to march, to sleep in the crowded forecastle afloat, to make camp ashore, to give the best of their peoples' songs and customs to strangers; to try to gain new scholarships for new boys at Hampton—this is the gift of these Negro and Indian students to their school.

❡ Hampton Institute stands to-day for all that aids in training members of undeveloped races to become earnest, industrious, Christian citizens. It teaches them the dignity of labor, the happiness of service, and the value of moral and physical cleanliness.

❡ Building schools, teaching children, making homes tilling lands, and leading communities, they have labored since Hampton began.

❡ We are seeking investments in lives One hundred dollars, a full scholarship, will give a boy or a girl one year of training at Hampton.

❡ Will you take stock in a life ?

A flyer for *Hampton Afloat and Afield,* 1914. (Courtesy of Hampton University Archives)

A young Charles Holston Williams
at Hampton Institute. (Courtesy of
Hampton University Archives)

The African Quartet, composed of Hampton
students from Sierra Leone, Natal, and
Liberia. (Courtesy of Hampton University
Archives)

Men of the Hampton Creative Dance Group, posed on the campus in African costumes. (Courtesy of Hampton University Archives)

Men of the Hampton Creative Dance Group in *Fangai Man.* (Courtesy of Hampton University Archives)

The Hampton Creative Dance Group in *Middle Passage*. (Courtesy of
Hampton University Archives)

Women of the Hampton Creative Dance Group in *City Called Heaven*.
(Courtesy of Hampton University Archives)

Women of the Hampton Creative Dance Group in *Finding a Way Out.*
(Courtesy of Hampton University Archives)

5

Asadata Dafora

AFRICAN DANCE WAS A SEMINAL INFLUENCE on the choreography of black concert dancers of the 1930s. In dances such as
Ritual, African Themes, and *Jungle Wedding,* Hemsley Winfield and
Edna Guy presented their interpretations of African culture during their
1931 concerts. They did not have firsthand knowledge of African dance,
however, and their choreography was based on expressions of their subjective feelings about African themes and subject matter. Charles
Williams, on the other hand, was able to expand his knowledge of
African dance by supplementing his own research with the input of
his African students.

There was, however, one artist, Asadata Dafora Horton, who established himself as the preeminent purveyor of African dance and culture in America during the thirties. Dafora was the first native African artist to exert a strong influence on American concert dance and
American culture in general. His work may be thought of as a contin-
uation of the influence African art had been exerting on American and
European art and culture for decades. The success of Dafora's efforts
to bring African dance to American audiences was not a fluke but the
product of a cultural confluence that involved several different artistic movements.

In the visual arts, for example, cubism—one of the most important movements in the history of Western painting—was heavily influenced by European interest in African sculpture. At the turn of the century, the admiration of African art by French avant-garde painters came about, first of all, because of its accessibility. Beginning in the mid-nineteenth century, European nations became increasingly interested in collecting art from their colonies. This was often motivated by a desire to understand the cultures of the colonized subjects, so that the knowledge could then be used to the colonists' benefit.[1] Large numbers of artifacts from Africa and Oceania were brought to newly established ethnological museums where, for the first time, they could be viewed by the general public, private collectors, and artists. Although these objects were initially frowned upon because they did not adhere to the naturalistic, representational canons that had dominated European art since the Renaissance, they eventually gained popular approval, and the appreciation of primitive sculpture reached a high point in Europe between 1915 and 1925.[2]

Parisian painters were ahead of the public and ethnologists in their appreciation of primitive art. As early as 1905 the *fauve* artists Vlaminck and Derain and, later, Matisse began collecting African art.[3] By 1907, when Picasso created his first works relating to African sculpture, he had admired African art for some time. He did not view it—as some others did—as a quaint relic of primitivism but as a highly skilled art of compositional purity with its own original vocabulary. In part under the influence of this art, his work during the 1910s and 1920s marked the development of cubism.[4]

European fascination with Africa also influenced the performing arts during the 1920s. A prime example existed in the repertoire of the avant-garde ballet company Les Ballets Suédois (1920–25), during its short existence one of the leading exponents of dance modernism. Founded by a wealthy landowner, Rolf de Maré (who also produced *La Revue Nègre*, the show that introduced Josephine Baker to European audiences in 1925), Les Ballet Suédois presented the African-influenced ballet *La Création du Monde* in 1923.

The ballet, which was described as bringing "black African art into the Western theater for the first time,"[5] was a collaboration among some of Europe's leading artists. Their fascination with Africa and African America was summed up by the writer Kay Boyle, who said that the ambition of the moment among Blaise Cendrars (the poet who wrote the libretto for the ballet) and his friends seemed to be to become as African-Negroid as possible.[6] Among those who collaborated on *La Création du Monde* were the composer Darius Milhaud, the choreographer Jean Börlin, and the painter Fernand Léger.

Milhaud had frequented music halls and jazz clubs in Paris, traveled in Latin America, where he studied folk and popular music, and spent time in America, where he haunted Harlem's jazz clubs. Léger's cubist paintings had been influenced by African art. Jean Börlin (who had choreographed an African-influenced solo, *Sculpture Nègre*, in 1919) did not attempt to use movement that approximated authentic African dance in *La Création du Monde*. It was not the dance, in fact, that dominated the stage but the Afro-cubist costumes, masks, head-pieces, and moving scenic elements, which were designed by Fernand Léger to create a theater of total movement in which the dancers were considered on a par with the other theatrical elements.

During the 1920s, the rage for blackness was simultaneously sweeping Europe and America and affected blacks and whites alike. Black visual artists in America became more concerned with the African antecedents of their art, and black intellectuals such as Alain Locke became avid collectors of African art. Locke wrote about the aesthetic issues surrounding the African heritage of African Americans, and he was aware of "an essential enigma in [the] culture-building enterprise" of intellectuals and artists during the Harlem Renaissance.[7]

Locke acknowledged that the African had a rich expressive tradition in graphic and sculptural forms, but that black Americans did not have an artistic tradition that was comparably as strong. Yet, he was "convinced that African art held a key to Afro-American artistic expression."[8] The knowledge of the arts of Africa could free African Americans from imitating European traditions. Black artists could develop new idioms based on their rightful inheritance just as European artists such as Picasso, Braque, Brancusi, and Lehmbruck "were liberated through African sculpture to powerful restatements of human form."[9]

Locke's ideas were reflected in the works of artists such as Richmond Barthé, whose bronze sculptures *African Dancer* and *Feral Benga* captured the deep rhythms of Africa in sinuous human forms. Barthé's interest in capturing movement is clearly apparent in these works. He used the dancer Randolph Sawyer as a model for one of his most ambitious projects—a sculpture memorializing the poet James Weldon Johnson to stand at the 110th Street entrance to Central Park—which was never realized because of the shortage of metal during World War II.[10]

Other artists, such as Aaron Douglas, one of the best known painters of the Harlem Renaissance, developed a style of drawing that echoed African iconography. Douglas created drawings with rhythmic vitality that fairly jumped off the pages of black publications such as *The Crisis* and *Opportunity* and white magazines such as *Vanity Fair* and *Theatre Arts*. Angular stylization, stark forms, and black silhouettes echoed the decorative, nonrepresentational art of Africa. His were truly powerful statements reflecting the synthesis of Africa and African America. His images conveyed an ageless modernity, the sense of something very ancient and primal as well as something startlingly contemporary.

Whereas African plastic art, and the art that was patterned after it, was attracting serious attention during the early twentieth century, authentic African dance was not held in equally high esteem. It was primarily presented at international exhibitions and world's fairs, as it had been since the late nineteenth century. In Europe, exhibits such as the "Kaffir Kraal" (or African village) at the 1889 Earl's Court Exhibition in London blended ethnography and entertainment.[11] The practice of exhibiting human beings as well as artifacts from other cultures was a unique kind of cultural appropriation that was characteristic of colonial Europe and had its counterpart in nineteenth-century America.

One of the earliest American presentations of African performers at exhibitions offers an interesting perspective on how African cultural influences found their way into African-American theater. In 1883, six years prior to the Earl's Court Exhibition, a group of performers from Dahomey failed to arrive for the opening of San Francisco's Midwinter Fair because their ship was delayed. Two black entertainers, Bert Williams and George Walker, who had recently begun collaborating as a vaudeville comedy team, donned loincloths and feathers and temporarily substituted for the missing Africans. As soon as the ship arrived, the two entertainers were out of a job, but they remained to observe the Dahomean performers, and they decided that if they were ever able to produce a show of their own they would include African characterizations.[12]

Twenty years later when they starred in the first all-black show performed at a major Broadway theater, *In Dahomey* (1903), they brought their version of Africa to the American stage. The show dealt with African themes and characters only in a peripheral way, but it was a smashing success in New York and in London. It was, however, Williams and Walker's second show, *Abyssinia* (1906), that fulfilled the team's desire to bring a meaningful interpretation of Africa to the American stage. As Allen Woll points out, "The Africans of *Abyssinia* were depicted as representatives of an ancient and praiseworthy culture, and Americans were the targets of humor."[13]

Later, less-flattering depictions of Africa appeared in plays such as *Taboo*, which was noteworthy as one of Paul Robeson's first stage appearances. Written by Mary Hoyt Wiborg and produced by Isadora Duncan's brother, Augustin, at the Sam Harris Theatre in New York in 1922, the play included a dream sequence in which Robeson appeared as an African king. Photographs show him in pseudo-African garb and a ludicrous fright wig.

There were other shows in which white performers portrayed Africans. In *Golden Dawn*, a 1927 musical drama of interracial romance and miscegenation, a white dancer, Jacques Cartier, performed an African witch-doctor dance in full body makeup. Interestingly enough, Countee Cullen, the reviewer for *Opportunity*, singled him out for special mention.[14] Cartier, who had performed in the *Ziegfeld Follies of 1923* and the *Greenwich Village Follies of 1923*, became well known for his African dances and performed them in two Hollywood films during the early 1930s.

After decades of European and American artists' using African images as inspiration for their work, after exhibitions and world's fairs, and after various interpretations of Africa on the theatrical stage, there is little wonder that a native African armed with extensive knowledge of both his own folk culture and Western theatrical art could embark upon a successful career that would be described as the "beginning of an entirely new and healthy adaptation of the pure African tradition of ritual dance, costume, and music."[15]

Asadata Dafora was born on August 4, 1890. He was a native of Freetown, Sierra Leone, West Africa, a settlement that had been founded by British abolitionists and philanthropists in 1787 as a haven for freed and runaway slaves. His great-great-grandfather returned to Africa after living as a slave in Nova Scotia, where he had adopted the surname Horton from his master. Dafora spoke of the auspicious meanings of his African names in a 1934 interview. The name Asadata indicated that he was born on the day of a great festival and destined to become famous; and Dafora, the name of his great-grandfather, meant that the bearer had vision.[16]

He grew up in a privileged environment. Several members of his family were distinguished in their community because of their education, their multicultural background, and their political connections. His father, the town treasurer, was educated in England. His mother studied in Vienna and Paris and became an accomplished pianist, and his great uncle was knighted by Queen Victoria.[17] The Dafora family's African heritage in combination with their European education provided a broad cultural background that eventually shaped his art. As a child in Sierra Leone, Dafora received a Western education at the English colonial Wesleyan School, but he also had an abiding love of and interest in African cultural traditions. Years later, he alluded to the early discovery of this interest in an interview with the critic Margaret Lloyd. He spoke of his childhood experiences of running away from home on numerous occasions to follow the native festivals, which lasted for days and nights in the countryside.[18] As a young man, he traveled throughout West Africa, studying dance, music, folk tales, and languages (he familiarized himself with twelve African languages), and he eventually used the accumulated knowledge as the foundation for his art.

When Dafora was twenty years old, he made his first trip to Europe. He began his performing career in a Berlin nightclub where he danced for enthusiastic audiences. He was encouraged to form a dance group, which he later described as composed of white dancers "made up to look colored."[19] Around the same time—between 1910 and 1912—he began to pursue other musical interests by studying at the La Scala Opera in Milan and touring England, France, and Germany with productions of *Aida* and *L'Africaine*.[20]

After serving in the West African Frontier Force of the British army, he made several more trips back and forth between Europe and Africa as he continued to study and perform. "After a maze of European experiences," Lloyd wrote, "after seeing European dance and other art forms, he realized the distinctive beauty of African art and culture, and resolved to devote his life to setting it before people."[21]

Dafora arrived in New York in 1929, at the age of thirty-nine. Before pursuing his goal of bringing African art to the American public, he made a brief but unsuccessful attempt at a career as a concert singer. His first concert was given at the Mother A.M.E. Zion Church on 137th Street on January 26, 1931.[22] The program—"A Unique Joint Recital"—billed him as a lyric tenor under the name Austin Dafora Horton. He shared the stage with his cousin from Sierra Leone, Madeleine Graden (Princess Musudee).[23]

Finding little success as a concert singer, Dafora began to formulate plans for presenting African culture to American audiences and took his first steps toward achieving that goal. With the help of the Native African Union, an organization of Africans living in New York, he began training and rehearsing a group of dancers, drummers, and singers and seeking opportunities to present them to local audiences. In an early New York *Age* account of one of the group's performances at Madison Square Garden, his company was referred to as the "West African Jabawa male troupe." The program—on October 7, 1933—consisted of songs and dances from *Zoonga*, an African opera he had begun writing. The newspaper article also said that the group had recently performed at the Little Theatre of the West 135th Street YMCA, at the Experimental Theatre, and at Mountain Lake, New Jersey.[24]

Dafora's early performances were not particularly well received. Some observers considered his work "too high-brow" because it did not fit their preconceptions about the "savagery" of African performance. He did, however, begin to gain some access to New York's black cultural establishment when he and his company appeared at Town Hall on November 25, 1933. The Urban League benefit program included such black stars as Bill "Bojangles" Robinson, the Hall Johnson Chorale, and the actress Rose McClendon, who had recently appeared in *Porgy*.[25]

By this time, Dafora was forty-three years old, a comparatively late age to begin establishing a dance company and artistic credibility in New York. Not one to be discouraged by such issues, Dafora expressed a different point of view, which kept his visions and his enthusiasm alive: "In my country," he said, "we do not talk of age. We have a saying, 'Every man has his time.' I do not think of how old I am, but of my 'time.' This may be it."[26]

His time arrived when Anne Kennedy, the business manager of the Unity Theatre, saw his drummers and dancers perform at Madison Square Garden. She was impressed and delighted by what she saw and invited him to perform on March 4, 1934, at her theater, a small make-shift space on East Twenty-third Street that had formerly been John's Beauty Parlor. Shortly afterward, she encouraged him to create an evening-length work, and he began rehearsals for *Kykunkor*, his dance-opera.[27]

The all-male company Anne Kennedy had initially seen consisted of Africans such as Abdul Assen, who had participated in Dafora's first New York shows. After leaving New York to perform at Chicago's Century of Progress in 1933, Assen had returned to rejoin the group, which was now called the Shologa Aloba Singers and Dancers. It is not certain when female dancers began to be recruited for the company, but it was probably not until preparations were being made for *Kykunkor*. They, unlike Dafora's first male performers, were not Africans and did not have prior training in African dance. They were African Americans who received most of their dance training from Dafora. He had attempted to use a few dancers from revues but found it difficult to adapt their "American-made 'jazz'" style to his objective of presenting authentic African art.[28] With the exception of Frances Atkins, who had appeared with Hemsley Winfield's company, the women he chose had little performance experience.

Dafora based *Kykunkor* on the folklore of the Mendi, an ethnic group neighboring his own Temne people, and set it near the village of Kam-lawoo, Sierra Leone. In the following synopsis (which I paraphrase from a souvenir program of the production)[29] it is clear that his choice of material was rife with opportunities to highlight the dance, music, and drama of West African culture:

> The story takes place in a "maidens'" village where young girls are taken to be initiated through the rites of womanhood. The curtain rises upon a scene of young women preparing food under the watchful eye of the Oto-bone, or chaperone.
> Drum beats announce the arrival of Bokari, a young man from a neigh-boring village who has come to choose a bride. He gallantly presents the

Otobone with a gift, then makes his choice from among the young women who have danced the Bundo, or Maidens' Dance, for him. Bokari and his chosen are left alone to become acquainted as they dance the Susu, an engagement dance. They also dance the Alogobole, which expresses their growing love for each other.

The Chief conducts the wedding ceremony and afterward dances happily while sternly admonishing the drummers to keep good rhythm. Following this, Bokari and his bride dance a wedding dance, which is interrupted by Miramu, the Witch Woman, who has been sent by a jealous rival to spoil the occasion. Although Bokari shouts his defiance at her, she succeeds in casting a spell upon him, and he sinks unconscious to the ground.

Everyone in the wedding party sings to elicit aid from the gods. The Devil Dancer dances around Bokari to lift the spell, but to no avail. Finally, the Witch Doctor is summoned, and after tremendous effort he succeeds in drawing out the evil spirit.

The third and final act centers around several dances that express the renewed joy of the wedding party. A maiden dances herself into a frenzy; the Eboe, or eccentric dancer, fairly outdoes himself. The men perform a challenge dance; and the finale is a Jabawa, or festival dance. As the curtain closes, Bokari and Musu Esami dance together ecstatically along with the other young couples.

Dafora created his work by skillfully combining African and European performance traditions. From his African roots he drew upon the rich tradition of festival art. As Martin Banham points out in his book *African Theatre Today,* in its original setting this art functions not simply as entertainment or diversion but as a symbol for seasonal rhythms, a vehicle for ritual efficacy, and a means of religious communication.[30] The retention of a sense of these spiritual functions helped shape the unique structure of *Kykunkor* and also accounted for the opera's powerful impact.

Dafora filled out the framework of his story with authentic songs and dances that he had committed to memory during his travels among various African ethnic groups. He reshaped the material to serve new functions that were determined by the maxims of Western theater. In a traditional setting, for example, the order of songs, dances, and spoken material would have been determined by the exigencies of a particular community's ritual needs. To accommodate a Western theatrical production, however, the material was presented in three acts and shaped to fit the logical needs of a dramatic plot that adhered to the Aristotelian structure of beginning, middle, and end.

The proscenium stage was another factor that affected the spatial structure of dances, which otherwise would have had the free-ranging use of village and countryside in their original settings. Likewise, material that might have occurred in religious rituals lasting for days was condensed into the space of a few hours. Dafora realized that he had to adhere to European theatrical precepts, to a certain extent, if he wanted to achieve his goal of having African art accepted as serious art according to Western standards.

Since there is no record in Dafora's own words of how he created the details of *Kykunkor,* one can only speculate about the similarities between certain elements of his dance-opera and the themes that run through many Romantic ballets—the amorous encounter between a prince (in this case a chief's son) and a maiden, a wedding scene or some other celebration that includes a royal entourage and functions as a pretext for danced *divertissements,* the sudden arrival of a supernatural being who heightens the dramatic situation, and a joyous finale of many dances. One might contend that some of these are universal themes that appear consistently in the folklore of different cultures around the world. But one must also take into consideration Dafora's familiarity with different types of European art. It is likely that he had familiarized himself with ballet scenarios as well as operas during his travels in Europe.

What is known is that Dafora was the composer, librettist, choreographer, director, and leading man of his production. He faced the formidable task of teaching approximately eighteen dances and twenty songs to his cast. Though his company had performed some of the material on previous occasions, he had to do a considerable amount of reconstruction from memories of his early days in Africa. Fortunately, he had an able assistant, a pianist named Margaret Upshur, who spent hours notating the songs as he sang them to her.

Before mounting *Kykunkor* for Anne Kennedy, Dafora presented it at several other places, including the Congo Room of Harlem's Saratoga Club on March 24, 1934. The anonymous reviewer for the New York *Age* called it an event "that well nigh should draw some praise in its attempt to bring something new to Harlem."[31] He felt that the artistry in the work was masterful, and, if given the right setting and production elements, the show would "take New York by storm for its originality and color."[32]

Kykunkor opened at the Unity Theatre on May 5, but the ecstatic predictions of the Harlem reviewer did not come true until four days of almost empty houses had passed. After Anne Kennedy prevailed upon John Martin to attend the May 8 performance, he published a supportive review the following day; the box office was deluged with requests for tickets, and enthusiastic audiences began to throng the tiny theater. Artists such as George Gershwin, Theodore Dreiser, Helen Tamiris, and Charles Weidman became regulars.[33]

In Martin's first review he observed, "The performance is eminently worth seeking out, not only by those who are interested in dancing, but by anyone who likes genuine and exciting theatre-art." He went on to speak of "amazing songs and dances" and said in conclusion, "Here, by all means, is one of the most exciting dance performances of the season."[34]

Other critics also found much to praise. John Mason Brown of the *New York Post* was impressed with the "furious vitality of the production."[35] One exception was Lincoln Kirstein, who was ambivalent. After he praised the performances of three male dancers, he went on to say that he found the overall production "interesting, although it [was] neither a consistent dramatic whole, nor an 'authentic' piece of anthropology, nor an 'artistic' experience." In closing he said, "So much of it is unrelieved and hard to look at. Nevertheless, one visit is more rewarding than any other recital that has been presented this spring."[36]

Whatever the critical reception, *Kykunkor* began to catch people's attention and attract consistently enthusiastic audiences. The production's tremendous magnetism was due in part to the fact that very little authentic African dance had been seen previously in America. Consequently, critics struggled to compare it to something with which they were familiar. Martin, for example, spoke of the production as the visualization of *The Golden Bough*, the seminal work on religious cults and ancient myths written by the anthropologist James Frazer in 1890.[37]

Another reason crowds were drawn to the Unity Theatre was the intense energy that infused the production, an energy created by the polyrhythmic vortex of music and dance. This, in fact, was the element most often mentioned by critics. Martin said, "Through-out the action, three drummers sit at the side of the stage beating out hypnotic rhythms sometimes of extraordinary composition. Against this background the beautiful voices of the singers rise from time to time, but more often the terrific vitality of the dancers vents itself."[38] John Mason Brown made similar observations: "Its dancing is possessed of an amazing primitive energy. . . . Its dancer-singers are tireless performers. . . . They never lose their energy, their sultry symbolism, their savage strength, and their joyous response to the ever-haunting and intricate thumpings of the tom-toms. . . . Interesting—and certainly different—as the whole program is, it is the four tireless drummers at one side of the crowded stage who give the most astonishing and compelling performance of the evening."[39]

The critics' consistent fascination with the drummers as well as the dancers suggests that they had never before witnessed such explosive energy produced by the special symbiosis that exists between dancers and musicians in traditional West African dance—what the cultural historian Robert Farris Thompson calls "the bright willingness to respond to change."[40] This relationship enables performers to exchange cues and leaves room for sparks of improvisation to ignite within the structure of the dance. These improvisational moments, in turn, enable the performers to "catch fire" in a way that is not often seen in more rigidly structured forms of Western theatrical dance. The energy that this symbiosis generates has the potential of taking the participants (as well as the observers) across the threshold into the altered state of consciousness called possession.

In his second review, on May 13, Martin was impressed by the semblance of ritual possession that was created on stage. He spoke again of the "extremely skillful drummers, who become almost possessed as the action progresses by the very hypnosis of their own playing." He continued, "It is, indeed, this possession that gives the performance its unique quality."[41]

Critics especially pointed to Abdul Assen's portrayal of the witch doctor as an instance of a theatrical performance that created the illusion of true possession. Martin was utterly amazed at the verity of Assen's falsetto incantations and his animal ecstasy as he cast the devil out of the bridegroom. He further commented that the abandon and improvisational vitality of the scene was characteristic of the best parts of the production.[42]

But it was Kirstein's discussion that, again through its ambivalence, pointed out the quandary in which some critics found themselves. After calling Assen "a Mohammedan witch-doctor accidentally on a New York stage," he continued, "This performance develops into a frenzy of self-hypnosis, diabolical gaiety, anguish, and success which is fiercely dramatic because *it is experienced* [my italics] . . . but it is always more of a black sacrament than a good performance."[43]

Although he had begun his review by saying that the production was neither "an 'authentic' piece of anthropology, nor a dramatic whole, nor an 'artistic' experience,"[44] he still seemed to be powerfully moved by it. Yet he did not want to call it a good performance in the traditional Western theatrical sense; and he was hard pressed to know what else to call it. His emphasis upon what *Kykunkor was not* indicated that it was hard for him to categorize it; this further points out the production's uniqueness as a theatrical experience without precedent.

In reviewing Dafora's early work, critics seemed to concentrate primarily on the visceral excitement of the performances. Although many agreed that dance was an important part of the production, there was little written description of the actual choreography or movement style. It was not until several years later, during the 1940s, that critics began taking markedly different approaches to Dafora's work. The passage of time diminished their concentration on the novelty and excitement of his choreography. Writers such as Edwin Denby began taking a more analytical look at the dance itself.

Denby wrote a detailed article describing the style and technique of Dafora's work after viewing a Carnegie Hall concert in 1943. Denby was especially impressed and surprised to find that in one scene—apparently recycled from *Kykunkor*—in which a suitor chooses his bride from a line of village maidens, the movement reflected a charming ceremoniousness, a gentle manner, elegance, and lightness of play that reminded him in spirit of an eighteenth-century pastoral.[45]

He found the choreography to be built upon simple floor patterns and the repetition of small detailed movements such as sharply syncopated steps, arm variations that created secondary rhythms, and shoulders that also moved in independent rhythms. This, he felt, resulted in a remarkably lucid style in which the various parts of the body were separately defined.[46] (Robert Farris Thompson describes this technique as "a remarkable process in which the dancer democratically imparts equal life and autonomy to each dancing portion of his frame.")[47] The isolated movements were, however, orchestrated into a polyrhythmic visual whole, which, according to Denby, made the dance soar above the drum accompaniment. He praised Dafora for his striking dance intelligence, the excellent proportions and sequences of his dances, and his performing ability, all of which indicated his dances were not "savage or accidental, but were the outcome of a consistent and highly cultivated dance tradition."[48]

Besides the fact that Denby seemed to be a more descriptive writer than most of the critics of his time, his tone as well as that of others such as Walter Terry and Margaret Lloyd indicates that, during the 1930s and 1940s, Dafora began to achieve his goal of having African art accepted by the arbiters of "high" Western culture. In this way, as Lynne Fauley Emery points out, Dafora began to prove that "Black dancers working with material from their heritage could be successful on the American concert stage."[49]

After *Kykunkor's* New York run, which included stints at several other theaters including the Chanin, it toured New England and New Jersey during the late summer, and in December of 1934 it reopened in New York for a short period.

By the end of 1935, most members of Dafora's Shologa Aloba had been absorbed into the Federal Theatre Project of the Works Progress Administration (WPA). As part of the federal government's response to the massive unemployment and social upheaval caused by the Depression, the WPA was one of several programs designed to put Americans back to work. Roosevelt's New Deal had established a number of relief programs: the Federal Emergency Relief Administration (FERA) in 1933, which included community service theater projects; the Civil Works Administration (CWA), also in 1933; and finally the WPA in 1935. In spite of numerous internal and external problems, the arts projects of the WPA (the Federal Theatre Project, the Federal Music Project, and the Federal Writers Project—and eventually the Federal Dance Project) met with widespread success. As part of the Federal Theatre Project (FTP), Dafora's dancers became known officially as the African Dance Troupe.[50] His primary undertaking with the FTP was the choreography he created for one of its most successful productions—an adaptation of *Macbeth* with an all-black cast. The story of what became popularly known as the "voodoo" *Macbeth* is filled with all the intrigue and controversy that seemed to be characteristic of the FTP's short history. Those who recalled the drama behind the production told stories that were as exotic as the lush Caribbean island that became the setting for Shakespeare's play.

This unique version of *Macbeth* was the second production of the WPA's Negro Theatre Project in New York. (The first was Frank Wilson's *Walk Together Chillun!* which was also the first full-scale project of any type mounted by the FTP of New York.) The Negro Unit, as the Negro Theatre Project was also known, was originally to be co-directed by Rose McClendon and John Houseman. McClendon, one of the greatest black actresses of her time, had appeared in *Porgy* and in the Pulitzer Prize–winning play *In Abraham's Bosom.* Houseman, a close friend she chose to work with her, had gained a certain reputation for working with black artists because of his controversial but highly acclaimed production of Gertrude Stein and Virgil Thomson's opera, *Four Saints in Three Acts.* Shortly after the Negro Theatre Project was established, McClendon died, and Houseman was left in charge of establishing Harlem's Federal Theatre Unit.

Assisted by two black aides—Edward Perry, who had been his stage manager for *Four Saints,* and Carlton Moss, who helped him navigate the unfamiliar territory of black cultural politics—Houseman spent his first month assessing hundreds of applicants. Some of them had theatrical backgrounds, but many more had simply heard that there were jobs available that offered an alternative to being on the dole.[51] Houseman considered mounting several types of productions but finally decided on dividing the company into two contingents. One group would present "plays written, directed and performed by and for Negroes, in Negro locales and, preferably, on contemporary Negro subjects" (an objective that echoed W. E. B. Du Bois's statement concerning the purpose of black theater) while the other group would present "classical" productions.[52] Houseman was concerned that all-black productions of classical plays might become travesties of the originals. So he decided that he would need directors with outstanding creative powers. For the first of these productions, he contacted his friend Orson Welles, who had first impressed him in the role of Tybalt in a New York production of *Romeo and Juliet*. Welles—then twenty years old—had also begun to distinguish himself as a radio performer, but *Macbeth* was to be his first major directorial project. He immediately accepted the position, and his wife, Virginia, suggested the first production, *Macbeth*, set in nineteenth-century Haiti, with voodoo priestesses replacing the witches.[53]

From among the 300 hopefuls who auditioned, a cast of approximately 137 was chosen and began rehearsing in Harlem's refurbished Lafayette Theatre. The cast members had varying degrees of theatrical experience ranging from impressive to none. Among the more experienced actors, several were singled out in later accounts of the production for their colorful pasts as well as their professional capabilities.

Jack Carter, who was cast as Macbeth, was of mixed parentage. Depending upon whose version one accepted, he was either born in a French chateau and brought up in the lap of luxury as the offspring of a black American chorus girl and a European nobleman, or he was the son of a famous white actress and her servant.[54] At six foot four, Carter was a strikingly handsome man who was notorious for his heavy drinking and his fiery temper. His credits included the role of Crown in the original cast of *Porgy*. And he was purportedly an ex-gangster who had served time in prison for murder.[55]

Edna Thomas, who had the role of Lady Macbeth, had appeared in many stage productions including *Lulu Belle* and *Run, Little Chillun'*. Genteel by nature, she was noted for the literary and theatrical salon that she regularly held at her Harlem apartment and for being one of "the circle of handsome women"[56] attending A'Lelia Walker, Harlem's millionaire heiress and socialite. One writer described Thomas as "a beautiful lesbian with a passionate attachment to a European lady of considerable means."[57] Thomas, like Jack Carter, was extremely light-skinned, and both of them used makeup to darken their complexions for *Macbeth*.

Other experienced members of the cast included Canada Lee in the role of Banquo. He had seriously studied the violin, become a jockey, and been a prize-winning lightweight boxer before turning to acting

in 1933. The role of Hecate was played by Eric Burroughs, a graduate
of the Royal Academy of Drama. Lawrence Chenault, whose career
spanned minstrelsy, vaudeville, and the all-black films of Oscar Mi-
cheaux, appeared as one of the noblemen.

Several of the other performers had been associated with various
aspects of theater, including concert dance. Ollie Burgoyne, Leonard
Barros, and Beryle Banfield—all formerly with the Winfield company—
were among them. Archie Savage, who later became one of Katherine
Dunham's leading soloists, distinguished himself in the role of Siward
and was long remembered for being thrown off an eighteen-foot para-
pet every night. Another dancer, Clarence Yates, served as co-chore-
ographer with Asadata Dafora. Yates brought with him to the production a number of dancers that he and Randolph Sawyer had been
training during the preceding months.

Welles worked with his diverse cast from midnight to dawn after
finishing his radio broadcasts each night. As he began shaping his
heavily edited version of *Macbeth,* the play became a suspense thrill-
er in which the leading characters were completely manipulated by
the forces of evil. In Welles's interpretation, Macbeth did not struggle
with his conscience but could only surrender to the preordained patterns that were set into motion by the forces of darkness—Hecate, the
witches, and the voodoo hosts.

Welles created a theatrical experience that focused on spectacle rather
than psychological subtleties—a moiling, convoluted horror story rich
with sound, movement, and colorful visual effects. In using off-stage
sounds (thunder, voodoo drums, shrieking incantations, maniacal
laughter) to underscore and heighten the drama of the play, he borrowed
techniques he had learned from his radio experience. His use of lighting to create visual illusions that shifted the audience's focus from one
part of the stage to another presaged his work in cinema. As a director, he also displayed a choreographic sense of stage movement that
enabled him to incorporate his choreographers' material to its fullest
advantage.

Dafora and Yates were in charge of different aspects of the choreography, each of which highlighted major themes in the play. Yates choreographed act 2, scene 1, a gala ball scene for Macbeth's coronation
that replaced the original banquet scenario of Shakespeare's play. The

ladies of the court, decked out in their brilliantly colorful gowns designed by Nat Karson, shimmered as they were swept about by noblemen who were equally colorful in their exaggerated uniforms festooned
with ropes of outsized gold braid and fantastically huge epaulets. To
Virgil Thomson's arrangements of nineteenth-century Joseph Lanner
waltzes, Yates choreographed symmetrically patterned dances that
reflected the orderly aspects of Macbeth's world.

As the scene progressed, the lords and ladies drifted away, leaving
the stage to the confrontation between Macbeth and Banquo as the
sound of drums replaced the lilting waltzes. The murder of Banquo took
place, and Hecate was seen dragging his body away as the witches
hovered like vultures high up on the battlements of the castle. Their
chant of "Fair is foul and foul is fair" completed the ominous moment.

The waltz music was heard once again—this time quiet and distorted.
Finally the music burst forth, the lights came up on the ballroom once
more, and the dancers reestablished the previous mood. Lady Macbeth
persuaded her husband to dance, and they were seen waltzing among
their guests, but their dance became a *danse macabre* when Macbeth
saw the ghost of Banquo looming before him.

Welles's illusionistic weaving of contrasting elements—pounding
drums and lilting waltzes, witches and beautiful noblewomen, shim-
mering light and murky darkness—delineated the underlying conflict
between the superficial facade of a civilized society and the rampant
evil of "a world steadily consumed by the powers of darkness."[58] As
Richard France notes, "The contrast is both striking and complete in
every respect; in ambiance, in terms of space and sound, they are two
entirely different worlds. Within the palace walls a layer of civilization, however treacherous, exists; while just outside, the jungle lies
in waiting."[59]

The jungle outside was Dafora's domain. In addition to the three
witches, he created choreography for nine witch-women, eight witch-
men, nine voodoo women, and eight voodoo men, all of whom Macbeth engaged during his forays into their tropical netherworld. The
main scenes for the witches and their entourage were in act 1, scene
1, when—amidst a barrage of thunder and lightning—they cast their
initial spell upon Macbeth, and in act 2, scene 2, when Hecate leads
Macbeth back into the jungle.

It was in the latter scene, which followed the court ball, where the contrast between the play's two worlds was most effectively delineated. As Macbeth approached, the three central witches appeared to be suspended in midair. (They stood on a raised platform three feet above the stage and were isolated by the lighting.) Ominously silhouetted against Nat Karson's painted drop of huge expressionistic palm fronds, garbed in robes and fantastic headdresses, they loomed above three drummers seated behind a huge cauldron. The remainder of the witches and voodoo celebrants formed two concentric semicircles (one of men and one of women) around the three central witches, the drummers, and the cauldron.

Macbeth was confronted by seven possessed figures that taunted him. The semicircles became full circles of sinuous bodies dancing wildly around the cauldron while the drums increased in tempo. The ritual reached its climax with the celebrants swirling like a whirlpool around Macbeth, the three central witches, and the drummers. The finale also used flashing lights to intensify the chaotic effect.

Though not impressed by the overall acting in the production, Brooks Atkinson of the *New York Times* described the witches' scene as one of the most effective moments in Welles's transposition of Shakespeare's play from Scotland to Haiti:

> The witches have always worried the life out of the polite tragic stage. . . . But ship the witches down into the rank and fever-stricken jungle of Haiti, dress them in fantastic costumes, crowd the stage with mad and gabbing throngs of evil worshippers, beat the jungle drums, raise the voices until the jungle echoes, stuff a gleaming naked witch doctor into the cauldron, hold up Negro masks in the baleful light—and there you have a witches' scene that is logical and stunning and a triumph of theatre art.[60]

The review most often pointed out by those who remembered the events surrounding *Macbeth* was by Percy Hammond, whose writings tended to adhere to the right-wing Republican leanings of his newspaper, the *Herald Tribune.* Hammond wrote, "What surprised me last night was the inability of so melodious a race to sing the music of Shakespeare. . . . The actors sounded the notes with a muffled timidity that was often unintelligible. They seemed to be afraid of the Bard, though they were playing him on home grounds."[61]

His review was remembered not only for its mocking tone but also because of the events that occurred not long after it was published. According to Houseman, Dafora was extremely upset by the article and came to see him the next day accompanied by Abdul Assen and his drummers. They all agreed that the review was "the work of an enemy," and then Dafora and his men withdrew in stony silence.[62] There were varying accounts of what happened next, including stories of Abdul Assen fashioning a voodoo doll and Dafora and his troupe drumming and chanting all night in the theater after the next performance. What is clear is that Hammond died a few days later of what was reported to be pneumonia.

The entire rehearsal period and performance of the Lafayette Theatre *Macbeth* was full of similar stories of supernatural occurrences, political rumblings that engaged factions ranging from Harlem's Urban League to the Communist Party, and pitched battles among Welles, his cast, and his associates. Much of the drama and intrigue surrounding the play's production was spontaneous, but some of it was orchestrated by Welles, whose lust for publicity was driven by his enormous ego.

The result of it all was that, in spite of (or because of) all the controversy, *Macbeth*, which officially opened on April 14, 1936, was a huge success—Harlem's grand theatrical event of the decade. On the day of the premiere, the Elks Lodge band marched in full uniform through the streets of Harlem with a banner announcing the production. That night, the Lafayette Theatre glowed with floodlighting, thousands of people thronged the streets, and luminaries from uptown and downtown society were present.

It played for ten weeks in Harlem to standing-room-only crowds and then moved downtown to the Adelphi Theatre on Fifty-fourth Street, where it played for eight weeks. After its New York triumphs, it toured nationally on Federal Theatre stages in Detroit, Cleveland, Dallas, Chicago, Hartford, and Bridgeport. It became a vehicle that successfully transported Welles's interpretation of Afro-Caribbean culture to America audiences.

After *Macbeth*, Dafora was no longer associated with the Federal Theatre Project. The following year, however, the tradition of his African dance-operas was continued within the FTP. *Bassa Moona: The Land*

I Love, a production that was blatantly derivative of *Kykunkor,* opened at the Lafayette Theatre on December 7, 1937. It was written, directed, and choreographed by two Nigerians, Norman Coker and Momodu Johnson. It was a far more lavish production than *Kykunkor* since it, like *Macbeth,* drew upon the resources of the federal government. Consequently, it made use of some of the best scenic and costume designers in New York and a cast of forty actors and thirty dancers.

Bassa Moona told the story of an African king who angers his people by selling rubber from sacred trees to white invaders. The king's son-in-law challenges him and finally restores his people's god to them. For the most part, the plot was a pretext for including familiar scenarios such as a princely betrothal, appearances of a witch-woman and devil man, and the casting and breaking of spells. There were some additional scenes of West African village life, ceremonial preparations for war, and a coronation scene, all of which were obvious attempts to surpass the theatrical limitations of *Kykunkor.*[63]

Taking a cue from the publicity that accompanied the purported supernatural occurrences surrounding the production of *Macbeth,* Momodu Johnson created his own black-magic press releases. There was a report of the drummer who committed a sacrilegious act, mysteriously died, and whose ghost followed the cast of the show from one theater to the next. (The show played at the Lafayette, Ritz, Daly's, and Majestic theaters between December 7 and February 1.) Johnson baited the press further by explaining that his drums were made of the skins of sacrificed virgins.[64]

John Martin remarked that *Bassa Moona* was better staged and smoother than *Kykunkor,* but it lacked the impact and spontaneity of it predecessor.[65] The production was another vehicle that brought African dance-drama to the American public. The government's practice of touring its most successful productions and offering very low ticket prices again provided a diverse national audience with a semblance of African art presented in a theatrical form that Dafora had created.

Dafora's next major project was in March 1937 when he participated in the *Negro Dance Evening* with Edna Guy, Alison Burroughs, and Katherine Dunham. Clarence Yates, who shared the choreographic credits for *Macbeth,* also performed in the concert. As mentioned earlier, it was a significant event that featured the dances of the black diaspora, and Dafora received the highest critical praise of all the participating artists.

By August 1938, Dafora had produced his second major dance-drama, *Zunguru*, at the Davenport Theatre on East Twenty-seventh Street. Martin observed that it lacked the novelty and surprise of *Kykunkor*, since other groups in the meantime had explored similar material. He added, however, that the new dance-drama used an approach entirely different from those of its predecessors.[66] Several things distinguished *Zunguru* from *Kykunkor* and *Bassa Moona*. Dafora used English dialogue instead of the African dialect of his earlier production. He also chose to abandon the folk tales he had used in his earlier work and drew upon themes that had parallels in his own experiences. His leading character, Sooree, the prince of Kaduna, Nigeria, returns to his homeland after a five-year stay in Europe where he has received a modern education. He is greeted with apprehension by his elders, who frown upon his new ways. The situation is complicated because of intertribal friction between his father's tribe and a neighboring one. Fortunately for all concerned, Sooree intercedes to settle the dispute, unites the tribes, and becomes the leader of the newly formed confederation. The story ends on a final note of felicity when he marries the daughter of the opposing chief.

After choreographing another project in June 1939—the dances for a production of *The Emperor Jones* starring Paul Robeson at the Ridgeway Theatre in White Plains, New York—Dafora presented a reworked version of *Zunguru* in 1940. In his review, Walter Terry noted that the show was tighter and swifter than its 1938 version; and he complimented Dafora on the improved lighting, costuming, staging, and "electrifying" dances.[67] Among the changes Dafora made, he reestablished his earlier practice of using African dialogue instead of English.

Like *Kykunkor*, the show had to be moved from one small theater to another to keep it before the public. It first opened at the Hudson Guild Neighborhood House at 436 West Twenty-seventh Street on March 17 for a few performances. It moved to the Cherry Lane Theatre on March 20 for five performances and ended up at the Chanin Auditorium on April 8. Reviewing the Chanin performance, John Mason Brown of the *New York Post* made a weak attempt to be positive by observing that Dafora's singing in the new version of *Zunguru* was "curiously moving at times." But he ended his review with a paragraph of unbridled patronization that compared the performance to a midway side-show act; this, he concluded, in another half-hearted attempt to balance his viewpoint, was all the more piteous because of the rare moments when it was genuinely good.[68]

In the first of two reviews, John Martin said he found it paradoxical that the dance-drama appeared to be more lucid now that its lines were spoken in African dialect instead of the English used in the original 1938 production. He was also much more impressed with the newer version of *Zunguru* and found that it had undergone "so many fundamental changes as to be virtually a new piece."[69] Three days later, in his second review, he pointed out the rare opportunity that presented itself to New York dance audiences. With Dafora performing at the Chanin and Katherine Dunham's first Broadway review, *Tropics and Le Jazz Hot*, at the Windsor Theatre, dance enthusiasts had an unusual opportunity to compare "two totally different approaches to a common racial heritage in the arts."[70]

The simultaneous appearances of the two companies was also a happy coincidence for Martin because it gave him a stunning opportunity to continue to elucidate his theories on the racial aspects of theatrical concert dance: "Miss Dunham's work is considerably more sophisticated than Mr. Dafora's and far more objective. This is entirely natural, for she is American born and bred. The primitive sources of Negro culture are found by her only by diligent searching, and are put upon the stage only by means of the conscious processes of art. There is in her compositions, accordingly, an element of comment that gives them point and flavor."[71]

Martin went on to point out that Dafora had lived in America long enough to know that he had to adapt and formalize his work. He commented that Dafora had fulfilled that task in a clean-cut and intuitive manner. His adaptation was most apparent in the music when there were "conspicuous . . . outbursts of obviously European harmony . . . and only a trifle less so in the dancing and deportment of a fairly large proportion of the cast."[72]

Impressed by Dafora's theatrical sensibility, Martin compared the elemental directness and simplicity of his setting to the formality of

Greek theater.[73] Since he concluded his article on a positive note that pointed out Dafora's "conscious" manipulation of theatrical techniques, one wonders why he made his earlier distinction between Dafora and Dunham in matters of sophistication and objectivity. It seems that the most important reason Martin considered Dunham's work superior was that she was "American born and bred" and therefore more capable of interpreting her material through the "conscious" processes of art associated with European-American aesthetics.

During the early 1940s, Dafora continued to produce his dance dramas and gained substantial support from a Harlem cultural organization composed of native Africans, most of whom had originally come to America as students. The African Academy of Arts and Sciences, founded by Kingsley Ozumba Mbadiwe in 1943, attracted Dafora's interest because its primary goal was strikingly similar to his own—to encourage the appreciation of African culture among Americans and among Africans themselves.

In the same year it was founded, the academy began producing a series of African cultural festivals in which Dafora and his company were the main feature. The first of these, an African Dance Festival performed at Carnegie Hall on December 13, consisted of a dance-drama that used much of the music and dance that had been featured in *Kykunkor* and *Zunguru*. The material, as John Martin pointed out, was well worth seeing again, especially since it was so beautifully performed.[74] He felt that Alma Sutton, who had appeared in most of Dafora's concerts, was magnificent in *Dance of Blessing*, but a young guest artist named Pearl Primus "literally stopped the show." Within the context of the story, she appeared as a visitor to the village who performed two dances. Both consisted of her own choreography, which was described as being dignified and dramatic in *African Ceremonial* and markedly Caribbean in the other work.[75] The reviewer for the *Dance Observer* made the interesting observation that Primus, whom he classified as a "genuine modern dancer," was at the same time the most "ethnic" of the artists.[76]

Two distinguished guests appeared during intermission and gave brief speeches in support of the African Academy's idealistic goals. Eleanor Roosevelt, who had a long record of defending the rights of black people, spoke of goodwill and brotherhood among nations. Her friend and compatriot in the battle against racism, the black educator and civil-rights activist Mary McLeod Bethune, delivered a similar message.

The African Academy's second festival at Carnegie Hall occurred on April 4, 1945. African Dances and Modern Rhythms was a departure from Dafora's usual format. He was responsible only for the first part of the program, "Festival at Battalakor," set in seventeenth-century West Africa. The balance of the program (like his earlier collaboration with Guy, Burroughs, and Dunham) was structured around the theme of the historical continuum of black dance and music from Africa to the New World. This part of the program included artists who per-formed the music and dance of the Caribbean. Princess Orelia and Pedro, who were best known for their nightclub appearances, per-formed dances of Cuba and Brazil. The Duke of Iron, a calypso singer, represented Trinidad, and Josephine Premice performed Haitian dances. Bill Robinson and the jazz musicians Mary Lou Williams and Maurice Rocco represented the United States. Martin observed that Robinson's tap dances were, for the first time on record, performed to the accom-paniment of seven African drummers.[77]

When the African Academy presented its 1946 festival, A Tale of Old Africa, one reviewer, Irving Kolodin of the New York Sun, questioned the authenticity of the material that was presented. He found that the performance—which resembled the 1945 program in that it included a number of artists besides Dafora and his company—featured so much material "in the Caucasian manner" that it was difficult for an observer to believe that any of it was authentically African. He continued, saying that the spirit and primitiveness of Dafora's earliest work seemed dis-tant indeed.[78] Kolodin's comments raise interesting questions about how Dafora's work may have diverged from its African roots during the seventeen years he had spent in America. Though these questions are difficult to answer conclusively, it may be assumed that he had been influenced, to some extent, by the artistic and social environment surrounding him.

In addition to surrounding influences affecting his work, there may have been other factors involved. One writer for the Dance Observer speculated that Dafora purposely featured the most dynamic and ex-citing aspects of African dance movement during the early part of his career in order to capture the attention of those who first came to see his performances, and that later (during the early 1940s) he began to incorporate subtler forms of movement that were just as African but appeared "less-authentic" to those who were expecting only unbridled primitive energy.[79] If this were true, it might have influenced Kolodin's reaction to the 1946 production. If by "in the Caucasian manner" Kolodin meant that Dafora's work was borrowing a certain subtlety and refinement from Western art, he was taking a much narrower view of African dance than did other writers, such as Edwin Denby, who repeatedly spoke of subtlety and refinement as inherent and authentic aspects of Dafora's performances.

A look at another review of A Tale of Old Africa reveals how opinions about the authenticity of Dafora's work varied from one critic to another. Walter Terry was a critic who could reflect upon African dance in light of his firsthand experiences on that continent: "In their dancing I saw again boys and girls dancing on the shore of the Gold Coast . . . the flash of a torch, the whisper of running feet cutting through an African night. The validity of 'A Tale of Old Africa' not only provided memories for those who knew that rich continent and its richly gifted peoples, but it also provided others with a glimpse of a culture alien to some of us but worthy of our interest and our fostering."[80] In view of his long-standing desire to bring the beauty of African art to American audiences, Dafora, no doubt, hoped that everyone would respond to the authenticity and importance of his work as appreciatively as Terry did.

In 1946 and 1947 Dafora and a small company of dancers undertook several extensive tours across the United States. Sponsored by civic and cultural groups and black educational institutions such as Fisk University, Howard University, and Hampton Institute, he continued to be America's leading purveyor of African dance and music during that decade. He also produced another of his dance-dramas, *Batanga*, in New York in 1949.

The settings for his performances shifted markedly in the 1950s and 1960s. There were fewer performances in legitimate theaters and concert halls and more performances at nightclubs, zoological gardens, fairs, and expositions. Dafora had previously refused much of this type of work, but declining public and critical interest in his work and the appearance of younger artists and newer companies led him to accept whatever bookings he could find. After traveling to Sierra Leone for a brief period in 1963, he returned to America where he died in 1965.

His achievements during the first two decades of his career in America parallel those of other major concert artists, both black and white. He was vitally committed to pursuing an aesthetic based on the technical brilliance of an established dance tradition. His unique contribution was that he changed the tradition by removing the dance from its ritual usage and shaping it to fit the priorities of a Western theatrical setting. In doing this, he created a hybrid theatrical form—African in spirit and content, Western in structure and function—which, like so much black art in the New World, could not be categorized as being singularly African, American, or European but existed in the unique beauty of its synthesis. Because of its initial dynamism and freshness, Dafora's work was enthusiastically received by a wide audience in America and was consequently an important influence on the development and acceptance of African-American concert dance.

6
Katherine Dunham

DURING THE MID-1920S, when Hemsley Winfield was just beginning his theatrical career with little theater groups in Yonkers and with the National Ethiopian Art Theatre in Harlem, another teen-ager was about to embark on a similar path. But unlike Winfield's, her career would not be cut short. Instead, it would span seven decades and establish her as the preeminent contributor to the black concert dance tradition.

The significance of Katherine Dunham's career cannot be judged by her contributions in any single area of the dance arts. By her own admission, she was not a particularly outstanding dancer, nor was her choreographic career characterized by a series of breakthroughs that led her toward fresh new aesthetic vistas. In some respects, her work became formulaic, and she recycled a good deal of her choreography over the years. What is most significant is the breadth of her career—inside and outside the field of dance. The depth of her vision led her—more than any other artist of her time—to study the connections between dance and other cultural phenomena and to translate her findings into theatrical art. Though the white pioneers of modern dance engaged in studies of movement that stressed the relationships between psychological and emotional impulses and expressive movement that could be used in dance performance, Dunham went several steps further. Beginning in the early 1930s and using her training as an anthropologist, she lived with, observed, and studied the dances of people in New World black cultures. Her examination of the relationship between form and function in dance took place in settings that became her laboratory for the study of living rituals. Her closeness to the people she studied and her participation in their rituals and dances provided her with a depth of understanding that was invaluable. This, in turn, enabled her to use elements from non-Western folk cultures and transpose them into unique art for the world stage.

Of the artists who have been discussed in these pages, Dunham was unique in the way that she was perceived by critics and audiences. By the mid-1940s, because of the groundbreaking work of Winfield, Guy, Williams, and Dafora, Americans had become more accustomed to seeing black dance presented as serious art. Like early European-American concert dancers, these artists had prepared the way for new perceptions of dance. Critical and audience reactions based upon old stereotypes about black performers were still strong; however, Dunham gathered a new array of forces to combat those stereotypes. Using dance as the main focus, she created a total theater experience that depended heavily on the sophisticated use of elements such as costuming and lighting. In these areas, her concerts far surpassed the efforts of the black artists who had come before her. High production standards made her someone to be reckoned with. In her best reviews, she and her company were spoken of as a revelation.

As her performance career gathered momentum, she gained more and more attention in the press because of the scholarly credentials that made her a fascinating anomaly to many of those who wrote about her. The fact that a woman—especially a black woman—who was invited to lecture at universities and anthropological societies could, at the same time, present a sensuous, glamorous image on Broadway stages and in Hollywood films sent writers into fits of journalistic ecstasy.

Speaking of this in 1941, Dunham found it interesting that the publicity she received on any given day referred to her as both "the hottest thing on Broadway" and "an intelligent, sensitive young woman . . . an anthropologist of note." She continued: "Personally, I do not think of myself as either one of these extreme phenomena. But eager reporters, confronted by the simultaneous presence of two such diverse elements, have often failed to grasp the synthesis between them. . . . Now that I look back over the long period of sometimes alternating, sometimes simultaneous interest in both subjects, it seems inevitable that they should have eventually fused completely."[1]

Much that was written about her was sensational, but the resulting popular recognition of the Dunham image opened doors for her, enabling her to garner more serious attention for her work. Dunham very likely manipulated her unique image as a performer/scholar to benefit her career. But, most important, she worked hard, faced down her detractors, published her research, established a school, and toured the world with a large company of dancers. Accomplishing these things in the face of racism and sexism was a feat that doubly testifies to the seriousness of her endeavors.

Katherine Dunham was born on June 22, 1910, in Glen Ellyn, Illinois. Her mother, Fanny June Taylor Dunham, was a very fair-skinned woman of French-Canadian and American Indian descent. She was a notably beautiful, charming, and intelligent woman whose position in the black community was enhanced by the fact that she was an assistant principal in the Chicago Public School System. Katherine's father was a tailor's apprentice when he met Fanny June, who was twenty years older than he and had five children of her own from a prior marriage.

The family's life in Glen Ellyn had its idyllic moments. Mrs. Dunham was an accomplished musician who could often be found in the parlor playing the small organ or the harp that she kept there. Young Katherine had fond memories of music wafting through the house when her mother, accompanied by her father on guitar, would entertain guests or simply play for her own enjoyment.[2]

The quality of life for Katherine and her brother, Albert Dunham Jr., who was six years older, began to deteriorate when their mother died after a lengthy illness. Their father was forced to sell the house in Glen Ellyn to pay off accumulated debts, and shortly afterward he became a traveling salesman. The two children were boarded with his sister, Lulu Dunham, in a dreary Chicago tenement.

The aunt was a kind and generous woman, but she tried to make ends meet by constantly moving with her two young wards from one small apartment to another. After the Dunham children had been shuttled between relatives several more times, their father sent news that he would be returning with his new wife, Annette Poindexter Dunham. The children greeted the news with apprehension, but when they finally joined their new stepmother in Joliet, Illinois, they found her to be kind, considerate, and devotedly attentive to their needs. As years passed, they found her to be more loving than their father.

Albert Dunham's household regained a semblance of stability as he poured his energy into establishing a new business, the West Side Cleaners and Dyers, housed in a building where the family lived in several adjoining rooms. The initial signs of family accord soon faded, however. There were constant financial problems created by the struggle to maintain the business; and in spite of the new wife's substantial contributions to the family's welfare, she could never recreate the special aura that had surrounded Fanny June Dunham. Because of his attachment to his first wife, Albert Sr. always carried a store of resentment concerning his lost dreams. The situation was exacerbated by the fact that the father and son became increasingly antagonistic toward each other, with the stepmother taking the side of Albert Jr.

The boy tried to work hard and appear to comply with his father's wish that he eventually take over the family business, but his self-assured nature and brilliant intellect were hard to suppress. "He was," as his sister later described him, "one of those rare people born into philosophy, and scholarship came to him far more naturally than the usual forms of social intercourse."[3] These qualities only bred further resentment in his father.

Though Katherine shared some of her brother's intellectual curiosity, there was another part of her that thrived in a world of make-believe adventures. She wanted to be an explorer and charted imaginary expeditions into the depths of Africa.[4]

She was extremely curious about people and supplemented her imaginary trips with real excursions to different neighborhoods around town. When she had occasion to travel further, she keenly observed the sights and sounds she encountered. After traveling with her stepmother and a friend to St. Louis, for example, she remembered the music that drifted from doorways on Chouteau Street in the black neighborhood. She felt a deep stirring, a possession by the indigenous music of the community—the blues—that made her deeply aware of her racial roots for the first time.[5]

But there was another aspect to the young girl's life that would eventually combine with her world of imagination and her keen interest in human behavior. Her participation in physical activities such as basketball and track became an increasingly important part of her daily routine, and she soon discovered dance. She first studied with her high-school gym teacher, Phoebe Ann Kirby, who taught a kind of free-style movement based upon the concepts of Emile Jaques-Dalcroze and Rudolf von Laban. Katherine participated in the school's Terpsichorean Club as an extra and became an "eager wood nymph, a willing tree, and an obliging scarf bearer."[6] Inspired by watching the more advanced dancers perform, she grew more interested and her parents permitted her to attend special dance classes that met after school.

Her first opportunity to create her own dances came when she volunteered to organize an evening of entertainment for a church fundraiser. She was encouraged by a local matron and former chorus girl who contributed costumes and musical scores from *In Dahomey* and *Shuffle Along*. As originally planned, Katherine was to act as mistress of ceremonies, read verses before each number, accompany a vocal solo sung by her father, and perform several solo dances. Though her enthusiasm presaged the energy with which she would later assume numerous responsibilities as a director-choreographer, the tasks proved to be too much for the young girl. By the evening of the performance, Katherine had worked herself into such a state of nervous exhaustion that several substitutes had to assume some of her duties, and she was left to struggle through her Oriental and Russian dances.[7]

In spite of the Dunham family's outward appearance of normalcy—their participation in church and school activities and their conscientious attempts to keep the family business thriving—familial bonds began to unravel again, primarily because of the father's growing bitterness and his frequent violent outbursts. The relations between father and son deteriorated to pitched battles, and Katherine and her stepmother eventually moved out of Albert Dunham's house.

Albert Jr. had been the first to find a permanent escape route from the domestic traumas. He accepted a scholarship to the University of Chicago where he began majoring in philosophy. He stayed in touch with his sister, encouraging her to seek a life outside of Joliet. Her opportunity came when she filled out an application for the Civil Service examination that he had mailed her, and she was accepted as an assistant librarian in the Chicago suburb of Hamilton Park. With her new job as a means of support, she also entered the University of Chicago.

In 1929, soon after she moved to Chicago, Dunham became involved with a little theater group organized by her brother and one of his friends, Nicolas Matsukas. The Little Theatre Group of Harper Avenue became a meeting place for the local avant-garde, which included visual artists Charles White and Charles Sebree (who later danced in one of Dunham's early Chicago companies), actors Ruth Attaway and Canada Lee, and other black artists and intellectuals such as Langston Hughes and Alain Locke, who passed through Chicago from time to time.[8] Dunham's first acting role at the theater was in a dramatization of F. Scott Fitzgerald's story *The Man Who Died at Twelve O'Clock*.[9]

The little theater group came to an end when Albert Jr. married in September 1929 and moved with his new wife to Cambridge, Massachusetts, where he continued his academic studies at Harvard. Katherine was upset by the departure of her closest friend, her brother.[10]

Her interest in dance began to exert a stronger influence over her life, and she found that teaching dance could be an additional means of support during the economic hard times of the Depression. As she became more deeply involved, she studied Oriental dance with Vera Mirova, participated in a lecture series sponsored by the Chicago Dance Council, and became active with local modern dancers.[11]

One of Dunham's earliest fruitful associations in the Chicago dance community was with Mark Turbyfill, who had studied with Andreas Pavley and Serge Oukrainsky and become a lead dancer with the Chicago Opera Ballet. In addition, Turbyfill was a gifted poet and painter, a self-styled renaissance man whose career also included performances with Ruth Page and Adolph Bolm and collaborations in several experimental dance projects.[12]

The critic Ann Barzel remembers him as "very much a part of the artistic and social life of Chicago's 'golden age,' with its exciting Chicago School of Literature, lavish opera company, flourishing symphony orchestra, and repertory ballet company directed by Bolm. Turbyfill had a studio in the row of storefronts at the edge of Jackson Park near the University of Chicago."[13] He had been entertaining the notion of forming a Negro ballet company for some time, and his studio was not far from the Little Theatre of Harper Avenue.

Dunham took her first ballet lessons with Turbyfill, and he later remembered her standing at the barre, "the only black in a line of young women."[14] As he got to know her, they formed an alliance based on their mutual interests. The two artists struggled to recruit dancers and interest the black community in their project. Moving from one rehearsal space to another, they were able to use Bolm's studio for a while until the landlord began to complain about the black students attending the classes. The result of their collaboration was a group they called Ballet Nègre, which performed at the Chicago Beaux-Arts Ball in 1931. On this occasion, Dunham presented her first notable choreography to the Chicago public. (The work, *Negro Rhapsody*, is often mentioned in reference to this period of Dunham's career, but there is no description of it.) After a year of trying to keep the group of dancers together, meet expenses, and find studio space, she and Turbyfill abandoned their project.

During these formative years as a dancer and choreographer, Dunham became associated with another artist whom she later credited with being very influential in the development of her dance career, her teacher Olga Speranzeva. After studying ballet in Russia and modern dance with Mary Wigman in Germany, Speranzeva came to the United States with a Russian musical revue, the Chauve Souris, which was famous for its lavish costumes and scenery and its ethnic flavor. Speranzeva remained in America, opened a school, and began sharing the experiences of her colorful theatrical background with her students.

Speranzeva was very active in the Chicago dance scene, performing with Adolph Bolm and with her own Art Dance Trio, which consisted of herself and two other dancers, Bernice Holmes and Drucilla Schroeder.[15] Dunham remembers her teacher as "the 'maestra' who would lead me through her 'Chauve Souris' variety show experiences, her Kamerny Theatre dramatic Polish, Karsavina and Preobajenskaya classical ballet technique, her Russian gypsy affiliations and her own non-conformist attitudes into a style and decision of my own."[16]

As described by Ann Barzel, one of Speranzeva's early performances was noteworthy for its unintentional titillation: "She [Speranzeva] presented a program starring Dunham. . . . The show included a ritual dance about an African sun goddess, a synthetic but effective piece. What many who saw it remember most was that four attractive young black women carried in the portly sun goddess on a litter, and while undulating to African rhythms their strapless upper garments slipped and they finished the dance topless but looking great."[17]

Another concert, a presentation of the Negro Dance Group, occurred at the Abraham Lincoln Center on March 2 and 4, 1934. Listing Luda Paetz-Speronzeva (one of several names that can be found for Speranzeva) as the director, the printed program noted that the group "was originated by Katherine Dunham for the purpose of bringing to the concert stage not only the highest developments of classical, modern and character dancing, but also to express the folk themes and folk ballets. Mme Speronzeva . . . inspired by Miss Dunham's enthusiasm for a Negro ballet[,] has made the realization of this aim a definite part of her dance future."[18]

The program consisted of ten dances performed by the group of nine women. Dunham performed several solos including *Arabienne*, choreographed by Vera Mirova. Among the other dances there was a trio, *Berceuse*, danced to Stravinsky music, and a group dance, *Two Spirituals*.[19] A flyer for the concert includes several interesting photographs that show Dunham and her dancers dressed in long dresses, looking more like typically austere modern dancers of the time than like the colorfully costumed Caribbean characters they would later portray.[20]

While working with Speranzeva, Dunham struggled to pursue her studies at the university and continued teaching dance in the community. It was again through the assistance of Mark Turbyfill that she met Ruth Page, ballet director of the Chicago Grand Opera. Page invited her to perform in a ballet, *La Guiablesse*, which was first performed at the Auditorium Theatre for the Chicago World's Fair during the summer of 1933.

Set in Martinique, *La Guiablesse* was initially conceived by Page and Bolm on a return voyage from a tour of South America. At that time, they were both reading a story by Lafcadio Hearn based on a native legend of a beautiful she-devil who lures a young man away from his lover. Bolm suggested that Page write the libretto and choreograph the ballet.[21] Upon returning to New York, Bolm contacted the African-American composer William Grant Still, who began composing the music in 1927, though the actual ballet would not be produced until seven years later.

In the 1933 production, Page danced the lead role of the she-devil in a cast of thirty-five black performers, including some of Dunham's earliest dancers, notably a very young Talley Beatty. The ballet was performed for a second time on November 30, 1934, when the Chicago Grand Opera presented several programs that were nationally publicized as being "the first attempt in American opera to devote an entire evening to ballet."[22] Since Ruth Page was occupied with choreographing *Hear Ye! Hear Ye!*, a new ballet to be presented on the same program, the restaging and the lead role of *La Guiablesse* were turned over to Dunham. The male lead was danced by Jordis McCoo, who at the time was married to Dunham.

Edward Moore of the *Chicago Tribune* praised the ballet. "This time," he wrote, "the principal part was danced by Katherine Dunham. It was an astonishing performance. . . . The ease and grace that the negro group put into their evolutions, the eloquence of their swaying bronze bodies, made a perfect performance of this tale of the Martinique siren."[23] Page was so pleased with the way *La Guiablesse* was performed that she gave the ballet and the costumes to Dunham. Dunham's fledgling company, by this time called the Negro Dance Group, was beginning to perform in the Chicago area in small concerts and in other productions such as a pageant of Negro history at Soldier Field.

As Dunham's visibility increased in the Chicago arts community, a set of fortuitous circumstances brought her work to the attention of the Rosenwald Foundation. Established by Julius Rosenwald, the chief stockholder in Sears, Roebuck and Company, the foundation was noted for its philanthropy in support of African-American causes. From the 1920s through the 1940s, Rosenwald gave a large portion of his vast fortune to "New Negro enterprises of university endowments, law and medical school construction, and graduate fellowships."[24] A member of the board of the foundation, Mrs. Alfred Rosenwald Stern, had attended one of Dunham's performances and suggested that she present a proposal.

In preparing her proposal, Dunham began to formalize her ideas concerning the relationship between dance and other sociocultural elements. When she first began studying at the University of Chicago, she had not declared a major, and her approach to these interests was mostly intuitive. Later, she enrolled in a class taught by one of the leading ethnologists of the time, Dr. Robert Redfield. Her ideas began to crystallize, and she decided to major in anthropology. She became tremendously excited when her studies began to confirm her feelings that dance was more than just a physical activity, that it was an integral part of a people's social structure.[25] Redfield was known for his research in folk and peasant cultures. He believed that traditional societies offered unique opportunities to study the "congruency, balance, and close interdependence" of cultural institutions and beliefs.[26] For Dunham, he became a mentor and a major influence upon her decision to pursue academic studies in anthropology as well as a performance career in dance.

In 1935, after presenting her written proposal and performing before the Rosenwald committee, Dunham received a grant to do field work in Jamaica, Trinidad, Martinique, and Haiti. She also received an additional sum that enabled her to study with Melville Herskovits, head of Northwestern University's African studies department, before she departed for the Caribbean.

Herskovits, who was in the process of laying a methodological foundation for the study of African retention and acculturation processes as they affected blacks in the New World, had done extensive fieldwork in Africa and the Caribbean and would later publish his theoretical findings in *Myth of the Negro Past* (1941). This pioneering study revealed his lifelong dedication to using scientific scholarship in the pursuit of humanistic goals. To use his studies to enlighten people about the rich African heritage of blacks would, he felt, "influence opinion in general concerning Negro abilities and potentialities, and thus contribute to a lessening of interracial tensions."[27] In this respect, his ideas reflected the sociological positivism that had become a part of the philosophies of the Harlem Renaissance intellectuals W. E. B. Du Bois and Charles Johnson. These ideas also became an important part of Katherine Dunham's philosophical motivation in her scholarly and artistic work. Speaking of this several years later she said, "There is no doubt but what we are doing is creating a better understanding of, and sympathy for, the American Negro. From the beginning, I aimed at sociological as well as artistic targets."[28]

After a thorough study of fieldwork techniques, Dunham—armed with letters of introduction from Melville Herskovits—began her Caribbean travels. Her first stop was Jamaica where she stayed for six weeks with the Maroon people. Living in isolated mountain villages, these descendants of escaped slaves had defiantly clung to their old, African-based traditions. Through her studies of the Maroons, Dunham gained a firsthand awareness of the tenacity of Africanisms in New World blacks. She observed dances that were a synthesis of African and European elements. For example, the villagers still used traditional African movements, but they combined them with steps and figures from seventeenth-century European quadrilles that they had learned from plantation owners. A similar type of synthesis would become the primary characteristic of her choreography.

Dunham continued her research by traveling to the islands of Martinique and Trinidad and finally became absorbed in the culture of Haiti. There, with the assistance of the anthropologist Jean Price-Mars, she was able to study peasants in isolated mountain areas. Their culture, like the Jamaican Maroons' culture, was very similar to that of their African ancestors.[29]

In her book *Dances of Haiti*, first published in 1947, Dunham explained the strategies she used to gain the Haitian people's confidence in order to see and participate in their danced rituals. At first, she simply let them know that she liked to dance, and, because of the importance of dance in their society, they accepted this as a reasonable explanation.[30] But, as she grew to understand the Haitian villagers more, she realized that being an African American placed her in an advantageous position. She found that they recognized her as a descendant of Africa whose ancestors hailed from *Nan Guinin* (faraway Guinea), but she belonged to a group that needed special attention: "There was great and protective interest in the recognition of 'Guinea' blood ties and great concern for my ancestors, who had not received the proper ritual attention because the group of slaves taken farther north had been cut off from their brothers in the Caribbean and had forgotten these practices. . . . Fortified by [the] mutual love of rhythmic expression, by some facility in the pursuit itself, and by the ancestral tie, observation and actual participation were not too difficult."[31]

As she became more familiar with the details of Haitian culture—
the rich tapestry of African and Catholic elements in *vaudun* religion,
the elaborate pantheon of spirits, and most of all, the dances through
which these spirits manifested themselves—the country and its people found a special place in her heart and in her aesthetic development.
Eventually, she was initiated into the *vaudun* religion as a priestess,
an experience she wrote of in her book *Island Possessed* (1969), and
in 1949 she established a home in Haiti where she resided as often as
her busy schedule permitted her.

After eighteen months in the Caribbean she returned to Chicago,
where one of her first performances was at the office of the Rosenwald
Foundation at Forty-ninth Street and Ellis Avenue. Accompanied by
Melville Herskovits playing Haitian rhythms, Dunham danced the
sacred dance of Damballa for a select audience that included her other professor, Robert Redfield.[32]

She soon began reorganizing her school and the group of dancers she
had left behind. Speranzeva had continued to work with them during
her absence. Several months later, Dunham received the first opportunity to present her choreography before a New York audience. She
was invited to participate in the *Negro Dance Evening* sponsored by
the Ninety-second Street YM-YWHA on March 7, 1937. There she
came in contact with other black dance artists—Alison Burroughs,
Edna Guy, Clarence Yates, Archie Savage, and Asadata Dafora.

Inspired by the collaborative project in New York, Dunham returned
to Chicago, where she continued to incorporate the material gathered
during her fieldwork into her choreography. Critics such as Edward
Barry of the *Chicago Daily Tribune* increasingly recognized the unique
character of her work. Reviewing a performance in June 1937 that was
a benefit for victims of the Spanish Civil War, he spoke of her dances
as being "nothing less than a revelation." He also commented that the
effectiveness of her work was due to the high quality of its execution,
not to some natural ability of the dancers.[33] Dunham often spoke of
her battles to overcome the misconceptions represented by the latter
point of view. During her early teaching in Chicago, she had even found
that some of her black students did not continue their studies because
they accepted the idea that technical training was unnecessary for
them, while some local white dancers told her that she was "inhibit-
ing natural talents" by training her black students too rigidly.[34] Such

attitudes only made her more determined to develop a system of dance training that would help combat these misconceptions.

Barry was also impressed by the ritual elements he saw reflected in the "sheer monotony," the "impassive faces and motions of the dancers," which suggested "immense powers and darkly realized forces."[35] In these comments, he was responding to the live drum accompaniment and repetitious movements Dunham used to create an insistent rhythmic pulse in her dances. In Haiti, Dunham had observed that the drums that summoned the spirits were the major instrument for inducing altered states of consciousness among participants in rituals. She had begun to recreate the feeling of religious ecstasy, the hypnotic, trance-like quality of the rituals she had observed. As Barry inferred, these elements, when successfully transposed for the stage, resulted in a powerful theatrical statement.

The next major phase of Dunham's career was made possible through the federal government's WPA program. She first received a nine-month assignment with the Federal Writers Project, where she organized several writers and anthropologists to undertake research showing the relationship between the stress of oppression and the growth of religious cults in urban environments.[36] Her findings in this project were further affirmation of the cultural congruence between people of the African diaspora. In many of the religious groups she studied in the Chicago area, she noted that the ideology was Christian but the patterns of religious behavior were purely African, similar to those she had observed in the West Indies: "The rhythmic percussion-type hand-clapping and foot-stamping, the jumping and leaping, the 'Conversion' or 'confession' in unknown tongues which is a form of possession or ecstasy (induced, in some cases, by a circle of 'saints' or 'angels' closing in upon the person in rhythmic motion of a dance), the frequent self-hypnosis by motor-activity of the shoulders—all these African forms are present."[37]

Continuing with the WPA, she next became involved with the Chicago branch of the Federal Theatre Project, where she, along with three other dancers, Grace Graff, Kurt Graff, and Berta Ochsner, contributed to a dance evening entitled *Ballet Fedre* at the Great Northern Theatre on January 27, 1938. Robert Pollok of the *Chicago Daily Times* said, "The show was clearly stolen . . . by 'L'Ag'Ya,' a fiery folk ballet set in Martinique."[38]

According to the historian VéVé Clark, there are a number of reasons why *L'Ag'Ya* is of special significance in the Dunham repertoire. It was her first full-length ballet based on material gathered from her trip to the Caribbean; it incorporated staged versions of traditional West Indian dances such as the creole mazurka, the beguine, myal, and majumba. It was also Dunham's favorite work, which remained in her repertoire for two decades and became a centerpiece for revues such as *Tropical Revue* (1944), *Bal Nègre* (1946), and *Caribbean Rhapsody* (1950).[39]

L'Ag'Ya, named after the Martinician fighting dance that is related to the French savate and the Brazilian capoeira, was set in the eighteenth-century fishing village of Vauclin. It told the story of a young woman, Loulous, her lover, Alcide, and a rejected suitor, Julot. Seething with jealousy, Julot visits the King of the Zombies to obtain the "cambois," a powerful love charm, which he later uses to paralyze Alcide and to make Loulous dance the majumba, a sacred dance of possession. As she dances, she begins to remove the several layers of petticoats she is wearing. Julot is about to embrace her as she reaches the last one, but Alcide breaks free from the spell and separates them. The villagers encourage the two men to settle their dispute by engaging in the ag'ya. The combative dance ensues, and Julot finally kills Alcide. The ballet ends with the mournful Loulous hovering over her lover's body.

The Caribbean dance motifs used in *L'Ag'Ya* reveal how Dunham used the dances of different cultures within the context of her own choreography. The creole mazurka, a Caribbean dance based upon the Polish mazurka, which French colonists brought to the islands, is one example. Dunham used the stately dance in a festival scene to represent the orderly aspect of village life. In contrast to this European-derived dance, she used the "smooth bump and grind of the Martinician beguine"—an erotic dance of fecundity—to foreshadow the passions that would bring the ballet to its tragic conclusion.[40] In Clark's words, "The form of the ballet is *creole* in every sense of the term; that is, it is born of the American sensibility and mixes African and European elements."[41]

By the late 1930s, Dunham was continuing to explore the blending of African, European, Caribbean, and American dance elements. For example, she was further synthesizing creole dance forms (which were themselves a synthesis) with ballet and modern dance. Her use of percussionists began to assume an even greater importance in her productions, an importance that echoed their role in West Indian cultures. Speaking specifically of the ag'ya dance form, she says that the player of the drums indicates the movements of the dance, the advance and the retreat, the feints, and leaps.[42] She also states that the fascination of ag'ya is not in the lust for combat, but in the finesse of approach and retreat, the almost hypnotic tension as the performers whirl at each other in simultaneous attacks.[43]

During the creation of *L'Ag'Ya*, Dunham also first collaborated with John Pratt, whom she married in 1939. (Her first marriage, to Jordis McCoo, had been brief and ended in divorce.) Pratt was a costume designer, a painter, and a commercial fabric designer who was also employed with the Federal Theatre Project. Throughout her career, the color and vitality of his costumes and scenic designs drew the highest praise from critics and audiences alike and were an invaluable asset to her theatrical success.

By 1939, Dunham was drawing the attention of a number of people who were interested in promoting her professional career. Among these was Louis Schaffer, director of New York's Labor Stage, which had been founded in 1936. His goal was to present relevant working-class drama and "to be instrumental in developing a new kind of theatre, alive and responsive to the important trends in current American life."[44] Sponsored by the International Ladies' Garment Workers Union, the theater initially drew its performers from the ranks of workers in the garment trades. Schaffer, who believed that working-class theater need not be humorless, began producing a musical revue called *Pins and Needles*, which opened in 1937 and had a long and exceptionally successful run. He had seen Dunham's earlier performance at the YM-YWHA, and he asked her to return to New York to choreograph some of the dances for the show.

There seems to have been little that was noteworthy about her choreography for *Pins and Needles*. One segment was called *Bertha the Sewing Machine Girl*. Another, based on a biblical theme, was called *Mene, Mene, Tekel*. Two things were important about her participation in the show, however. Her involvement with the production enabled her to learn more about the theatrical construction of a musi-

KATHERINE DUNHAM   143

cal revue, the format that would become characteristic of most of her work. And by working in New York for an extended period of time, she was able to bring together the necessary elements to mount her first critically acclaimed production on Broadway.

With the money she earned from *Pins and Needles*, and with additional assistance from Louis Schaffer, Dunham choreographed and starred in *Tropics and Le Jazz Hot*, which opened on February 18, 1940, and ran for thirteen consecutive Sundays at the Windsor Theatre.

The production consisted of a kaleidoscope of dances, instrumental music, vocal selections, and dramatic vignettes drawn from many cultures. A suite of dances, *Primitive Rhythms*, borrowed elements of Polynesian, Cuban, and Mexican culture. *Peruvienne, Bahiana, Island Songs,* and *Tropics* represented South America and the Caribbean islands. The dances of urban and rural black American culture were featured in *Le Jazz Hot* and *Bre'r Rabbit an' de Tah Baby*.[45]

The response to *Tropics* was sensational. Walter Terry described the performance as "the occasion that saw the Negro dance come into its own at last. . . . Katherine Dunham has proved herself the first pioneer of the Negro dance."[46] Though he did not like the *Bre'r Rabbit* suite, John Martin was also beside himself with praise. Dunham's work, he said, was "a revelation . . . the basis of a true Negro dance art."[47]

Terry, however, could not help alluding to an idea that was popular among critics of the time. He said that one of the primary breakthroughs of the evening's performance was that it stayed away from "alien techniques." In his second review of the program Martin concurred: "Miss Dunham has apparently based her theory on the obvious fact so often overlooked that if the Negro is to develop an art of his own he can begin only with the seeds of that art that lie within him. . . . Yet in the past (and even in Miss Dunham's present company in certain instances) there have been those who have started out by denying this heritage and smoothing it over with the gloss of an alien racial culture that deceives no one."[48] More specifically, he mentioned Talley Beatty's "distressing tendency to introduce the technique of the academic ballet" into the performance.[49]

Martin expressed the ambivalent viewpoint that usually surfaced when he wrote about black dance artists. On the positive side, he came out strongly concerning Dunham's effectiveness as an artist, noting that "never before in all the efforts of recent years to establish the Negro dance as a serious medium has there been so convincing and authoritative an approach."[50] But his commentary was double-edged, praising the production on one side and detracting from it on the other. After mentioning the program's simplicity and lack of "self-importance," his compliments, sincere though they appeared, trotted out all the stereotypical images of black performers: "This is quite in character with the essence of the Negro dance itself. There is nothing pretentious about it; it is not designed to delve into philosophy or psychology but to externalize the impulses of a high-spirited, rhythmic and gracious race. That Miss Dunham's dances accomplish this end so beautifully can mean only that she has actually isolated the element of a folk art upon which more consciously creative and sophisticated forms can be built as time goes on."[51]

Dunham's life was extremely busy during the run of *Tropics*. She worked at a hectic pace and juggled several roles, a practice that became characteristic of her activities over the next decade. She taught and rehearsed the company, and she lectured on her West Indian research at the anthropology departments of Columbia, Yale, and New York University. While *Tropics* ran on weekends at the Windsor Theatre, she and her dancers continued to perform in *Pins and Needles*; and they also managed to present concerts at the YM-YWHA.

In the midst of her busy New York activities she also made trips back to Chicago. During one of these, she visited her professor, Robert Redfield, and talked to him about the conflict she felt concerning whether or not to continue her anthropological studies, in view of an offer to appear in a Broadway show, *Cabin in the Sky*. She told him that she did not know what to do, and he replied, "Why can't you just do both? Why are you so worried about which is which? If you're sincere in both, you'll never stop being one or the other anyway, so go right ahead."[52]

Cabin in the Sky, which opened at the Martin Beck Theatre on October 25, 1940, brought her more acclaim than she had ever received before. Based on a story by Lynn Root, the humorous and poignant musical told the tale of Little Joe Jackson (Dooley Wilson), a man of questionable morals, who dies but is given a six-month reprise on earth to correct his errant ways. During that time, The Lawd's General (Todd

Duncan) and Lucifer, Jr. (Rex Ingram) battle for Joe's soul, and he is repeatedly tempted to stray from the path of righteousness.

The cast was outstanding. Ethel Waters, who by this time was a veteran of vaudeville, the Cotton Club, movies, musicals, and revues, was praised for her acting, singing, and dancing as Petunia Jackson, Joe's wife. Petunia steadfastly tries to save her husband's soul, but the seductress Georgia Brown, played by Katherine Dunham, constantly thwarts her. Dunham's performance was described with words such as "sizzling," "fascinating," and "torrid." As a dancer-actress, she projected the ultimate sensuality that her character called for.

She and her company, which served as the show's chorus, were praised by John Beaufort of the *Christian Science Monitor* for the excellence of their training.[53] Kelcey Allen of *Women's Wear Daily* commented effusively, "Pushing . . . hard for first honors in 'Cabin in the Sky,' is Katherine Dunham, one of the greatest dancers (white or colored) in the world."[54]

Comments such as these (and the overall attention the press paid to Dunham and her company) did nothing to allay the growing tension between her and Ethel Waters, who had top billing.

John Martin was impressed but more reserved. He felt that Dunham's performance was commendable in her first exposure in a medium (the Broadway musical) that was not noted for its "free creation." He also found her characterization of Georgia Brown interestingly revealing in comparison to the roles she had created for herself in her own repertoire. Though she performed exceptionally well, he felt her acting and dancing in *Cabin* was two-dimensional, whereas similar characters of her own creation were "never without comment, presenting the character and telling a wealth of secrets about it at the same time."[55]

George Balanchine staged and directed the production. There was, however, other dance material in the show besides his. John Martin explained that Balanchine "wisely allowed the dancers throughout to make use of great quantities of their own type of movements, many of them right out of the vocabulary of their concert repertoire."[56]

Balanchine also offered an explanation of how the choreography for the show came about. He felt that there was no need for him as a white man to invent movements that were supposed to characterize Negroes, so he sketched in "dispositions of the dancers on the stage"; and "the rest almost improvised itself."[57] He continued: "I was careful to give the dancers steps which they could do better than anyone else. No one can do certain hanging, fluent, smooth jumps the way these boys can. . . . No women trained in classic ballet hold their arms as beautifully as these girls. There are few dancers in the world whose lack of self-consciousness means more intense and disciplined audience projection, rather than less."[58] Even though it is clear that he was crediting the success of the dancers' work to more than his own choreography, he still implied that its success was due to innate ability rather than to their prior training.

One of the dancers who appeared in the musical, Talley Beatty, added insight concerning how Dunham's choreography became a part of the production. According to him, the show's producer, Martin Beck, was not pleased with Balanchine's work and fired him just before the production opened. Most of Balanchine's choreography remained, but during previews Dunham added some of her own choreography to complete several scenes.[59]

Cabin in the Sky ran until March 1941 and then toured the country. After the show closed in San Francisco the following summer, Dunham and her company remained in California, where they performed in nightclubs and concert halls in several cities. It was not easy for her to keep her dancers together during this period, but the critical and popular acclaim they received attested to their artistic growth as a company. Viola Swisher of the *Hollywood Citizen News* pointed out their uniqueness on the current dance scene because of "the coupling of a throbbing vitality and perceptive intelligence which results in a living art."[60] The reviewer for the *Los Angeles Examiner* praised Dunham for her wealth of talent: "Miss Dunham is not only a dancer of great skill and grace, but her songs of significant vibrancy and sauciness add much to her performance."[61]

Several members of the company were repeatedly singled out for their stunning performances. Among these were Talley Beatty, Carmencita Romero, Roger Ohardieno, Lavinia Williams, Laverne French, Carmela El-Khoury, Lucille Ellis, and Tommy Gomez. The group also included two recent recruits who would distinguish themselves in their own ways. Syvilla Fort would soon direct Dunham's New York school and go on to become one of the most respected teachers in that city, while Janet Collins would become the first nationally recognized black ballerina.

Besides success on the concert stage, Dunham's West Coast stay provided her and her dancers with opportunities to appear in several films. Warner Brothers produced *Carnival of Rhythm* (1941), a short film devoted entirely to the company. In 1942, she created choreography for Paramount Pictures' *Star Spangled Rhythm*, starring the comedian Eddie "Rochester" Anderson, and that same year her company was also featured in Universal Pictures' *Pardon My Sarong*, starring Bud Abbott and Lou Costello. In 1943, she and her company appeared in one of their most successful films, *Stormy Weather*, which was produced by Twentieth Century–Fox and starred Lena Horne and Bill Robinson.

Despite the lucrative engagements and the pleasant climate that reminded Dunham of Haiti, she became tired of California. Fortunately, the opportunity for her to move on occurred when Howard Skinner, director of the San Francisco Opera and Symphony, introduced her to Sol Hurok and suggested that he sponsor her on his concert circuit.[62] After seeing one of her rehearsals, Hurok agreed. The result was *Tropical Revue*, which left California in early 1943 to tour the northern United States and Canada and then opened on Broadway at the Martin Beck Theatre in September of that same year. The production's six-week run was a record-breaking length for an all-dance production on Broadway.

In its touring version and in the version that opened in New York, *Tropical Revue* was one of Dunham's most important creations because of its sophistication and refinement. In some respects it was similar to *Tropics and Le Jazz Hot*. It included suites of dances, such as *Primitive Rhythms*, which had appeared in the earlier production. There were, however, dances such as *Rites de Passage* that revealed new dimensions of Dunham's artistry. Though some of these dances had been seen in California and other parts of the country, they were new to New York.

The program consisted of a seamless flow of music, dance, and theater—Dunham's version of the musical revue format that she had been refining for the past three years. Part of this refinement, according to Hurok, was due to the fact that he took over her management and began to help her present her concert pieces in a way that would make them more successful in Broadway and road theaters. He added singers and a jazz ensemble to her piano and percussion accompaniment. "As an entertainment form" he said that "[*Tropical Revue*] rested somewhere between revue and recital."[63]

Whether the transformation of the company was primarily Dunham's doing or Hurok's, John Martin was obviously perturbed when it returned to Broadway. He repeated the same criticism that he had used in reviewing her characterization of Georgia Brown in *Cabin in the Sky*—her work lacked comment; and it had, furthermore, lost some of its integrity. As he put it, "Now both that comment and that integrity appear to be sacrificed in a degree to conform to what Broadway expects the Negro dance to be."[64]

Critics had often berated black artists for engaging in "Harlem highjinks" and praised them for presenting material that—in their constantly shifting opinions—was perceived as being more artistic. Apparently, Martin felt that Dunham was moving dangerously close to the former: "There are already scads of dancers who can do that sort of thing by the yard while artists of insight are comparatively rare."[65]

Denby, as usual, saw things differently, particularly in regard to Dunham's individual dancing: "Her dancing is representational, she acts her dance, so to speak. One admires her projection, her stage presence. She does not force herself on your attention, she allows herself to be seen. Her gestures are provocative and yet discreet and she can even keep a private modesty of her own. As a dance entertainer, she is a serious artist."[66]

In matters of choreography, he had additional insights. He felt that her strongest instinct as a choreographer was "for the decorative values of abstract dancing." But her "handling of the dramatic values of abstract form" was more uncertain.[67] Denby observed that Dunham faced a particularly sticky problem in preparing her ethnologically based dance material for the stage: "The movement is based on African dance elements but the choreographic plan is that of the American modern school." The latter, he felt, was distinguished by a constant quest to use the stage space in different ways. But in African dance, inventive floor patterns were less important; performances gained their strength from individual improvisations on thematic material and dynamic repetitions of movements. Denby felt that Dunham had not reconciled these different values in her work.[68] When he spoke of the lack of conciliation between African dance and Western choreographic techniques, he was specifically referring to *Rites de Passage.*

Two years earlier, Dunham had attempted to clarify her ideas concerning how concepts and elements of performance from different cultures could be reconciled. In an interview she again spoke of form and function:

> In making use of field training to choreograph for my group, I found persistently recurring in the back of my mind in some form or another "function." . . . The cultural and psychological framework, the "why" became increasingly important. . . . As in the primitive community certain movement patterns . . . were always related to certain functions, so in the modern theater there would be a correlation between a dance movement and the function of the dance within the theater framework. And certainly a broad and general knowledge of cultures and cultural patterns can be advantageously brought to bear upon the problems of relating form and function in the modern theater.[69]

In *Rites de Passage,* Dunham again combined a semblance of the cultural functions of dance with the theatrical exigencies of the concert stage; but this time, she attempted to make a more universal statement. Unlike dances such as *L'Ag'Ya,* which she had built around references to a specific culture (in that case Martinique's), in *Rites* she used her theatrical elements to create a mythic society that was neither African nor West Indian. It was an idealized black society surrounded by an aura of timelessness.

The dance was composed of three sections. The first section, *Fertility,* was an initiation rite that depicted a young man and woman being introduced into the mysteries of sexual selection and procreation. The second section was also an initiation rite, that of a young boy being prepared for manhood by a group of warriors. *Death,* the final section, recounted the death of a chief and his people's reaction to it. Her chosen themes provided the structure for the dance. Each functioned theatrically as a self-contained dramatic situation; and each situation showed how rituals functioned within a traditional society to demarcate important periods of transition—for the individual or for the group—from one social status to another.

Within the context of the overall dance, the *Fertility* section is a striking example of how Dunham blended more traditional African and Afro-Caribbean movement with her own original movement to create a continuum from fieldwork to theater. In the opening of *Fertility*, she invented repetitive-movement motifs that were used to create a sense of dramatic anticipation. In the dim lighting, barely visible dancers can be seen moving minimally.[70] Two women stand facing each other, raising and lowering their fists in a pounding motion. The movement is a mimetic gesture based on the task of grinding grain with a huge mortar and pestle. But it also echoes the sexual symbolism of the gestures of two men nearby. Seated on the floor, the men engage in a stylized movement dialogue in which they extend their arms toward each other, circle two fingers, draw their elbows down to their sides, and then forcefully thrust their arms out with fists. Other men enter and join in the movement dialogue.

Though the gestures are obviously phallic, they lack sensuality. The men, keeping a measured rhythm, seem intensely involved in the physical action, and yet they also seem emotionally distant from their activity. Their hypnotic concentration and the ceaseless repetition of their gestures create a portentous atmosphere. Dunham created motifs that showed the multivocality of ritual gestures as the men (and to a lesser extent the women) commune with each other and engage in an incantation that summons the gods of fertility. At the same time, the movement sequence functioned theatrically to create a sense of dramatic anticipation in the audience and to set up the next segment of the dance.

As the dance continues, more men and women enter. Two of them—the primary initiates—begin a slow duet at center stage. They establish another motif, this one based on more authentic Afro-Caribbean movement. They move in intricately woven patterns of pelvic thrusting, withdrawing, and circling. The two change positions several times, relating to each other in different facings, but their pelvic movements remain constant.

As the duet continues, the other men and women frame the two central dancers and form ever-shifting patterns. Sometimes they divide into male and female groupings with two lines facing each other. The men steadily advance toward the women, thrusting through space with violently aggressive leg and arm gestures. The women hold their ground; their movement is also forceful, but they tend to stay in place and let different parts of their bodies ripple sensuously. At other times, the dancers divide into couples.

The focal man and woman do a series of steps and turns that alternately move them apart and then back together again. All the while, the rhythmic tempo and complexity of their pelvic undulations increase until they meet center stage. He places his hands on her waist, and she places her hands on his shoulders. They continue their pelvic contractions, lowering themselves until the woman is on her knees and the man is in a wide stance with his legs deeply bent. The balance of *Fertility* becomes a propulsive interplay between the two central characters and the group. The man pursues the woman as she weaves between the other dancers. At the end of the dance, the men form a circle around the couple, kneel, and direct the finger/arm/fist-thrusting gesture toward them.

Dunham had observed a dance quite similar to the duet described above during her stay with the Maroon people of Jamaica. It was a myal dance in which an old man (the shaman or "doctor") entices an evil spirit out of a woman:

> They were facing one another. [The woman] circles around the doctor, hesitant, advancing and retreating. Her eyes were fixed, mouth clamped shut tightly, body rigid. The doctor squats in front of her. . . . As he advances slowly toward her, his pelvis begins to move. . . . They hesitate in front of each other, swaying. Then she eludes his embrace with a sharp convulsive bend and is on the other side of the circle, taunting, enticing. . . . They are face to face, bodies touching, both of them squatting now with arms pressed to sides, elbows bent, and widespread fingers quivering violently.[71]

Whereas the myal dance used sexual movement to evoke curative powers, Dunham used similar movement to represent the fecund power of a mating ritual.

In the duet and the group sections of *Fertility* the most prominent feature of the choreography is the pelvic movement. But in these sections the dancers—like the men who engaged in the phallic gestural conversation—seem to distance themselves from their activity, as if hypnotized by the rhythmic repetition of the movement. By having the dancers create a feeling of detachment, Dunham commented upon the serious nature of the events occurring on stage and drew attention to interpretations of the movement that were different from those that were familiar to American audiences. Dunham was well aware that in African and Caribbean cultures, movement that appeared to be sexual in nature could simultaneously serve other functions. It could express a worldview in which sexual activity, procreation, and the life force that runs throughout the natural world are all joined in a spiritual continuum.

In *Fertility*, Dunham was attempting to show that bodily movement could be imbued with intense metaphysical meaning. Her intention of bringing these concepts into the theater was often misconstrued, as indicated by the critical response to *Rites de Passage.* The most glaring example of this occurred in Boston, where *Tropical Revue* opened a few days after leaving New York.

The notoriety of the production preceded its opening in Boston. As one columnist put it, "For the past few months the wires between Boston and New York have been fairly sizzling with excitement over Katherine Dunham's 'Tropical Revue.'"[72] Elliot Norton of the *Boston Post* wrote one of the most acerbic commentaries:

> There has been nothing quite like this "Tropical Revue" in Boston in recent years. Some of it is colorful, indisputably brilliant, quaintly charming, and some of it is downright offensive and needs to be drastically altered at once in the name of good taste and common decency. . . . Since she is presenting the dances of the tropics, Miss Dunham and her associates present many "native" numbers. Since many of the natives of all the lands involved seem to be concerned with love in its less civilized manifestations, there is more than one dance that is frankly erotic. Of these, one in particular is inexcusable, though it was staged with something like genuine artistic skill. . . . This one, which the programme admits is not copied after any native dance, but is merely hypothetical, is altogether too explicit. It is danced by men and women, all scantily clad, who gyrate and posture in a continuously offensive way.[73]

For Norton, who could not reconcile the notion of serious art with material that appeared to be sexual in nature, *Rites* was little more than lascivious entertainment masquerading as art. By categorizing the dance as such, he dealt with it in a way that reflected a prejudice about black theater that had hung on since the 1920s. Among white producers, it was considered taboo to portray a black man and woman in a meaningful intimate relationship. Whether one liked the shows or not, disparaged them or praised them, productions that showed black performers intimately involved were acceptable as long as the image created could be interpreted as crude and animalistic. Earlier shows such as *Lulu Belle* and *Harlem* capitalized on these types of images.

Dunham, however, was attempting to change perceptions about race, culture, art, and sexuality. No one quite knew how to handle it, particularly the city fathers of Boston, who sent their own shaman, John J. Spencer, the city censor, to exorcise the show. In spite of sold-out houses and thunderous applause, *Rites* was removed from the program after his viewing.

The revue continued to tour the country and returned to New York a year later, where it opened at the Century Theatre on December 26. By then critics and audiences had, as Margaret Lloyd put it, become "acclimated to the so-called tropical atmosphere, and accepted the undulating rhythms, not as a sign of moral undulant fever, but as sincere native expression."[74] Dunham had made a number of changes in the program including the addition of a reworked version of *L'Ag'Ya*. She again received general critical acclaim, and Edwin Denby described her as being "in the full bloom of her successful beauty and showmanship."[75]

Her next New York appearance, *Carib Song,* which opened at the Adelphi Theatre on September 27, 1945, was less successful, running for only thirty-six performances. She jointly directed the musical play with Mary Hunter and also choreographed and starred in it. *Carib Song* told the story—one that critics found to be flimsy—of an errant wife who dallies with a village fisherman, becomes pregnant, and is murdered by her husband. The musical's high points were achieved by outstanding individual performances such as Tommy Gomez's dancing as the Boy Possessed by a snake in a Shango ritual, Avon Long as the Fisherman, and Katherine Dunham (singing, dancing, and acting) as the Wife.

Prior to *Carib Song,* Dunham had taken an unprecedented step concerning her company's management. Sol Hurok had a standard practice of not refurbishing scenery and costumes once a show had become acclaimed and could coast along on the momentum of its prior success. Dunham could not accept this because she felt that it cheated her audiences and undermined her artistic standards. So she bought her contract from Hurok, paying for it in installments for several years.

The focus of her energies underwent other major changes during this period. She began the arduous task of codifying her ideas about dance and culture by establishing a school in New York. The school's first incarnation was in 1944 as the Katherine Dunham School of Dance. It was located in Caravan Hall in a studio that had been formerly used by Isadora Duncan.[76] By 1945, she had moved her school to 220 West Forty-third Street where it was housed on the top floor of an old Schubert theater. Soon it was renamed the Katherine Dunham School of Dance and Theatre. Finally, in the fall of 1946, the school was once more renamed the Katherine Dunham School of Arts and Research, and it included the Dunham School of Dance and Theatre, the Department of Cultural Studies, and the Institute for Caribbean Research.

By the time the school was fully developed, it had become one of the most ambitious educational projects ever established by a dance artist in terms of the breadth of its curriculum. The training offered included courses in dance history, notation, eukinetics, acting, visual design, anthropology, languages, philosophy, and religion. There was a faculty of twenty-nine, which included many past and present Dunham dancers, such as Lavinia Williams, Syvilla Fort, and Archie Savage. Other teachers included Todd Bolender and José Limón.

The school was a bustling affair with an electric environment where Papa Henri Augustin, Dunham's lead percussionist, held classes in one room, while she and her teachers inspired dancers in the studios, and other students busied themselves among the big tables in the sewing room.[77] There were students from Switzerland, Palestine, and Ireland, and white students made up a large portion of the student body.[78] Over the years, artists who would make their marks in a variety of fields attended the school; Marlon Brando, Jennifer Jones, Rudi Gernreich, Arthur Mitchell, and Peter Gennaro were among them. Most important, Dunham's school provided a home where her dance technique could be passed on to others.

As mentioned earlier, when Dunham first began studying and teaching, she had been influenced by Chicago artists such as Speranzeva, Turbyfill, Page, and Bolm. Consequently, much of her early training was ballet-based. She was also influenced by other artists who passed through Chicago. Among those performing, lecturing, and giving classes during the 1930s were Harald Kreutzberg and La Argentina.[79]

Dunham developed her dance technique—like her choreography— by synthesizing material from African-American, European-American, and Afro-Caribbean dance forms. By the early 1940s, her technique had begun to be codified. Thanks to one of her dancers, Lavinia Williams, there are early records of the structure of Dunham's classes during that period. In August 1942, at the Bodil Genkle Studios in San Francisco, Williams began keeping a series of notebooks that included line drawings and written descriptions of exercises.[80]

Williams says that Dunham included a full ballet barre in her classes every day and encouraged her company members to study with ballet teachers such as Karel Shook in New York and Mme. Sprenskaya in Chicago when the group was in residence in those two cities.[81] Williams notated barre exercises that were very different from the strictly classical exercises. Though these incorporated standard classical movements such as *tendus, developpés,* and *ronde de jambes,* they also stressed a non-balletic use of the body that emphasized Afro-Caribbean movements—pelvic contractions, hip isolations, and undulating back movements.

Williams mentioned another section of the typical class as "floor stretches . . . based on the basic modern dance technique's floor work, combined with breathing and flexing."[82] From the descriptions of the modern exercises she goes on to list, it appears that they were Graham-based. There is the likelihood that Williams herself, along with another dancer, Lawaune Kinnard, contributed Graham material to the Dunham classes since they had both studied with Graham before joining Dunham's company in 1940.

Center-floor exercises and progressions across the floor consisted of phrases of steps and movements from ballet, modern dance, and the dances of non-Western cultures. Of the latter Williams said, "Dunham used movements from ritual dances as exercises. She would break down the movements of such dances as *Yenvalou, Petro, Congo,* etc. from Haiti, or dances from Cuba, Brazil, Fiji Islands, Melanesia, Trinidad and Jamaica. She said then, as she does now, that she has been greatly inspired by the dances of Haiti."[83]

Few writers have thoroughly examined Dunham's influence and the consequent influence of African-derived dance on American modern dance. Millicent Hodson suggested in the late 1970s that Dunham's primary contribution was a liberated use of knees and pelvis, "a new vocabulary of movement for the lower body" that enriched modern dance technique.[84]

In a more recent essay, "Ethnic and Modern Dance," Gerald E. Myers discusses reasons why Dunham's work has not been seriously considered in terms of its contribution to the modern dance tradition. He says that since her work is of a type that has often been mistakenly categorized as "ethnic" dance—dance closely associated with specific cultural groups—it has been looked upon as something separate from the nonconformist, rebellious modern dance tradition, with its characteristic rejection of theatrical dance precedents.[85]

Continuing his analysis of the situation, Myers reminds us that Dunham's work was not simply a "re-creation of [dances] whose origins lie in the past." It was an original contribution that expressed "in contemporary additions and subtractions the artist's rebellious respect for the inspiration that tradition supplies."[86] In this respect, he contends that Dunham's contributions ultimately fall into the modern dance tradition:

> What pioneers such as Katherine Dunham . . . showed, in blending African/Caribbean elements into new modern dance styles, is a timeless truth: The innovative artist speaks with and through tradition but with and through an original voice. No matter how entrenched in an ethnic heritage, the modern dance choreographers absorb steps and gestures, rhythms and sounds, plots and themes—taken from an inspiring heritage—into a movement-speech distinctively their own. Bearing their personal timbre, their dances extend and not merely reflect a cultural legacy.[87]

Dunham herself gives us clues as to how her work influenced the modern dance tradition. Speaking of the mechanisms through which black cultural elements are absorbed into mainstream American culture, she states that black Americans were in a different situation than peoples of the Caribbean. Historically, their African retention had been less strong than in the more isolated cultures of the West Indies, but what cultural elements did remain were more likely to be absorbed into the mainstream of American culture. "The inevitable assimilation of the Negro and his cultural traditions into American culture as such has given African tradition a place in a large cultural body which it enjoys nowhere else. . . . The traditions are strengthened and re-emerge with new vigor."[88]

One of the primary individuals who strengthened these traditions and brought about their emergence in the modern dance tradition was Dunham herself. Through her national recognition as a concert artist and through the establishment of her school, Dunham brought to audiences, other artists, and students an array of movement possibilities that had not been seen or used before in contemporary dance.

While she poured her time and energy into the school, she still continued to create colorful Broadway productions. Her next revue, *Bal Nègre*, which opened in November 1946, was considerably more successful than *Carib Song*. This time, John Martin was more pleased with Dunham's return to Broadway. In his first review of the production, Martin called it Dunham's best show to date. Though he pointed out that its pattern and content closely followed that of *Tropical Revue* (*Bal Nègre* included works such as *L'Ag'Ya* from that revue and *Shango* from *Carib Song*), he said, "It surpasses its predecessor in taste, stageworthiness and general artistry."[89] A second review by Martin appeared ten days later. Overall, it was also complimentary, but, not one to let the Dunham men get away unscathed, he said, "Some of the boys should be reminded that they are not Russian ballerinas and that it would be nice if they would comport themselves accordingly."[90] *Bal Nègre* continued its run at the Belasco Theatre for more than a month, after which the Dunham Company embarked on its first major tour outside of the United States.

Mexico was its first stop. With invitations to meet the Mexican president, Miguel Aleman Valdes, as well as leading artists and intellectuals, Dunham received her first taste of international acclaim. In Mexico City the company performed at the Esperanza Iris Theatre for four weeks and then moved on to tour the provinces. Everywhere they went, the performers were received with stunning ovations, and newspapers carried daily stories about "La Katerina" and her dancers.

After Mexico, they returned home for a time to prepare for their first European tour. Dunham found that the enrollment in her school had markedly decreased. It had never been an economic success, and it proved to be a frustrating financial burden through the years. She poured most of the income from her touring back into the school to keep it going.

The European performance schedule opened with *Caribbean Rhapsody* at London's Prince of Wales Theatre on June 2, 1948. The company's critical reception was unanimously positive. Even critics who had generally poor opinions of modern dance praised the Dunham Company.[91] One critic wrote, "For the average spectator, perhaps, the high 'entertainment value' of her work may obscure its more solid qualities and keen intelligence, knowledge and artistry behind it. But the unity and beauty of her stage ensembles make some of our own ballet productions look more than a little primitive."[92]

Following the London performances, the company toured other British cities and then moved on to Paris where it received even more adulation. As in Mexico and Great Britain, the dancers were introduced to the cream of society, including artists such as Jean Cocteau, Josephine Baker, Mistinguette, and Maurice Chevalier. Paris, with its longstanding reputation for racial egalitarianism, was a favorite of the Dunham Company; so much so that several company members decided to remain and use the city as a home base for establishing careers in Europe. Among these were Eartha Kitt and Jean-Leon Destine.

The tour brought further success in Italy, Germany, the Netherlands, and Scandinavia and finally concluded in August 1949. It had been both an invigorating and exhausting experience for all involved, but for Dunham it was also a period of loss and extreme pain. Her brother Albert, who had long since completed his Ph.D and become a professor at Howard University, had died earlier that year, and her father died shortly after she returned to New York.

During the 1950s the Dunham Company continued to tour America and to take its unique cultural message around the world. There was a South American tour, a Jamaican tour, and a second European tour. There was also a tour of Australia, New Zealand, and the Orient. After disbanding her company in 1957, Dunham reestablished it for a third European tour in 1959.

Her programs continued to consist of dances from her old repertoire and new choreographic material presented in the format that she had used over the years. These were shows such as *Bamboche,* which toured the United States in 1962 and 1963 and featured the Royal Dance Troupe of Morocco in addition to the Dunham Company. As her company's popularity declined, and the sheer physical stress and financial burden of managing such a large enterprise took its toll on her, Dunham turned toward other projects that stressed her kinship with black cultures around the world. In 1965, she helped establish the Senegalese National Ballet, acted as cultural adviser to Senegal's president, Léopold Sédar Senghor, and helped organize the First World Festival of Negro Arts in Dakar.

It was also in 1965 that Dunham laid the groundwork for a project that she considered the last important phase of her career. After being invited to choreograph the opera *Faust* at Southern Illinois University in Carbondale, she visited the SIU campus at Edwardsville and decided to house her large collection of costumes, memorabilia, and other archival material there. Around the same time, R. Sargent Shriver, director of the U.S. Office of Economic Opportunity, suggested that she visit the nearby Illinois city of East St. Louis to investigate the possibility of establishing a cultural arts program in that economically depressed area.

Dunham was familiar with the effects of poverty and illiteracy because of the years she had spent in Haiti. But the appalling conditions in East St. Louis made an impression upon her that she could not ignore. She began drawing up a proposal for the Performing Arts Training Center. More than a year later, while traveling abroad working on various other projects, she received news that her proposed program in East St. Louis had been funded by the Rockefeller Foundation and the Danforth Foundation. She immediately returned to the United States and began the project.

She focused particularly on the population of black youths who were plagued by illiteracy, a high dropout rate from school, gang participation, and, consequently, a volatile relationship with the local law enforcement system. At a time when East St. Louis, like so many other urban areas in America, was exploding from the friction between militant young blacks and local police, Dunham became actively involved in channeling the energy of gang members into activities such as drumming, martial arts, and dancing. Her task was arduous, but she succeeded in establishing an institution that used art and culture as a tool for enriching the lives of young people who had little reason to be positive about themselves. Her approach was a variation on the old social positivism that had heralded the coming of the New Negro during the Harlem Renaissance. Her primary emphasis, however, was not on proving to the outside world that her people were worthy of an equal position in society; it was on proving to the individuals she worked with that art and culture and self-knowledge could foster feelings of self-esteem that could permanently change their lives.

Dunham's life's work always reflected the complexity of the interrelated interests, disciplines, and missions she pursued. For her, scholarly asceticism and performative extroversion were not mutually exclusive. The serious intent of a dedicated artist did not keep her from using the shrewd intuition that enabled her to captivate audiences from nightclubs to opera houses. The glamour associated with being constantly in the public eye did not cause her to lose sight of the social activism that informed everything she touched. During her early touring years, she had often protested against segregation in the theaters where she performed and in hotels where she had difficulty finding lodging for her company.

Her curiosity, humanity, and generous spirit led her in directions few American artists ever followed. Though her academic career did not, as the anthropologist St. Clair Drake put it, result in her "getting caught up in the Ph.D. processing machine,"[93] her scholarly contributions to the field of anthropology were considerable. She apparently did not finish her master's degree work at the University of Chicago, but the thesis she wrote, "The Dances of Haiti," was later published under the same title in Spanish, French, and English.[94] Along with her other books that recount her West Indian experiences, *Journey to Accompong* and *Island Possessed*, it provides important insight into the function of dance in Caribbean cultures. In addition to the rigors of her anthropological fieldwork, she always seemed to be taking nonartistic detours that led her to the hearts of people—probably her most enduring interest.

Because of these qualities, coupled with her establishment of a technical and aesthetic foundation that others could build upon, she more than any other black concert dancer was able to influence generations of young artists and propagate the artistic and humanistic principles that shaped her life.

Asadata Dafora as Bokari in *Kykunkor*, 1934; photo by Maurice Goldberg. (Asadata Dafora Horton Collection, Photographs and Prints Division, Schomburg Center for Research in Black Culture, New York Public Library, Astor, Lenox and Tilden Foundations)

Alma Sutton as Musu Esami in *Kykunkor*. (Asadata Dafora
Horton Collection, Photographs and Prints Division,
Schomburg Center for Research in Black Culture, New
York Public Library, Astor, Lenox and Tilden Foundations)

Abdul Assen and Asadata Dafora in the exorcism scene from *Kykunkor*. (Asadata Dafora Horton Collection, Photographs and Prints Division, Schomburg Center for Research in Black Culture, New York Public Library, Astor, Lenox and Tilden Foundations)

The witches scene in the Federal
Theatre Production of *Macbeth*,
1936. (Federal Theatre Project
Photograph Collection, Special
Collections and Archives, George
Mason University Libraries,
Fairfax, Virginia)

Katherine Dunham in an early solo, *Tango Motif on a Theme by Shulhoff* circa 1936; photo by Dorien Basabé. (Courtesy of Katherine Dunham Papers, Special Collections/Morris Library, Southern Illinois University, Carbondale, Illinois)

Dunham's Negro Dance Group in *Fantasy Nègre*, circa 1936; photo by Dorien Basabé. (Courtesy of Katherine Dunham Papers, Special Collections/Morris Library, Southern Illinois University, Carbondale, Illinois)

An early cast of *L'Ag'Ya* in Chicago; photo by Dorien Basabé. (Courtesy of Katherine Dunham Papers, Special Collections/Morris Library, Southern Illinois University, Carbondale, Illinois)

Katherine Dunham and Vanoye Aikens in *L'Ag'Ya*; photo by
Maurice Seymour. (Courtesy of Katherine Dunham Papers,
Special Collections/Morris Library, Southern Illinois Univer-
sity, Carbondale, Illinois)

Katherine Dunham in *Tropics and Le Jazz Hot*, 1940. (Courtesy of
Katherine Dunham Papers, Special Collections/ Morris Library,
Southern Illinois University, Carbondale, Illinois)

Katherine Dunham and Roger Ohardieno in *Barrelhouse*, 1938. (Courtesy of Katherine Dunham Papers, Special Collections/Morris Library, Southern Illinois University, Carbondale, Illinois)

Pearl Primus in *African Ceremonial*, 1943; photo by Gerta
Peterich. (Dance Division, New York Public Library for the
Performing Arts, Astor, Lenox and Tilden Foundations)

Pearl Primus and Joe Nash in *Playdance*; photo by Gerta Peterich.
(Dance Division, New York Public Library for the Performing Arts,
Astor, Lenox and Tilden Foundations)

Pearl Primus performing *Dance of Thanksgiving* during trip to Zaire.
(Dance Division, New York Public Library for the Performing Arts,
Astor, Lenox and Tilden Foundations)

7

Pearl Primus

IN 1943, PEARL PRIMUS EMERGED as an important new artist on the New York dance scene. Although she shared some characteristics with the black concert artists who preceded her, in many ways she was a strikingly original artist who brought a new dynamism to the field of dance. Her initial appearance was as a solo performer, one distinction that set her apart from the other black artists discussed here; most of them had first appeared with companies of their own. Perhaps her earliest solo performances caused those who saw her to focus more intently on the individual qualities she brought to the stage.

Early photographs of the young performer convey images that are unique for the period. Unlike the pictorial records of her contemporaries, which capture the earthbound quality of early modern dance, many of the performance photographs of Primus show her suspended in midair, bursting with kinetic energy and seemingly oblivious to the forces of gravity. As critics and audiences constantly noted, she had a special affinity for being airborne.

Margaret Lloyd's description of Primus's performance of *Hard Time Blues* attests to the artist's fascination with flight: "Pearl takes a running jump, lands in an upper corner and sits there, unconcernedly paddling the air with her legs. She does it repeatedly, from one side of the stage, then the other, apparently unaware of the involuntary gasps from the audience. . . . The dance is a protest against sharecropping. For me it was exultant with the mastery over the law of gravitation."[1]

As a dancer, Primus was distinctive in other ways. When her style is compared to that of the other leading black dancer of the period, Katherine Dunham, it is clear that one of the few things they had in common was their use of dance elements from Africa and the Caribbean. Dunham's performance style reflected a glamorous and sensual persona. Primus, on the other hand, was more elemental, more visceral. When she danced, she wrenched movement from the air and then brought it down to its earthy conclusion. At other times, she imbued stillness with the elegant primal austerity of an African woodcarving.

Dunham surrounded her own striking physical presence with a company of dancers whose beauty seemed to take up where her own left off. Primus's early works did not depend upon a group, and when she did use other dancers during the early days of her career, they were few. Over the years, much of her work continued to be choreographed for herself or for small groups of dancers.

Primus was born in 1919 in Port-of-Spain, Trinidad, and her family moved to the United States when she was three years old. In an early interview, she described her childhood in New York as growing up "in a narrow circle that embraced church, school, library and home."[2] She lived with her family at Sixty-ninth and Broadway, where her father, Edward, was a building superintendent. She considered herself fortunate that the racial prejudice that later became the subject matter of many of her dances did not adversely affect her during her early childhood.[3] As a child, she became keenly interested in Africa and made a vow that she would travel there some day. "I grew up in a home," she said, "where discussions about Africa were everyday occurrences. My father and uncles had been in various countries of Africa, either as merchant seamen or as soldiers."[4]

After attending Public Schools 94 and 136 in New York, she attended Hunter College High School and later received her undergraduate degree in biology and pre-medical sciences from Hunter College. While attending college, she excelled in track-and-field competitions and other sports, displaying the athleticism that would become a unique physical signature of her later performances. From Hunter she went to New York University where she studied health education for a while, but she returned to Hunter College to work on a M.A. degree in psychology. Finding that she became too emotionally involved in the psychiatric cases she was required to study, she transferred to Columbia University, where she began graduate studies in anthropology.

The first glimmer of recognition that dance would be the guiding force in her life occurred when she became involved in a dance group sponsored by the National Youth Administration, a government job training program for young people. While working in the wardrobe department of a NYA project, she was approached by one of the vocational advisers who suggested that she become an understudy for a program that was in preparation, *America Dances.* Pressed into service for one of the performances, she was outstanding.[5]

The NYA dance experience was inspiring but short-lived. In 1941, after the program disbanded, she moved on to the New Dance Group (the politically activist dance collective and studio that had been founded in 1932), having heard about auditions for a scholarship there. She was the only black student at the time and so inexperienced that when someone suggested she warm up before class she replied, "What do you mean warm up? I'm warm already. It's not hot in here."[6] In spite of her unfamiliarity with dance studio decorum, she impressed her teachers with her outstanding talent and began her studies with fellow Trinidadian Belle Rosette, a specialist in Caribbean dance, and the modern dancers Jane Dudley, Sophie Maslow, and William Bales. She was also encouraged to study with Martha Graham, Hanya Holm, Doris Humphrey, and Charles Weidman. Graham called her a "panther," and Weidman called her "his little primitive." In retrospect, Primus remembered their words as affectionate appellations used to describe the "burst of joy" she was trying to express through dancing.[7]

Her first performance in a professional atmosphere took place on February 14, 1943, when she appeared at the Ninety-second Street YM-YWHA on a program entitled *Five Dancers,* which she shared with Nona Schurman, Iris Mabry, Julia Levien, and Gertrude Prokosch. Her part of the program consisted of *Strange Fruit,* which portrayed a woman's pained reactions to a lynching; *Rock Daniel,* a jazz-inspired piece; *Hard Time Blues,* a dance protesting the plight of southern sharecroppers; and *African Ceremonial.* To gather material for *African Ceremonial*—based upon a fertility rite of the Belgian Congo—Primus had researched her material by consulting books, looking at photographs, and visiting museums. In addition, she had checked the authenticity of her movement with African students who were attending Columbia University. She also relied upon the expert advice of two percussionists, Norman Coker, who had performed with Asadata Dafora and had coproduced *Bassa Moona* with Momodu Johnson, and Alphonse Cimber, a Haitian artist who accompanied classes at the New Dance Group. Both men proved to be invaluable colleagues during Primus's career.

When John Martin published his review of the YM-YWHA concert the following week, his enthusiasm for the young artist established the positive support that he would extend to her over the coming years. He said, "If Miss Primus walked away with the lion's share of the honors, it was partly because her material was more theatrically effective, but also partly because she is a remarkably gifted artist."[8] He had not been similarly impressed since Katherine Dunham's arrival on the scene three years earlier. In many ways, he was more impressed. He could not think of another Negro dancer who was Primus's equal in technique, composition, artistic integrity, personal vitality, and charm.[9]

Her next performance venue was not a concert hall but a jazz club. In April 1943 she approached Barney Josephson, the manager of Cafe Society Downtown, to audition for his Greenwich Village establishment. When he saw the young woman primly dressed in a pleated skirt, socks, and shoes, he started to send her away; but after she showed him the few newspaper reviews she had received for her first YM-YWHA performance, he said, "Oh, are you that kid they wrote about in the Times? Okay, we'll try you out for ten days."[10]

Instead of ten days, her stay at Cafe Society lasted ten months. During that time, she continued to choreograph new dances, such as *Jim Crow Train*, another of her protest dances, and *Study in Nothing*, a humorous dance to the music of the jazz pianist Mary Lou Williams. She performed two or three fifteen-minute shows each night. The performance space was small and her repertoire of African, modern, and jazz dances was strange fare for the jaded audiences she faced; but she won them over with her talent, her earnestness—and, as Margaret Lloyd described one of the dances she performed, her beauty:

"The Negro Speaks of Rivers," to the poem by Langston Hughes and music by Sarah Malament, is one of Pearl's best. It is beautiful with undulating rhythms over deep-flowing currents of movement that wind into whirl-pool spins. She pivots on one knee or circles the stationary bent leg with the free leg, leaning her body in a long slant away from the traveling foot. The pale soles flash, the brown toes clutch and grasp, the dark fingers spread wide, the whole body sings: I've known rivers ancient as the world And older than the flow of human blood in human veins. . . . My soul has grown deep like the rivers.[11]

While Primus was appearing at Cafe Society, John Martin singled her out as the most important newcomer of the dance season. He remarked that the distinction did not usually go to a dancer who had been on the scene so briefly, but it was warranted because of her "vigorous and authentic" talent.[12] He mentioned only a few limitations in her dancing, which he credited to youth and inexperience. He spoke of her strong points as being her "inward power," her sense of drama, a talent for comedy, and "a really superb technique."[13] The last of these accolades was particularly remarkable coming from Martin, who had never been very generous with compliments concerning the technical abilities of black dancers. "There is no doubt," Martin continued, "that she is quite the most gifted artist-dancer of her race (she is Negro) yet to appear in the field." He concluded—in what surely must have been a first for him—by saying that it was unfair to classify her merely as "an outstanding Negro dancer" since she was, by any measure, "an outstanding dancer without regard for race."[14]

Bolstered by Martin's glowing comments, Primus continued her appearances at Cafe Society and also appeared as a soloist with Asadata Dafora and his company at Carnegie Hall on December 13, 1943. The following month, she shared a YM-YWHA program with another newcomer, Valerie Bettis. Edwin Denby spoke of this January 23, 1944, performance as being "the most dramatic recital that any young dancers have given this season."[15] He found the meaning of Primus's dance gestures completely clear and the "dramatic form and the dramatic point" of her dances appropriate within the limitations of her technique.[16] Lois Balcom, the reviewer for the *Dance Observer*, did not share his positive point of view; she said, "As a choreographer, her weakness is in a naive literalism of gesture and an unrestrained, undisciplined throwing of herself about."[17]

After presenting other concerts in New York (a YM-YWHA return engagement in April 1944 and a performance at Hunter College in June that she shared with Randolph Scott), Primus began a phase of study that led her closer to the anthropological roots of her dance material. Putting aside her performing for a few months, she spent the summer of 1944 living among rural blacks in the South. There she became more acutely aware of the economic oppression, fear, and degradation that resulted from racial prejudice. She also found rhythmic patterns, songs, and movements that were akin to their African antecedents. Though cultural retention from Africa was generally weaker in the United States than in other parts of the Western Hemisphere, she found that it was very much alive in the dozens of small churches she visited in Georgia, Alabama, and South Carolina. The experience affected her deeply and added new dimensions to works like *Strange Fruit* and *Hard Time Blues.* Vivid, first-hand knowledge began to replace intuitive feelings and information gathered from books.

As described in Jean Ruth Glover's account, Primus disguised herself as a migrant and picked cotton with the local workers; she spent time reflecting on her demeaning experiences as she traveled from one job site to another on Jim Crow trains and buses. In addition to providing material for her notebooks, her travels also supplied her with material for dances that she would later create, such as *Slave Market* and *Steal Away to Freedom.*[18]

After returning to New York, she became more actively involved than ever in concert work. For her Broadway debut, on October 4, 1944, at the Belasco Theatre, she supplemented her solo repertoire with dances she choreographed for four men—Joe Comadore, Thomas Bell, Albert Popwell, and James Alexander. She used them in *Ague,* an African ritual, and in *Slave Market.* There was also a duet, *Mischievous Interlude,* featuring Popwell, whom Denby called "very brilliant."[19] As for Primus, the critic had some reservations about her overall dancing. Though he still found her "exceptionally gifted" and "thrilling," he also found her to have a self-conscious tendency to "ham" her protest dances—compromising their dramatic integrity.[20]

One of the most interesting commentaries (actually a series of articles that was published in two consecutive monthly installments in the *Dance Observer*) was written by Lois Balcom. One or more New York critics, it seemed, wrote an annual status report on black dance and dancers. It was Balcom's year, and, as reflected in her earlier reviews of Primus, she seemed determined to oppose the generally positive views taken by other critics. She took on all comers who classified Primus as a "great Negro dancer" and said that it was a pity the young artist would never achieve the potential she showed because she had been seduced by trying to fulfill audiences' (and some critics') preconceptions about what a Negro dancer should be.[21]

According to Balcom, Primus was playing to the expectations of a particular type of audience by giving them the African, jazz, and black protest dances they expected. This same type of audience was infatuated by Primus's "natural skill and good intentions." And they did not have the foresight to temper their enthusiasm with an awareness of "the disciplined eloquence of which she might be capable after seasons of artistic growth."[22]

But there was another type of audience (which was, of course, where Balcom positioned herself). This audience was aware that a good modern dance artist should make an individual statement in which each dance assumed its own form without depending upon preconceived formulas.[23] To please this audience, to reconcile good Negro dancing with good modern dancing, Primus would have to stay away from stereotypes.

Balcom placed Primus in a position where she had very few places to turn to validate her aesthetic existence. Balcom dismissed her African dances because they were not authentic. They were stereotypical approximations, and they were derivative. She dismissed her jazz-influenced dances because they reflected the "forced gaiety" white audiences had come to expect from black artists. And her black protest dances (which were of the modern dance genre) were undisciplined; they were not taut and economic in expressing the emotional richness of her race. In other words, she simply wasn't a good modern dancer. With all these doors closed to her the only narrow space for Primus to squeeze through in her search for artistic identity was—as Balcom vaguely put it—to blend her racial memory and individual awareness, to realistically understand audience preconceptions, to speak for her race in contemporary terms with passion and discipline.[24]

In an interview prior to the Broadway debut that inspired Balcom's lengthy commentary, Primus spoke of the deep places where she sought her inspiration. Her words revealed the particularly poetic and spiritual sensibility that would characterize her writing and her artistry throughout the years.

> I see Africa as the continent of strength; it is a place with ancient civilizations, civilizations wrecked and destroyed by the slave-seekers. I know an Africa that gave the world the iron on which now it moves, an Africa of nations, dynasties, cultures, languages, great migrations, powerful movements, slavery . . . all that makes life itself. This strength, this past, I try to get into my dances. . . . And when I think of my people here in America too, I see something that they have to see clearer, that whites have to know about. I see the long road we have trod, the movements for freedom we have been in, from the slave revolts that dot our early history, up to our participation in the Revolutionary War.[25]

Shortly after her Broadway debut, Primus presented a concert at the Roxy Theatre in December 1944. She re-choreographed her solo *African Ceremonial* for an expanded group of fourteen dancers. Martin found the opening passage for the ensemble so "striking and vital" that he was all the more impressed with Primus's ability to match its dynamism in a solo section for herself.[26] Primus used the Roxy's huge stage effectively by having her dancers move up and down ramps and by performing a solo for herself atop a high altar from which she dramatically descended at the conclusion.

During the next year, Primus collaborated with several other artists on joint concerts. *India-Haiti-Africa* was a multi-ethnic program that she shared with Hadassah and Josephine Premice at Times Hall in January 1945; and in February she appeared with her former teacher, Charles Weidman, in a joint concert at the Central High School of Needle Trades.

Her first appearance in a Broadway musical took place the following year in a revival of *Show Boat*, choreographed by Helen Tamiris. Adapted from a novel by Edna Ferber, with memorable music by Jerome Kern and Oscar Hammerstein, this American musical classic had been produced in 1927 and again in 1932. When it opened to glowing reviews at the Ziegfeld Theatre in January, Primus was a featured soloist in two production numbers—*No Shoes* and *Dance of the Dahomeys*. The show ran for most of that year and then began touring. During the early part of the tour, at a time when Tamiris was unavailable to re-stage the choreography, Primus successfully took over the job.

Primus was not able to give her full attention to her concert appearances while she was working on *Show Boat.* Consequently, she left the show to begin a national concert tour. Beginning in November 1946, the tour took her to southern, northeastern, and midwestern colleges and concert halls. Her repertoire included several new dances such as *To One Dead,* a solo for herself, and *Myth,* based on a Melanesian version of the Pygmalion story. The latter dance was performed by Joe Nash and Jacqueline Hairston, the other two members of Primus's small touring company. She also re-choreographed her solos *Afro-Haitian Play Dance* and *Caribbean Conga* for Hairston and Nash. Both dancers complemented Primus by reflecting her vital energy and dramatic style. During the tour, when the company performed in Boston at Jordan Hall on January 17, 1947, the two were spoken of as "dancers of grace, style and variety, able, like Miss Primus, to go from capricious foolery to impressive symbolism."[27]

After concluding her tour, which consisted of some twenty-five concerts, Primus was invited by Ruth Page to dance in a 1947 revival of the opera *The Emperor Jones.* She danced Hemsley Winfield's witch doctor role, and Lawrence Tibbett recreated his role of Brutus Jones.[28] She also appeared at Jacob's Pillow Dance Festival in early August of the same year and presented several new works—an Afro-Cuban *Santos* and two spirituals, *Goin' to Tell God All My Troubles* and *In That Great Gettin'-up Mornin'.*[29]

Primus tried her hand at choreographing a Broadway show in late 1947. Between its October previews in Philadelphia and its opening at New York's International Theatre on December 5, the show went through several name changes. First it was called *Calypso,* then *Bongo,* and finally *Caribbean Carnival.* The indecision about the show's title apparently paralleled the indecision about what it was supposed to be. Brooks Atkinson said the production (which was billed as "the first Calypso musical ever presented") could not make up its mind whether it was a musical show or a dance recital.[30]

Atkinson praised the dancing in the show for being "accomplished and original." He particularly liked the Haitian ritual dances that comprised most of the second act.[31] The show had a strong cast led by Primus and Claude Marchant, with additional support from Josephine Premice, but its weak libretto kept it from achieving much success. *Caribbean Carnival* closed after only eleven performances.

Her lack of success as a Broadway choreographer was soon overshadowed by the turn of events that would lead Primus into the next phase of her career. She had applied for a Rosenwald Fellowship in hopes of acquiring funds to help her keep her company together and continue to build a repertoire. Her application had been turned down because the foundation had recently ceased its philanthropic activities. Just by chance, after a performance at Fisk University, Primus was approached by Dr. Edwin Embree, the president of the Rosenwald Foundation. He asked her when she had last traveled to Africa. Amazed to find that she had never been there, he initiated a chain of events that rectified that situation. In spite of the organization's dormancy, he arranged to make an exception for her so that she could receive a grant—the foundation's last and largest—to study and live in Africa for approximately a year.

After a return engagement at Cafe Society, Primus began a journey in December 1948 that took her to Nigeria, Liberia, Senegal, Angola, the Gold Coast, the Belgian Congo, and French Equatorial Africa. A young black woman (she was twenty-nine years old) traveling through Africa alone in search of her spiritual and aesthetic roots must have been an exceptional sight. Primus studied the dances of more than thirty ethnic groups. Since beginning her studies of anthropology at Columbia University several years earlier, she had become familiar with field research techniques, which included the use of still photography, motion pictures, and line sketches. When she was permitted, she took part in the tribal dances and studied with experts in the countries she visited.

The most striking validation of the kinship between her own dancing and the dances of Africa could not, however, be detailed in the languages of the body sciences, or ballet, or modern dance, which she also used to help record her observations of movement. It could not be measured by the techniques of the social scientist. It was most accurately reflected in the personal responses she received from the people with whom she lived and studied. The people she visited were amazed at the similarities between her dancing and their own; they believed her to be an ancestral spirit. In Nigeria she was called "Omowale" (child returned home). Her approach was heralded from village to village by talking drums that announced, "Little Fast Feet is on her way."[32]

In her own mind, the questions detractors such as Balcom posed concerning the authenticity of her dancing soon faded as she discovered the tremendous variety of movement in African dance. Although there were some dance patterns that were common in many areas, she found that there were also major dance distinctions among ethnic groups that existed within a few miles of each other.[33] There was no all-inclusive African dance style or technique that could be used as an easy reference to summarily include or exclude a dance as being "authentic" or not. To do so was simply inaccurate.

She found that the people of Africa used their bodies to convey every conceivable emotion and to amplify the major events of their communities as well as the minor occurrences in their everyday lives. "The result," she said, "is a strange but hypnotic marriage between life and dance."[34] There were "abstract ceremonials, fertility dances, dances of the aristocracy, children's dances, and dances of birth, puberty, death, and motherhood. Acrobatic, social, hunting dances were to be found, as well as ballets narrating story and legend, ecstatic dances, humorous dances and many others."[35]

She learned the distinctions between the traditions of trained African performers and those individuals who "just danced." The latter group included villagers who had learned ritual dances when they were children; later, they continued to dance because they enjoyed "speaking with their bodies."[36] Professional dancers, on the other hand, had been trained from childhood and apprenticed to master dancers. They learned traditional dances with exact precision and then were encouraged to elaborate upon the tradition through their own individuality: "The young dancer is taught his purpose, his function. He is told that he is not one, but that he is the entire tribe. His body is an instrument with which he can speak for his tribe and through which God can speak. This body must not be abused, but must be kept in readiness at all times."[37]

Through corresponding with John Martin, Primus was able to convey her impressions of Africa to people back home. Several months after she had departed, he published excerpts from one of her letters in the *Times*. "Their dancing," she wrote, "is losing the strength and freshness which they claim my dancing has." After reporting that many of the traditional dance forms were dying out, she continued: "I am fortunate to be able to salvage the still existent gems of dance before they, too, fade. . . . In many places I started movements to make the dance again important. . . . I saw dances which had not been done for twenty-five years; I saw some which will not be seen again for twenty years."[38]

Primus's travels in Africa had significant effects on the direction of her career. When she returned to America, her activities such as teaching and conducting lecture-demonstrations took on a new importance as she began sharing her rich experiences. In lecture-demonstrations such as *Dark Rhythms,* she used a small ensemble of performers to present Caribbean and African dances, gave informative talks about the cultures they represented, and spoke of the cultural continuum of the black diaspora. This format became an important part of her programming throughout the balance of her career.[39]

On the concert stage, she returned to using a male ensemble to capture the vitality of the dances she had seen, and she used her firsthand experiences of African dancing to create new works. There was *Fanga,* based on a dance of welcome from Liberia, *Egbo Esakpade,* which reflected the elegant court dances of Benin, and a dance that featured tribal masks, *The Initiation.* She also began combining individual dances into suites, such as *Excerpts from an African Journey;* these made stronger statements as theater pieces than the shorter, unrelated dances she had formerly presented.

She reserved one of the dances she had learned in Africa, *Impinyuza,* as a solo for herself. The dance was usually performed by towering Watusi warriors, but performing it had a special meaning for her because it had been taught to her by the king of the Watusi, who adopted her as his chief dancer. In a later interview, she described the religious significance of the stately dance that reenacts how the Creator strode upon the earth: "Where He walked, the earth, being soft and new, sank in. What stayed up were the hills and the mountains. Where His feet went were the valleys; the rivers sprang behind Him. . . . And that is what they are dancing about."[40]

In 1951, Primus embarked on a series of international tours. That year, again appearing with an ensemble of male dancers, she performed in London at the Prince's Theatre in November. The critic Cyril Beaumont found her dances ethnologically interesting but less successful as spectacle.[41] While in London she appeared before King George VI, and her European tour also took her to France, Italy, and Finland. In 1952 she toured Israel, where she and her company danced in theaters, for the armed forces, in settlements, and in immigration camps.[42]

After touring, Primus returned to her solo concert work and her anthropological studies, which took her to the West Indies in 1953. The time she spent in Trinidad was fortuitous in several ways. She was able to reestablish her ties with the Caribbean dancer and teacher Belle Rosette, with whom she had studied at the New Dance Group ten years earlier; and she met Percival Borde, a strikingly handsome Trinidadian dancer whom she married the following year. Together they began a long and fruitful collaboration that combined their artistic, educational, and administrative skills.

Primus spent the late 1950s appearing with her husband in their dance company, giving solo concerts from time to time, and continuing her work toward a doctoral degree that she had begun in 1953 in the Department of Educational Sociology and Anthropology at New York University's School of Education. During the next decade, she made several more trips to Africa; the most important of these was a two-year stay in Liberia that began in October 1959.

Under the sponsorship of the Joint Liberian–United States Commission for Economic Development, she and her husband were asked to establish and direct the African Arts Center in Monrovia, a project that was the first of its kind in Africa. They engaged in collecting and preserving dance material, teaching, and organizing professional performances.[43] Even though Primus had spoken of a tradition of professional dancers in recounting her earlier African experiences, there was no established performance tradition in the Western theatrical sense; consequently, part of her job was to create audience interest in indigenous art forms. Where these forms still existed, they were often taken for granted because they were such an integral part of the fabric of the people's lives. Primus felt that African cultural traditions had to be revitalized, nurtured, and recast in a Western theatrical mode so that they could survive the growing Westernization of African society. Primus and Borde were given free reign to structure the arts center as they saw fit. They gave their first public performance in March 1960 at the Monrovia City Hall where they performed along with dancers, drummers, and mimes from different Liberian ethnic groups.[44]

After ten months in Liberia, Primus returned to New York briefly, and John Martin published a lengthy article about the work she and her husband were doing. Quoting from a Monrovian newspaper, he stressed the fact that the Liberian government was behind the project completely:

> Africa has declared in no uncertain manner her avowed determination to speak for herself in all political affairs. Now, more than ever in the history of Africa, the need arises for the expression of her cultural heritage. This Liberia was wise enough to realize, for only through a people's culture can they really be understood. . . . As the oldest republic in Africa, Liberia is justly proud of her pioneering role and rightly deserves the honor of inaugurating this symbolic trend of interpretative expression of the human body.[45]

Upon completing their work in Africa, Primus and Borde returned to New York and opened the Primus-Borde School of Primal Dance on West Twenty-fourth Street. During the late 1960s and the 1970s, Primus taught at several educational institutions in the New York area and became involved in a number of special projects. One such project, sponsored by the U.S. Office of Education and the Unitarian Universalist Service Committee, introduced hundreds of elementary school children in New York City to the dances, music, and culture of Africa. The program stressed the importance of movement and dance as an educational tool that related to young people's overall learning abilities. This particular program was one of her special loves, reflecting her lifelong interest in conveying the importance of black culture to her own generation and to ensuing generations. It was also part of her final requirements for completing her Ph.D.

During the 1970s, Primus revived one of her dances, *The Wedding*, for the Alvin Ailey American Dance Theatre. In 1979, though basically retired as a performer, she danced on a program—also produced by Ailey—that honored black dance pioneers. In 1981, she appeared in one of her last concerts at the Theatre of the Riverside Church. A version of *Impinyuza* that was adapted for the men of the Ailey company was performed in 1990.

In some ways Primus's career seems enigmatic. At the height of her concert appearances, she was considered one of the most exciting dancers of her time. Her dynamism, dramatic flair, and kinetic magnetism were incomparable. The swiftness with which she caught the attention of critics and audiences indicated a special talent and charisma that distinguished her from other dancers of the 1940s. Yet she did not establish a long-lasting school or company. Perhaps the reasons she did not can best be found in the austere nature of her personality. In her approach to her work over the years, one perceives an extremely serious individual focused upon an artistic intent and engaged in a journey of cultural self-discovery that must be primarily undertaken alone:

> My career has been a quest . . . a search for roots. The journey has taken me deep into the cultures of many people in many countries of the world.
> Dance has been my vehicle. Dance has been my language, my strength. In the dance I have confided my most secret thoughts and shared the inner music of all mankind. I have danced across mountains and deserts, ancient rivers and oceans and slipped through the boundaries of time and space.[46]

One senses that she was a woman of a solitary, uncompromising nature who was not prepared to bend the integrity of her work to fit the exigencies of passing trends. On the other hand, neither her race nor her subject matter permitted her work to fit easily into the definitions of modern dance that were current during the 1940s and 1950s.

Through her unique personal and artistic style, however, Pearl Primus did create modern dances that captured the contemporaneous concerns of African Americans. She created West Indian dances that reflected another aspect of her heritage, and she created dances that were ultimately informed by her deep and loving involvement with the people of Africa.

In a sense, the movement in black concert dance from the 1920s through the 1940s had come full circle. There had been artists who had discovered their African and Caribbean dance roots either through research in whatever resources were available (books, photographs, museums) or by studying with Africans and West Indians who were in the United States. Dunham and Primus explored these roots by submerging themselves in the cultures where the dances were still a living tradition. There had also been a native African, Asadata Dafora, who brought his continent's rich cultural heritage to America and actively disseminated its elements to the American public. There had been African Americans who struggled to find kinship with the American modern dance movement. Most of the artists discussed here drew upon the vernacular roots of urban and rural American black dance traditions to enrich their choreography.

The resources these artists used in establishing their individual aesthetics were intertwined in elaborate ways. Artists' interpretations of African dances were informed by movement styles that could be traced to their African heritage. Afro-Caribbean dances drew part of their structure from European court and folk dances. Modern dance influences contributed their own kind of primal movement explorations.

In Primus—born in Trinidad, steeped in African-American and European-American culture, long a resident in Africa seeking the creative and spiritual font of the black diaspora—we find a fitting symbol of the circuitous ways in which black artists validated their individual existence and the existence of their people, their heritage, and their culture.

8
1950s–1990s: An Overview

THE ARTISTS DISCUSSED IN THE PRECEDING CHAPTERS made their marks on the concert dance stage as individual performers and choreographers, and each made distinctive contributions to the early development of African-American concert dance. Yet, when we look back on their achievements, from a perspective broadened by the intervening years, we can see more clearly the interrelationships between their individual works and the pattern that they form. We can also begin to assess their influences as a group of seminal artists whose innovations contributed to both art and culture in America. These artists established an ongoing tradition of their own while advancing the broader traditions of theatrical concert dance.

Among the distinctive features that define these artists as a group, their uses of thematic material, movement vocabularies, and music gleaned from the cultures of the African diaspora stand out as important aesthetic elements that these dancers brought to the concert stage for the first time. As innovators in this area, they developed syncretic processes of presenting vernacular, ritual, and folk material within a framework of European-American theatrical practices in an attempt to change perceptions about the aesthetic value of black dance and to focus positive attention on the beauty of the cultures they drew upon. In this respect, the artists shared an additional distinctive approach to

their creative work: they consistently fused their art-making endeavors with the common goal of effecting sociopolitical change for African-American people.

As we look back on the factors that influenced these artists during
the 1930s and 1940s, another major commonality becomes apparent.
They were committed to bringing together aesthetic and cultural elements that had historically been positioned as polar opposites. These
were elements divided into categories that had never been easily reconciled in mainstream American culture—non-Western/Western,
black/white, popular and folk art/serious art. Black dance artists such
as Winfield, Dunham, and Primus were members of a long line of
African descendants who had used cultural creolization as a means of
adapting to an environment that was complex, proscriptive, and for-
bidding. These artists were also aware of the strong impulse to synthesize elements from different cultures that had played an important
role in Western art since the turn of the twentieth century. White
European and American artists had repeatedly drawn upon diverse
cultural expressions in formulating aesthetic innovations in theater,
dance, music, and the visual arts. For African-American dance artists,
their African diasporan heritage of cultural syncretism could comfortably accommodate this European diasporan tradition of contemporary
artistic innovation. The resultant cultural mix was rooted in labyrin-
thine influences and counterinfluences.

African-American artists saw their efforts to create a unified aesthetic
out of different artistic traditions as an important part of their mission.
Each one worked his or her unique alchemy on diverse dance elements
as they undertook the multiple tasks of acknowledging differences,
celebrating commonalities, and bringing the results of their syncretic
experiments into the American cultural arena. The unifying process
was essential to them, part of a holistic, life-enhancing project to forge
a positive identity for black people in the midst of a social and political environment that was hostile and a cultural establishment that was,
at best, intolerant of racial parity in the arts.

These artists also shared commonalities with the European-American dance artists who were active during the same period. As we have
seen in previous chapters, African-American dancers became keenly
aware of the work of the early modern dance pioneers, adopted many

of their precepts, studied and performed with them during the rare occasions when they could, and drew upon the dance techniques and
styles those artists were developing. But the work of black artists was
a variation on the theme of discovering new theatrical dance expressions for the twentieth century. Like their white counterparts, they
wanted their dances to express a contemporary American ethos. However, they pursued this goal by creating theatrical works that used African-American, West Indian, and African movement iconography rooted in specific black experiences to convey universal human messages.
They created art that was multivocal as it articulated the interfaces of
different worldviews. At the same time, they attempted to disassoci-
ate their work from proscriptive stereotypes. This goal was too often
thwarted by critical appraisals that persisted in placing them in narrow categories that had as much to do with cultural politics as with
aesthetics. In the minds of many critics, the broad imprimatur of *universality* was reserved exclusively for European-American artists.

The preceding chapters of this book have shown that the politics of
racial and cultural difference were of utmost importance in determining who had access to the resources that facilitated the creation and
dissemination of art in American culture. For the early African-American dance pioneers, the struggle to pursue training in mainstream
studios and the biases that informed critical commentary about their
work were only two of many manifestations of racial conflict that
played out in artistic arenas. The struggles, negotiations, and eventu-
al accommodations that took place in the name of art were centered
around an essential bifurcation of American society that had its roots
in the complex history of black-white race relations. These factors, in
turn, presented black artists with the daunting task of solving the
conundrum of cultural differences and creating unity from diversity.
What resulted were dance expressions of unique power and eloquence
that laid the foundation for an African-American theatrical dance aesthetic that could be built on and extended in many directions.

Hindsight reveals the ways in which black artists contributed to and
changed mainstream theatrical dance, even though cultural arbiters
of the time constantly questioned whether or not they rightfully belonged to the evolving traditions. We have seen a number of instances
in which the work of black dancers was perceived as being only vaguely

related—or not related at all—to the modern dance innovation of the time. From this negative perspective, concert dance that incorporated elements that differed from mainstream aesthetics was viewed as an anomaly. One need only remember the controversy that arose when Katherine Dunham's *Rites de Passage* was performed in Boston to understand how extreme reactions could be to dance that attempted to cross cultural boundaries on the American stage. The sensuality of her dancers' movements was thought to be a subversive influence, and the fact that such movements were combined with recognizable material from modern dance and ballet only heightened the critics' ire.

In his essay "African-Americans and the Modern Dance Aesthetic," the historian and philosopher Gerald Myers discusses the marginalization of the work of black artists in the history of early modern dance. He writes:

> I think that even those who are quite familiar with the careers of Dunham, Primus, and their successors have not made enough of the point that their culturally blended works, while certainly modifying the modern dance tradition . . . were nevertheless continuing the spirit of the early modern dance aesthetic. Too often, one regrets, their multicultural dances were received as being separate and distinct from American modern dance, so that whereas Doris Humphrey, Charles Weidman, José Limón, and Erick Hawkins were taken to be doing mainstream modern dance, Dunham, Primus, and their progeny were judged to be doing something else.[1]

Myers's words bring to mind the unacknowledged foresight of innovators like Katherine Dunham, Asadata Dafora, and Pearl Primus. During the years since these seminal artists began their careers, the tradition of cross-cultural choreography has been continued and enriched by the African-American artists who followed in their footsteps, individuals such as Talley Beatty, Alvin Ailey, Jawole Willa Jo Zollar, Garth Fagan, and many others. As modern dance has evolved into a truly international art form, dance companies in America and around the world have been influenced by increasingly diverse elements from other cultures.

Myers has sorted through the interwoven ideologies that have always connected African-American artists to more than one aesthetic tradition; he discusses the dual heritage of these artists and refutes the idea that they somehow do not belong to the historical tradition of modern dance. Moreover, for a number of reasons, Myers considers artists such as Katherine Dunham and Pearl Primus clearly among those manifesting the "aesthetic and philosophical spirit of early modern dance."[2]

Like Isadora Duncan, Martha Graham, and others, black artists pursued personal "missions of meaning" that defined and dramatized their inner lives as they pursued self-definition through the ongoing invention of dance movement.[3] African-American concert dancers, like their European-American contemporaries, used deeply subjective explorations to express their visions of human existence in the modern world. But their subjectivity was, again, tempered by a unique sense of group consciousness that acknowledged the power of art to address the social and political concerns of the black community.

Over the ensuing decades, there would be African-American artists whose work echoed the Harlem Renaissance philosophy of sociopolitical and aesthetic conciliation and mediation, artists who stressed the importance of using their work to further the acceptance and understanding of black people in American society. However, during certain periods, black artists would modify this idea and use it in ways that reflected the exigencies of their individual artistic visions and the specific concerns that dominated their times. As the dance historian Halifu Osumare points out in her insightful essay "The New Moderns: The Paradox of Eclecticism and Singularity," the African-American dance artist has, over the years, continued to be "a reflection of his/her social era, serving as catalyst at one turn and as a willing community barometer at others."[4] She continues, "Today's black choreographers of the '90s reflect the 'seething, shifting' American social scene just as their predecessors."[5]

In the balance of this chapter, I will briefly discuss some of the ways that individual artists have, over the past five decades, extended, expanded, and diverged from the traditions that their predecessors established. As with the discussion of the earlier years of African Americans in concert dance, it is impossible to include all of the many artists who contributed substantially to the ongoing presence of black dancers on the concert stage. The many exclusions should not be interpreted as an oversight but only as an indication of the enormous amount of work that remains to be done to tell the complete story.

By the late 1940s, emerging African-American dancers could look to a brief but significant tradition of their own. This in itself created an environment that was quite different than that of their forerunners. Younger black dancers could study and perform with members of their own race. They were able to see the work of other African-American dancers to an extent not possible before. One of the most important second-generation black artists whose career exemplified these connections was Talley Beatty.

Beatty was born in Cedargrove, Louisiana, a small community outside of Shreveport. His family was forced to sell their property because of a racially motivated altercation with local townspeople. They moved to Chicago when he was nine months old, and it was there that he eventually had his first glimpses of concert dance. When he was twelve, he and a friend, Lester Harris, were roaming their South Side neighborhood when they came upon an old carriage house that Katherine Dunham had converted into a dance studio, at Vincennes Avenue and Forty-eighth Place. She noticed the young boys watching her class with interest, invited them in, and persuaded them to begin studying with her. Shortly afterward, she recruited them to perform in *La Guiablesse*, the Ruth Page ballet that Dunham was restaging for a performance at the Chicago Opera House in 1934. During the same period, Beatty was attending art classes as a scholarship student at the Art Institute of Chicago, but much to his family's dismay, he gave up those studies and began to concentrate on becoming a dancer.[6] His love for dance grew not only because of his early training with Dunham but also because she was a generous spirit who broadened her young students' horizons by taking them to see touring companies that performed in Chicago.

While Dunham was out of the country conducting her initial anthropological fieldwork in the Caribbean in 1935, Beatty studied with other teachers in Chicago. A Chicago critic, Cecil Smith, who had supported Dunham's attempts to form a company, arranged for him to enroll as a scholarship student at Edna McCray's studio in Orchestra Hall. However, Beatty was not permitted to take class in the same room as the other students. Managing to follow the exercises from McCray's office, which adjoined the main studio, he made the best of the situation and continued to study. At Kurt and Grace Graff's studio, he had a similar experience. There he was given private lessons in a dressing room while the regular classes met separately. In spite of these conditions, he had made considerable progress by the time Dunham returned, and when her reorganized company traveled to New York for the first time to participate in the *Negro Dance Evening* in 1937, he was a featured dancer. After returning to Chicago for a while, he was called back to New York to join the cast of *Pins and Needles,* which Dunham was choreographing.

Within the ranks of the Dunham company, Beatty was soon singled out in one way or another, either for his striking dancing or for his "serious dallying with ballet technique," as John Martin remarked about his performance in Dunham's groundbreaking production, *Tropics and Le Jazz Hot.* But Beatty was not one to be deterred by criticism. When he was rehearsing with George Balanchine for the 1940 Broadway production of *Cabin in the Sky,* he impressed the choreographer enough to be encouraged to seek further ballet training at his school. Unfortunately, when Beatty went to inquire about enrolling, he was told that the school did not accept Negro students. Unable to convince the receptionist that Balanchine himself had sent him, he left, so annoyed that he never mentioned the incident to Balanchine. When he told Dunham about it, she replied, "It serves you right."[7]

Beatty's scrappy personality led to an on-again off-again relationship with the Dunham company, and he finally left the group permanently in the mid-1940s. During one of his periods of absence from the company, he teamed with Janet Collins, who had also performed briefly with Dunham. (In 1951 Collins would distinguish herself as the first African-American ballerina with the Metropolitan Opera Ballet Company.) The two dancers appeared for a short time in California nightclubs such as Ciro's, and at the suggestion of one of their backers, they took the stage names of Rea and Rico DeGard in order to capitalize on their light skin and Spanish-looking features and to ensure themselves more work. Collins very quickly tired of the commercial venture and tried to convince Beatty to stay in California and join her in an extended period of preparation for a concert career. Beatty would not agree with the plan and returned to New York.

The following years were comprised of the typical patchwork of performance experiences that dancers find themselves creating in order to survive. In 1946, Beatty appeared in a minstrel-ballet, *Blackface,* choreographed by Lew Christensen and sponsored by Ballet Society, the organization that George Balanchine and Lincoln Kirstein established to encourage the production of new ballets. That same year he was featured in a revival of the Jerome Kern and Oscar Hammerstein musical *Show Boat.* As previously mentioned, this musical was choreographed by Helen Tamiris, and Pearl Primus figured prominently among the performers. The many other talented black dancers in the show included Alma Sutton, whom Beatty had met and greatly admired when she performed with Asadata Dafora on the *Negro Dance Evening* program in 1937. Beatty was even better acquainted with several of the male dancers in *Show Boat* since they had also been associated with the Dunham Company. Laverne French, Beatty's cousin from Chicago, had joined the company at the time of its first California tour, and Claude Marchant had been with Dunham since *Tropics and Le Jazz Hot* in 1940.

After *Show Boat,* Beatty began the phase of his career that would eventually establish him as a major choreographer on the international dance scene. In November 1946, one of the earliest performances of his own work took place at Charles Weidman's Studio Theater on a program presented by the Choreographers' Workshop, a group of young artists comprised of Beatty, Atty Van den Berg, Lavinia Williams, and Claude Marchant. In a review by Walter Terry, the critic made special note of the choreography's "intensity of movement," a characteristic that would become a hallmark of Beatty's work over the ensuing years. Terry also noted that the young artist was testing styles in search of a personal dance idiom; he continued, "the blueprint of an individual choreographic style [was] present, but the final structure was still in the scaffolding stage." Terry was most impressed with a duet, *Blues,* which Beatty performed with another Dunham dancer, Lavinia Williams. The critic closed his review by comparing Beatty's choreography with that of Claude Marchant, about whom he said, "This young artist has already found his style, quiet and introspective, almost Oriental in its serene traversal of even the most vigorous of movements."[8]

As Beatty searched for his individual choreographic style, he continued to draw on his experiences with Dunham. Commenting on a 1948 YM-YWHA concert, one critic said that some of the dances were "derived, lock, stock and barrel, from the style of Miss Dunham's folk ballet, though they are better composed, for the most part."[9] Beatty was never satisfied with creating dances that were derivative of his former mentor's work. The fact that he did so for several years was due to the encouragement of Albert Morini, who became Beatty's manager after seeing his group in rehearsal in New York. In order to capitalize on the tremendous popularity of Dunham's exotic revues, Morini convinced Beatty to continue in the same direction and mount a series of concerts entitled *Tropicana,* which premiered in Goteborg, Sweden, during the spring of 1949. Beatty and his small company of six dancers opened at the Stuart Theatre to audiences that applauded the cultural mix that Morini breathlessly described in the notes of the souvenir program:

> Taken as a whole, "Tropicana" is kaleidoscopic in its pulsating depiction of the Negro at work and at play, in the abandonment of religious frenzy and in the tense simplicity of religious awe. In locale, it ranges through the West Indies to the shores of South America and back to the Southland of the United States. Throughout, one feels the heartbeat of Africa, with its unexplored emotional recesses and its deep, almost mystical sense of passion. Outwardly, the Negro may seem a simple child of nature, but actually he leads a complex inner life which, the less influenced it is by the Western World, the more intuitive it is in its promptings. Only through the dance, through his intricate and highly elaborate rhythmic vitality, does he seem capable of expressing the many divergent outpourings of his soul.[10]

Tropicana consisted of dances with Cuban, South American, and Haitian themes, and it also featured a work by Ruth Page, *Canto Indio,* choreographed to music by Villa-Lobos. The dances based on African-American material included works such as *Boogie Woogie Improvisations* and *Blues Scenes* choreographed to music by Duke Ellington, W. C. Handy, and Count Basie, but one of Beatty's most memorable works on the program was *Southern Landscape* (1949). The five-part suite of dances was inspired by his reading of a book by Howard Fast, *Freedom Road,* that described the destruction of thriving black communities in the southern United States during the Reconstruction era. As Beatty remembered, "I was so horrified by the information I got from Fast's book—it was staggering. I couldn't believe man could be guilty of such horrible behavior."[11]

A riveting moment in the work was *Mourner's Bench*, a solo performed by Beatty that was a powerful meditation on the grief and desolation associated with great loss. The dance is a staple today in the repertoires of several companies such as the Dayton Contemporary Dance Company and the Philadelphia Dance Company (Philadanco) that have become archives for the works of black choreographers. *Mourner's Bench* remains as it was spoken of fifty years ago, "an outpouring eloquent in its movement that holds the audience in a grip of stunned and bated silence."[12]

The dance opens on a darkened stage with an isolated figure seated at one end of a long wooden bench. The starkness of the setting adds to the power of the piece, the power of unadorned truth. The relationship between the human figure and the eight-foot bench that stretches across center stage is one that is organic and animistic. There is the sense that a universal spirit connects the lone human figure and the wooden structure that supports his precarious balances, shelters his pleading gestures, and counterbalances his feints of protest. These exchanges—between a living body and an inanimate object that seems to project its own stolid life—compress a myriad of emotions into a brief period of time through movement invention that is breathtaking. At one point, for example, the dancer lies across one end of the bench with his head facing the audience and proceeds to feverishly roll the full length of the bench, braking himself by fanning a leg and coming to a seated position straddling the bench at the opposite end. The blur of movement that resolves itself with a punctuation of abrupt stillness is one of the many moments that makes *Mourner's Bench* an exquisite icon of modern dance.

Beatty and his company returned from Europe to tour the United States and Canada during the winter season of 1949/50; the following summer, the group toured South America and returned to Europe. They continued to tour extensively until Beatty disbanded the company in 1955. His heart had never been completely in the project. He later remarked that he never really enjoyed directing a company in the same way that Dunham enjoyed directing her company. Relieved of the burdens of administration, he began to concentrate exclusively on developing his own choreographic style. One of the earliest works that indicated the maturation of his distinctly individual approach to dance was *The Road of the Phoebe Snow.* The dance, which took its name from a passenger train on the Erie-Lackawanna Railroad, presented images of young and alienated men and women living in brutalizing urban surroundings. This theme would repeatedly find its way into Beatty's work over the coming years. More and more, the tempo and the dynamics of his choreographic language would reflect a tense, driven sensibility that physicalized the disruptive chaos—and the momentary joys—of modern society. In *The Road of the Phoebe Snow,* the structure of the dance was built on duets, trios, and ensemble dances that revealed the psychological and emotional turmoil of young lovers attempting to survive in a loveless environment.

During these years, many critics began to speak of Beatty's work as jazz dance, when in fact he was in the early stages of creating a seamless blend of jazz, ballet, and modern dance that was often performed to musical scores by leading contemporary jazz musicians. From ballet, he borrowed the rich vocabulary of turns and leaps, which his dancers performed with lightning virtuosity. He frequently used the lengthened lines of classical ballet, but he might quickly meld them into the floor-work of modern dance or the vernacular angularity of jazz dance. Beatty bent the virtuosity of ballet to his own will, approaching it with an extremely sharp attack that seemed to be full of an anger and a defiance that simultaneously reflected his subject matter, his underlying movement aesthetic, and his fiery temperament.

Without an artist's own explanation, one can only speculate about the inner motivations that shape his or her choreography. But it does not seem far-fetched to conjecture that Beatty's early experiences of rejection in the dance world influenced his approach to creating dance movement throughout his career. There is an almost obsessive-compulsive use of high speed, unrelenting attack, and sharpness in many of his dances. The breathless urgency of his dancers' virtuosity becomes a visual metaphor for the consummate technical proficiency of black dancers, as if Beatty were saying through them, "Yes, we can dance better than anyone else and do it twice as fast"; the lightning shifts from one movement technique to another make this statement even more resounding.

In an article by the dance historian Joe Nash, Beatty described the trials of black artists pursuing dance careers during the period when *Phoebe*

Snow premiered. As he spoke of the dancers who originally performed
the work, his words also seemed to reflect his own struggles:

> The variations were built on those fantastic dancers of the period—Dud-
> ley Williams, William Louther—who knew Graham. They later joined
> Alvin's company. There was Candace Caldwell, who loved ballet. The
> second duet was designed on her body. Georgia Collins could spin like a
> top. Others were Tommy Johnson, Joan Peters, Ernest Parham, Fred Ben-
> jamin, and Claude Thompson. It was a time when Louis Johnson, Alvin
> Ailey and myself used the same dancers for our concerts. In the opening
> dances of "Phoebe," the dancers are presenting themselves. They are say-
> ing look how beautiful I am, see what I can do, do I get the job? You sure
> don't. I was making a statement that no matter how good you are you will
> be pushed back. You see that in the ballet.[13]

The hard-driving through-line of his choreography can be taken as
a manifesto that projects a self-assertive image of black Americans who
prevail in spite of the barriers that are placed in their way. In this, he
had created his own variation on the artistic/sociopolitical philosophy
of his predecessors, but it was a variation with a much more defiant
message. Sometimes this approach was reflected in the subject matter that he chose, as in *Montgomery Variations* (1967), which was
another of his works that looked at racial discrimination and injustice,
or *The Black Belt* (1968), which was a further examination of the traumas of life in inner-city ghettos. But even when his dances were less
topical and more concerned with the sheer beauty of movement, he
still empowered his dancers with a high-strung edginess that spoke
volumes about the volatile nature of being black in America.

Until his death in 1995, Talley Beatty had an extensive career in
which he contributed to the repertoires of companies as varied as the
Alvin Ailey American Dance Theatre, the Boston Ballet, the Cullberg
Ballet, The Bat-Sheva Dance Company, and Ballet Hispanico. In addition, he choreographed numerous works for television and for musicals such as *Don't Bother Me, I Can't Cope* (1970), *Ari* (1971), and *Your
Arms Too Short to Box with God* (1977). Never too far from work that
reflected his vision of a black aesthetic, Beatty's choreography centered
around a dynamic style and technique that became a touchstone for
many African-American dancers and choreographers who came after
him. His unique dance expressions incorporated his racial heritage with

the philosophy of modern dance that encouraged artists to explore fully their individual sensibility.

Donald McKayle was an artist whose commitment to a dance career was also inspired by seeing the work of a pioneering African-American dancer. He was introduced to concert dance at the age of fifteen when a friend took him to see Pearl Primus perform at the Central High School of Needle Trades. Struck by the power of the performance, he was immediately drawn to the idea of becoming a dancer. His friend directed him to the New Dance Group, where he auditioned, received a one-year scholarship, and began to study with resident teachers Jane Dudley, Sophie Maslow, Pearl Primus, and William Bales. By the mid-1940s, there were new, though still limited, opportunities for black dancers to pursue careers in concert dance without having to face the full brunt of racial discrimination. Things had changed considerably during the twenty years since Edna Guy had searched for a studio that would admit her, and the ten years since Talley Beatty had suffered his own indignities in dance classes.

The New Dance Group had been founded in 1932 by dancers who declared themselves to be "artistic innovators against poverty, fascism, hunger, racism and the manifold injustices of their time."[14] The organization was part of an alternative dance community that placed as much emphasis on social and political consciousness as it did on purely aesthetic matters, and it had a policy of nondiscrimination that was strongly enforced. The welcoming environment and encouragement from his teachers enabled McKayle to progress quickly. His debut performance was in the spring of 1948 when he appeared in works by Jean Erdman and Sophie Maslow at the Mansfield Theatre. He continued his training the following summer at the American Dance Festival in New London, Connecticut, where he studied with Martha Graham. She offered him a scholarship and later invited him to tour the Middle East and Asia with her company during its 1955–56 season.[15]

The late 1940s and early 1950s were particularly fruitful years for young and aspiring black artists to become involved in the New York dance scene. The New Dance Group's close proximity to several other studios provided opportunities for McKayle to see a wide variety of performances and rehearsals of artists such as José Greco, La Meri, and Tanaquil LeClerq, who was rehearsing her first role in a Balanchine work.[16] Another factor that made the period particularly rich was the sense of communal support that was provided by the steadily grow-ing number of African-American dancers committed to pursuing con-cert careers. The field of modern dance was opening up more than was classical ballet, but even in the more discriminatory arena of ballet, artists like Louis Johnson were making their presence known. Even though there was no company that would make full use his phenom-enal talents, Johnson persevered, endured recurrent slights, and kept his eyes on a goal that would some day be attained. That goal turned out to be a career as a leading choreographer in concert dance, on the commercial stage, and in films.

Other artists such as Arthur Mitchell would find their solutions to racial prejudices in the dance world by inventively shaping their own destinies, as well as the destinies of those around them. After his groundbreaking career as the first black dancer with the New York City Ballet, Mitchell, along with his co-director Karel Shook, would estab-lish a community-based school and the internationally acclaimed Dance Theatre of Harlem. These institutions have since become ma-jor training grounds for dance and related arts, and they have guided African-American artists into that rarefied world of classical ballet in numbers that have never been achieved before.

Speaking of those years, McKayle remembered that even as some doors were opening, there were still battles to be waged in the differ-ent areas that African-American dancers were attempting to enter. In the commercial theater, these artists had to fight with unions to be allowed to audition for productions, and they resorted to picket lines to underscore their demands. In modern concert dance, when they were able to appear with companies that engaged in interracial casting, crit-ics spoke of the lack of theatrical verisimilitude based on the color of their skin. McKayle recalled the sheer waste of talent, the dancers "who came along before the great surge through, who gave up in desperation or continued in a bitter struggle, and are now too far beyond their prime in this art that idealizes youth." And he also remembered the group of artists "who had the wisdom and fortitude to leave this country and go to Europe."[17]

McKayle's involvement in the artistic milieu of the 1950s not only led him to broaden his perspectives in his chosen art, but also provided close interaction with black artists in other disciplines who were combining their social activism with their art. He became associated with a Harlem group, the Committee for the Negro in the Arts, that organized a performance in support of the blacklisted actor-singer Paul Robeson. For that occasion, McKayle choreographed one of his early solos performed to Robeson's booming vocal rendition of a spiritual, "Bye and Bye." The poet Langston Hughes, the actor Sidney Poitier, and the painter Charles White were among the other artists who were part of the stimulating environment. Through the group, McKayle also befriended Lorraine Hansberry, the playwright who later wrote the award-winning play *A Raisin in the Sun*.[18] McKayle would direct and choreograph a musical adaptation of the play, *Raisin,* in 1974.

In 1951, the premiere of his first successful group piece, *Games,* took place on a joint concert with Daniel Nagrin at Hunter College. It was a preview of the choreographic genius McKayle would continue to develop over the next decades. *Games* was inspired by his memories of growing up in New York neighborhoods. He used the imaginative world of children's play as a theme for his choreography. The work incorporated modern dance, vernacular dance, pantomime, and live vocal music (originally sung by McKayle and Shawneequa Baker) to create a theater piece combining light-hearted moments with the cruel realities of children's lives on the streets of the city. In the dramatic vignettes where the specter of urban violence looms in the background, the audience is reminded that the games the characters play are not only recreational, they are a training ground for developing skills need-ed to run the gauntlet of urban existence.

McKayle's delineations of human conditions and his emphasis on a kinetically visceral movement language were aspects of his choreog-raphy that became even more pronounced in his later works, such as *Rainbow 'Round My Shoulders* (1959). The convulsive, whip-lashing movements that he choreographed for his dancers encapsulated the dashed dreams and pained realities of men on a chain gang. The work's dynamic thrust came from choreographic motifs that displayed the unique capability of dance movement to convey meaning. It is in this sense that the movement in *Rainbow* shows how sinew and muscle fiber, the deep structures of the human body, can resonate with their own eloquent voice to approximate verbal expression. McKayle was always very clear regarding his intent to use his choreography to express messages revealing the inner depths of human existence:

> I always begin a project with the knowledge that I am dealing with people—with individuals, with human beings. And my approach is always visceral. I give movements that are visceral. Everything must come from within. And everything must have meaning. When I choreograph, I never use people merely to create a design. I mean, abstraction is always present in an art form, and I use it, but I have never used human beings simply as a design element. My work has always been concerned with humanity, in one way or another. Basically, I feel the beauty in man is in his diversity, and in his deep inner feelings.[19]

In addition to McKayle's commitment to work that delved into the serious concerns of the human condition, he also created dances that displayed the lighter side of his sensibilities. One of these was *District Storyville*, which premiered in 1962 at the Ninety-second Street YM-YWHA. Loosely based on the story of Louis Armstrong's early years spent hanging around the bordellos of the fabled red-light district of New Orleans, the dance presented a parade of colorful characters who gyrated, strutted, and slithered their way through a series of raucous—often hilarious—vignettes. Here were figures whose existence on the fringes of society enabled them to indulge fully in their transgressive eccentricities, and McKayle's finely crafted movement vocabulary heightened their theatrical delineations. The portraits included the stunningly elegant—but no-nonsense—madam of the bordello, the Countess; the hyperkinetic aspiring young trumpet player, Little Lou; and an array of sporting-house girls and their patrons. When he reviewed the first performance of the work, Walter Terry of the *New York Herald Tribune* expressed his obvious pleasure: "Crowning this wildly glorious event was the dancing. Mr. McKayle's movement designs—nostalgic in flavor but filled with brilliant invention both in full-scale virtuosity and in gesture—were in the hands of a remarkable troupe."[20]

McKayle's accumulating successes during the early 1960s included an opportunity to further his international recognition as a choreographer. Gian Carlo Menotti invited him to participate in the Festival of Two Worlds in Spoleto, Italy, where he presented *Games, Rainbow*, and a new work to the music of Ernest Bloch.[21] His company's subsequent European exposure included the performance of a program entitled *Black New World* that was presented in London in 1967 and was also performed in Wiesbaden, Hamburg, Zurich, Edinburgh, and other European cities. Throughout his career, McKayle continued to have an impact on the international dance scene by mounting works on companies such as the Bat-Sheva Dance Company in Israel.

McKayle's career has been further distinguished by the fact that he belongs to a group of choreographers who consistently maintain a foothold in both the concert dance world and the commercial entertainment world of Broadway shows, television, and film. As part of that group, he has often assumed the role of the director-choreographer who takes overall control of the different theatrical elements that come together on the musical theater stage. McKayle was the first black choreographer to join the ranks of artists such as Jerome Robbins, Bob Fosse, and Michael Kidd who take on the multiple duties of such a position.

One of McKayle's earliest Broadway performances was as a replacement for the injured Alvin Ailey in Harold Arlen and Truman Capote's 1954 production of *House of Flowers,* a colorfully exotic musical that centered around rival bordellos on a Caribbean island. Pearl Bailey and Diahann Carroll starred in the show, and the cast included an impressive list of up-and-coming African-American dancers—Louis Johnson, Arthur Mitchell, Carmen de Lavallade, Geoffrey Holder, and Albert Popwell. The talent in the show was one more indication of the growing network of black dancers that was being established in New York by the mid-1950s.

Another of McKayle's early theatrical experiences was in Jerome Robbins's groundbreaking 1957 musical *West Side Story,* in which he performed and served as dance captain. His first major success as a Broadway choreographer, however, was *Golden Boy,* a 1964 musical starring the multitalented Sammy Davis Jr. Based on a play by Clifford Odets, the show centered on a character named Joe Wellington, his struggles in the rough-and-tumble world of boxing, and his involvement in an interracial love affair. *Golden Boy* underwent numerous changes in its pre-Broadway performances, but McKayle's choreography was an element that changed little during the show's various incarnations. One of the scenes he created—a boxing ballet staged for Sammy Davis and Jaime Rogers—was consistently singled out for its innovation and its visceral dynamism. In an article that discussed the general decline in the quality of musical theater choreography, the critic Clive Barnes spoke glowingly of McKayle's work as an exception: "The best dancing as dancing on view this season on Broadway undoubtedly came from *Golden Boy.* . . . Here the whole choreographic concept had an originality, an integrity of approach, even a dignity that all the rest of the Broadway choreography lacks. It was also tougher, fizzier, and more exciting."[22]

As a director-choreographer, McKayle created works such as the aforementioned musical *Raisin,* which opened on Broadway in 1974. The story told of the struggles of a South Side Chicago family faced with the problems of moving into an all-white suburban neighborhood. The drama, first performed in 1959, was a timely exploration of the toll that contemporary racial strife could take on an African-American family. During the process of adapting the work for the musical theater stage, McKayle was well aware of the possible pitfalls. As he later mentioned, there was the problem of translating a story that takes place in the stultifying environment of a cramped apartment into a theater piece that could synthesize Lorraine Hansberry's powerful dialogue with music and dance movement in a way that embraced the audience.[23] The success with which McKayle achieved this end was reflected in an enthusiastic review, again written by Clive Barnes, who said that the production retained "all of Miss Hansberry's finest dramatic encounters, with the dialogue, as cutting and as honest as ever, intact."[24] Barnes continued:

> Broadway's first new musical of the season warms the heart and touches the soul. . . . [T]he score is not the most important aspect of the show. You hardly notice this, not only because of the exceptionally superior book, but also because of the enormous strength of the staging and the performance. Both are faultless. Director Donald McKayle comes to the musical theater as a ranking choreographer, but his skill with actors must now be unquestioned. The performances blaze—every single one of them.[25]

During the 1960s and 1970s, McKayle's extensive involvement in television productions ranged from choreographing awards shows to directing situation comedies. When he permanently relocated to the West Coast in 1969, he extended his professional reach even further to include choreography for movies such as *The Great White Hope* (1969), *Bed Knobs and Broomsticks* (1970), and *The Jazz Singer* (1980). Returning to Broadway in 1981 with *Sophisticated Ladies*, he directed and choreographed an eloquent and stylish paean to black entertainers inspired by the music of Duke Ellington and featuring a cast that included Judith Jamison, Gregory Hines, Hinton Battle, and Gregg Burge.

Over the years, not the least of McKayle's contributions has been his role as a committed and caring educator, an aspect of his career that he has shared with students at several prestigious schools including Juilliard, Bennington, the California Institute of the Arts, the American Dance Festival, and the University of California at Irvine, where he is currently a full professor. The length, breadth, and depth of McKayle's multifaceted involvement in the world of dance distinguish him as a model for artists of all colors. He is an exemplary individual who has crossed the superficial boundaries of "high art" and "low art" by consistently illuminating humanistic values; and he has struggled against the specious proscriptions that faced African-American artists of his generation. In these respects, he has continued to pursue a mission that was common to the black dance artists who preceded him—that of simultaneously transforming artistic practices and social inequities.

The work that Talley Beatty and Donald McKayle had produced by the late 1950s was clearly descended from the art of Dunham, Primus, and other seminal black artists of the 1930s and 1940s. However, the two younger artists had also begun to discover their own artistic directions, to shape an image of African Americans in modern dance that did not necessarily include the allusions to Africa and the West Indies that audiences had become accustomed to seeing in the work of Dunham, Primus, and Dafora. Neither did their dances, like those performed by Charles Williams's Hampton Creative Dance Group before them, become visual metaphors for the conservative philosophy of "social uplift." As they created their personal visions of black America that sometimes seemed to foresee the social upheavals of the 1960s, Beatty and McKayle exhibited a sense of urgency that was related to, but different from, that of their predecessors. For example, the nervous edginess that began to inform Beatty's subject matter and choreographic style reached beyond earlier references to social injustices and the pathos they inspired. His biting images of anger and frustration reflect-ed a point of view that was more confrontational than ameliorative.

Beatty and McKayle—along with Alvin Ailey, who as a young art-ist appeared on the New York dance scene a few years after them—were part of a determined group whose incremental artistic break-throughs slowly established a continuous and increasingly visible African-American presence in modern dance. Of the three artists, Alvin Ailey was the individual whose name audiences around the world would come to associate with the heart and soul of black culture as expressed through dance.

Ailey's achievements may be attributed to the fortuitous conjunc-tion of the individual experiences, artistic influences, and personal characteristics that slowly coalesced to shape his unique creativity. Among the factors that exerted an influence on him when he was a teenager in Los Angeles was his first sight of Katherine Dunham's dance company. The stellar aura surrounding Dunham, the exquisite sets and costumes, and the sensational dancing made an impression that stayed with him the rest of his life: "What Miss Dunham was doing was Afro-Caribbean. It was blues; it was spirituals; it touched something of the Texas in me. Her troupe danced in an elegant, excit-ing, stimulating style that made truthful statements about our cul-ture. . . . I was thrilled by the magic of Katherine Dunham."[26]

Beginning in 1949, another important experience that contributed to the development of Ailey's career was his association with Lester Horton. Horton's school and company brimmed with the creative in-novation that made it an exciting modern dance outpost on the West Coast. Colored by its founder's eclecticism, social consciousness, and eccentricities, the Lester Horton Dance Theatre drew its material from different cultures, and Horton would not tolerate racial discrimination among its members. In addition to classes in the dance technique that he was in the process of refining, the school also offered training in set, costume, and lighting design. Of equal importance, it introduced students to a world where improvisation was not only a way to explore movement, it was an essential tool for creating significant art with very limited resources. Somehow, in spite of meager finances, personal demons, and being outside of the artistic orbit of the New York dance scene, Horton managed to create his own world where Ailey and other developing talents like Carmen de Lavallade, James Truitte, and Joyce Trisler could thrive. After Horton's death in 1954, Ailey assumed the duties of company director and choreographer, moving a step closer to the artistic career that would dominate his life.

Ailey's innate personal characteristics were another important factor that enabled him to become a major contender in the dance world soon after he arrived in New York in the early 1950s. There was his striking physical presence (a valuable asset for any performer), his charismatic personality, and his creative genius fueled by curiosity and desire. All of these qualities helped shape a career trajectory that sped him—and those who joined him—toward the fulfillment of his dreams. After initial struggles and consequent successes, he founded a dance company that has performed continuously over the past four decades and a school that has trained generations of young dancers in a variety of dance techniques. The repertoire that he built over the years was another of his unique bequests to the world of dance. Early on, he decided that he wanted to establish a living library of American dance that was not only an archive for his own choreography but a storehouse for the work of other modern dancers of all races.

Both African-American and mainstream dance traditions have been enriched by Ailey's aesthetic contributions; outstanding among these is the highly theatrical performance style that has become his company's trademark over the years. Beginning with his earliest dancers, Ailey trained electrifying performers who could create a seamless interface between dramatic expression and virtuoso dance technique. He encouraged his dancers to bring the individual and idiosyncratic expressiveness of their personalities to the stage in a way that had not been seen before in modern dance performance. By the mid-1950s, dramatic characterization had become a staple of modern dance choreography, but Ailey's characters were not beings who existed apart from the realities of daily life. They were not representations of larger-than-life men and women drawn from literary sources or personifications that were studied representations of universal archetypes. Distancing the audience had no place in Ailey's aesthetic, and over the years there were detractors who increasingly showered criticism on the accessibility of his company's performances. His whole approach to the life of the stage was obviously different from the aristocratic hauteur of classical ballet, and it was also different from the studied seriousness of early modern dance or the iconoclastic and esoteric experimentation that later developed in reaction to it.

Ailey took a different route in delineating characters for the stage. His choreography—much like Beatty's and McKayle's—capitalized on the special ability of dance movement to establish a kind of visceral empathy between performer and audience, allowing dancers to reach out from the stage and draw viewers into a communal experience that often broke down barriers of contemplative aesthetic distance. The audience appeal of his early work was enhanced by his use of clearly defined characterizations, gestures, and bodily attitudes. He used movement material rooted in black vernacular dance as well as in the technical vocabulary of jazz, ballet, and modern dance. In continuing the syncretic traditions of African-American concert dance artists, he was particularly indebted to Dunham for giving him a vision of how to use colorful costuming, evocative lighting, and skillful programming effectively to enhance his choreography and create a distinctive and highly theatrical type of dance-drama. Ailey and Dunham were not afraid to embrace serious artistic intent and aesthetic refinement, technical virtuosity, spectacle, and theatrical entertainment as equally important components on the concert stage. In this sense, they were erasing the artificial boundaries that divided "high art" from "low art."

In a filmed interview after a performance of his signature work, *Revelations*, Ailey expressed his populist conception of the art of dance: "I always wanted to have the kind of company that my family could relate to; that my people in Texas could relate to; that my aunts and uncles on the farms, or wherever they're from, . . . could relate to and understand [that] the dance in particular is for everybody. . . . I believe the dance came from the people and that it should be delivered back to the people."[27] In spirit, his earliest works, such as *Blues Suite* and *Revelations*, were about those people and for those people, everyday black folks from his childhood. The joy and pain of their lives was expressed in Saturday night dances and Sunday morning church services that echoed an Africanist continuum between the secular and the sacred. Ailey drew on his experiences of small-town African America to delineate deep spiritual and emotional themes capable of reaching far beyond the specificity of time and place—1940s Rogers, Texas—

to connect with the feelings of all Americans, and all human beings. This was a palpably visceral connection that overcame the compartmentalization and the rigid dichotomies of contemporary American life, and from the outset this dismantling of barriers struck a positive chord with diverse audiences.

Though framed by the proscenium stage, the Ailey dancers who appeared in his initial New York performances at the Ninety-second Street YM-YWHA in 1958 established a tradition of infectious accessibility and an aggressively emotional openness that was new to concert dance audiences. These early concerts were enhanced by the music in works such as *Blues Suite* and *Revelations,* an additional element that contributed a feeling of familiarity to the performances and increased their positive reception. The blues, spirituals, and gospel music that Ailey used in these works, along with the jazz and pop music that he would use in a number of his later works, had—in one incarnation or another—long been an integral part of American culture to which people could relate regardless of their race and class. To witness Ailey's work as it placed black vernacular music in a concert dance context was to have a feeling of coming home to a vital part of American culture that was usually marginalized in the world of serious art—and it was a joyous homecoming. During the company's first international tours of the 1960s, audiences around the world often identified with this same familiar element and the vital humanism it conveyed.

By the 1970s, because of the continued refinement of his choreographic approach and the success that his work had achieved over the years, Ailey's company had become a popular icon of sorts. His concerts were well attended, and audiences felt free to be enthusiastically vocal at performances, exhibiting a kind of good-natured responsiveness that was rare in a concert dance environment. This popularity proved to have negative as well as positive results, especially in terms of how some critics perceived the company. Over the years, there were accusations of formulaic choreography that pandered to the least common denominator of popular taste, and the company was disparaged for having an overzealous performance style that tried too hard to please.

Mixed critical opinions about Ailey's work seemed to become more pronounced as time passed. Though this may have occurred for a number of reasons, I believe that in many instances it was due to critics' conflicted feelings concerning the intricately knotted issues of racial and aesthetic matters that eventually rose to the surface when the work of black artists was being discussed. This seems true particularly in view of the fact that several decades earlier, evolving critical responses to Dafora's and Dunham's work had elicited similar mixed messages. All three artists received a good amount of initial praise for the positive aesthetic values of their choreography. However, enthusiastic commentary came at the outset of each of their careers in part because critics were seeing dance that they simply had not encountered before. Many of them were clearly enamored with the novelty of the productions and were seeing for the first time black artists who set foot on the concert stage with a strong conviction in the seriousness and artistic merit of their work. Even by the time Ailey's company made its debut, this was still an unusual event; each time it occurred it was met with a certain breathless bemusement. Another source of novelty was the mixture of the familiar and the unfamiliar in the choreography. Although some of the elements were familiar, they were combined in new ways. The new configuration resulted in dance that was fresh and perplexingly exciting. Critics had little to compare the works to, and they were faced with new components that had to be fitted into their standard frames of reference.

One way that critics could contextualize the choreography of black artists was to view its extraordinary uniqueness from the perspective of the tenets of modern art. Innovation, a sense of the "new," and radical departures from aesthetic canons were, after all, distinguishing characteristics of modern art. As mentioned before, early modern dancers believed that the uncompromisingly subjective expressions of the individual artist should be at the root of artistic innovation; and this, in turn, would help establish a kind of theatrical dance that could be accepted as serious contemporary art. Black artists were no strangers to this idea. However, the route to innovation that Ailey and his predecessors chose in creating their new forms of dance presented a quandary for those critics whose perspectives were limited by preconceived ideas about categories of art. Ailey, like all of the black artists discussed here, ranged far and wide among cultural traditions in his subjective explorations. When he cast his net of imaginative possibilities, he drew in Europeanist artistic elements but at the same time captured African diasporan elements. For some critics the dance that resulted was ripe with contradictions. Most perplexing was the fact that it was dance whose serious intent was clear, yet it included choreographic material that did not fit comfortably into the categories of dance that were entitled to be placed on the highest rungs of artistic hierarchies.

From the accessible familiarity of its vernacular references to the infectious spirit of its religious material, Ailey's choreography placed elements from his African-American cultural heritage squarely on stage and declared *them* to be "high," and "fine," and worthy of serious appraisal. He made this statement in ways that did not adhere exclusively to European or European-American precepts, and in ways that were not African or West Indian in the same sense that Dafora's and Dunham's were. Ailey crossed the boundaries of aesthetic hierarchies and cultural dichotomies to create work that was replete with groundbreaking significance, and a major part of its significance lay in its political impact.

To mention the political nature of Ailey's work is not to suggest that explicitly political material was his primary focus, or that one should read agitprop messages into his choreography. Pointed political messages were more characteristic of African-American choreographers who came on the scene several years after Ailey's initial breakthroughs. The political nature of Ailey's work lay in the effect that it had on reshaping the aesthetic paradigms of those who saw it. It forced critics and audiences to broaden their perceptions of art and consider with new eyes the possibility that African-American dance could be cast in the mold of serious art. By valorizing his African-American cultural heritage and challenging existing aesthetic hierarchies, Ailey was effectively usurping the social and political power that was attached to privileged categories of art and claiming it as his own.

Even though artistic hierarchies are often thought of as purely aesthetic constructs that function independently of sociopolitical dynamics, they play an important role in supporting the interests of particular groups in a given social order. As the art historian Evan Alderson points out in his essay "Ballet as Ideology," dominant groups have a vested interest in reinforcing their ideologies by shaping the way that individuals perceive art. As he puts it, "These values become instru-

ments of social domination insofar as they are accepted by subordi-
nate groups as universal truths."[28] Ailey's work was anathema to this
process because it presented new images that could be perceived as
expressing universal truths, images that did not patently reinforce
prevailing aesthetic ideologies. The power of his art could be measured
by the enthusiasm of audiences' responses, if not by the consistency
of critics' support. His universal truths were based on his memories
of the heroism of everyday men and women who were black. Through
the incandescence of his artistry, his choreography projected them as
black archetypes that eloquently commented on the human condition.
Yet his men and women were not studied delineations that were larger than life or distant. It was their very commonness and accessibility that connected them to all members of the human family.

In earlier years, one way that African-American aesthetic elements
could become a part of "high art" canons was through the mediating
influence of white artists who reinterpreted and supposedly univer-
salized the material. The use of African diasporan art as a springboard
for innovation was a recurrent theme in twentieth-century art. (Pab-
lo Picasso's Africanist-cubist paintings, Helen Tamiris's danced spirituals, and Darius Milhaud's jazz-inspired compositions are examples
that have been cited earlier.) In these instances, the privileging influence of the artist's race was part of the imprimatur that validated
the transposition of "folk," "ethnic," or "low art" into "high art." But
by the 1960s, because of the struggles of earlier black dancers, the
fineness of his own work, and the changing social and political environment in America, Ailey could assume the reins of racial self-rep-
resentation to a degree that had not been achieved before. Though similar breakthroughs had been made before him, his additional steps
extended the continuum and advanced the struggle of black artists to
gain parity on the concert dance stage. The eclectic nature of Ailey's
art, his subject matter that kept his black heritage close to the core of
his work, and his goal of giving black dancers a place to thrive and grow
were all in the best tradition of those who had come before him.

From the mid-twentieth century onward, as the web of artistic cross-
influences in American modern dance became more complex, African-
American dancers increasingly found opportunities to participate in
racially integrated dance companies. They also had more chances to
form their own dance companies and continue to explore and define

their aesthetics. These new opportunities prompted new questions concerning the position of their dance artistry within the shifting contexts of African-American and majority American culture. As the decades passed and aesthetic traditions deepened and broadened, the directions that black dancers and choreographers would follow became even more diverse. Some of them would choose not to foreground their racial heritage and would declare that they were artists first who were secondarily black. This may have been an attempt to reject what was felt to be the burdensome obligation of having one's work constantly dominated by racial matters; the desire to free the creative process from various obligations is understandable. However, African-American artists who unguardedly assumed this position ran the risk of not taking into consideration the profound interconnectedness of art and race in America in all of its manifestations. If they blindly identified with a position that traditionally cast European-American artists as being aloof from racial and other sociopolitical influences, they might lose sight of the fact that such a position was, at its root, a political and social construct. This purportedly normative position was, itself, rooted in social and historical thought that equated whiteness with hermetic aestheticism, objectivity, and the imprimatur of universality discussed above. Conversely, blackness was equated with the inferiority of finite particularity that was associated with categories such as "folk," "ethnic," and "primitive" art. This construct was so solidly embedded in European-American aesthetics that it did not have to be spoken. It was understood that whiteness was a prerequisite for universality in art. Whiteness was the background against which all other points of view were projected in a dichotomy of superiority and inferiority.

For an African-American artist to aspire to a mainstream aesthetic that purported to be indifferent to its racist elements was certainly no better than being placed into the narrow confines of racial specificity. And, because of the threads of self-denial running through the former position, it was potentially a more detrimental alternative. To deny one's blackness, one's racial heritage, in this way was to deny the possibility of universality—the unique ability of art to reach diverse members of the human family in profound ways—*in* blackness. In the work of African-American artists such as Beatty, McKayle, and Ailey, audiences could witness—and, in a sense, participate in—the possibility of universality in blackness.

By the 1960s, another turn of events in the evolution of modern dance raised questions about the place of black artists in the performance arena. From the early twentieth century onward, the cyclical reconfiguration of dance aesthetics had been a powerful dynamic in theatrical concert dance. The impact of this influence can be traced from the experiments of European companies such as Les Ballets Russes and Ballets Suédois, through the work of artists such as Ruth St. Denis and Isadora Duncan, to later generations of artistic iconoclasts. Challenging the existing artistic status quo became one of the most salient characteristics of avant-garde artists. This thread of modern dance aesthetics was another element that African-American artists shared to a certain extent with their European-American counterparts. But in this instance, as in others I have pointed out, the African-American adaptation of the practice was different; it was a variation on the theme of cyclical aesthetic change.

The most radical impulses of avant-garde modernism in dance and in other arts emphasized the near dissolution of existing artistic practices. For example, the young white artists who began presenting joint concerts in 1962 as the Judson Dance Theater were committed to banishing the modes of theatrical presentation that had become standardized in the works of artists such as Martha Graham, Doris Humphrey, and José Limón. That an African-American presence was virtually nonexistent in the experimental environment of early postmodern dance leads one to consider a number of questions. For example, what were the factors that made the budding postmodern dance movement appear to be just as racially exclusive—even if for different reasons—as the segregated dance scene of the 1930s? What were some of the factors that caused most African-American artists to choose other directions?

If we look once more at Gerald Myers's essay, we can begin to fathom the reasons why black dancers were likely to follow the earlier tenets of modern dance instead of the paths of artists who were striking out in radically new directions. Myers writes:

What we need to remember, however, is that African-Americans continued this spirit of modern dance, this concern for giving dance moral, social, and religious meanings, during the late 1950s and to the present while much of the modern dance world, influenced by Merce Cunningham and the Judson Church group, took another course. The other direction led to movement for its own sake and in general a minimalist departure from the original aesthetic's focus on the "inner," "meaning," and the rest. Those taking this direction often disclaimed being modern dancers any longer. But whatever the merits of this disclaimer, the claim here is that African-Americans were among the influential few who, despite the change in fashion and the risk of being called passe, kept alive the traditional modern dance aesthetic.[29]

In a similar vein, the dance historian Halifu Osumare refers to an African legacy that compelled black artists to communicate in clear, humanistic terms, to "focus on functionalism in life and therefore in art." She continues, "It is not about dance for dance's sake, but it is dance to communicate to people, who in turn are part of the whole process."[30]

There are a number of other possible reasons why black artists remained closer to earlier modern dance traditions during the 1960s and the early 1970s, when others were exploring radically new approaches to choreography and dance performance. (The dance historian Sally Banes refers to the years 1960 through 1973 as the "breakaway period" of postmodern dance.)[31] Among these reasons is the likelihood that black artists were not enthralled with the idea of rejecting the traditions they had struggled so hard to become a part of just a few years earlier. They—unlike the coterie of white artists who were committed to aesthetic change—found little transgressive pleasure in dismantling the established practices of modern dance. On the contrary, most black artists continued to embrace the narrative, emotional, and dramatic elements of early modern dance. These elements enabled them to reach out to audiences and convey the immediacy of their concerns in ways that the esoteric and anarchic impulses of the breakaway postmodern artists did not. African-American artists could hardly relate to the notion that they needed to repudiate the hegemony of historical modern dance aesthetics because it restricted their creative freedom. Moreover, they were reminded, at every turn, of the tenuous nature of their involvement in the mainstream dance world that avant-garde white artists were rejecting.

Much of the discussion in the previous chapters has examined how black artists changed theatrical dance practices in ways that were never totally dominated by mainstream aesthetics. At the same time, the possibility of these artists' finding satisfaction in committing acts of aesthetic heresy was always mediated by the fact that they were categorically relegated to a position outside of the establishment, based on proscriptions that were, in large part, racial in nature. Their alternative aesthetics were not created through an "art for art's sake" approach that included self-reflexive commentary on mainstream traditions, or through a conceptual approach that radically redefined what a dance performance should be.

If we begin to examine the ways in which groundbreaking artistic movements in European-American art are related to other traditions, we can see the complexity of the issues that black artists considered in deciding whether to follow newer artistic trends. The role of avant-garde art in Western society has been one in which iconoclastic difference is a prized characteristic, its raison d'etre. Sally Banes makes the point that vanguard artists have consistently "turned to folk, popular, and exotic art as sources for breaking with mainstream values as well as for 'new' materials and techniques."[32] Susan Gubar makes a similar point in her book *Racechanges* when she cites Stuart Hall's comments on postmodern artists' concern "with a certain kind of difference," a fascination with the exotic and the ethnic.[33] The search for the "new," the "different," that which represents a radical departure from the status quo, leads avant-garde European-American artists away from entrenched artistic practices and toward the very same cultural expressions against which canonical art has been privileged. Since many of the cultural elements that are subsumed in the newer artistic expressions emanate from non-Western cultures, the shadowy presence of these elements represents another ironically convoluted way that racial constructs support artistic and cultural hierarchies. Perhaps, then, one of the true revelations of avant-garde artists is the discovery—whether purposeful or accidental—that the hegemony of the canons they reject is closely connected to the denigration of non-European-American art and culture. Again, one of the unspoken realities of the situation is that the effective transmutation of "folk," "ethnic," and "popular art" elements must be accomplished through the alchemy of a European-American consciousness.

From this perspective, one can further understand the reasons why

African-American artists chose other paths when confronted by new artistic trends such as the early postmodern dance of the 1960s. They surely sensed that these new trends were attended by an equally new kind of elitism, another attempt by the artistic mainstream—even if a divergent tributary—to maintain its exclusivity. Only this time it was the radical experimentation rather than the privileged elitism of canons that closed the European-American artistic domain to outsiders. Consequently, African-American artists continued to do what they had always done. In a response to the ironic vagaries of America's artistic and racial politics that buffeted them from all directions, they fought against the negative associations that majority America projected onto the difference of blackness. At the same time, they engaged in a subjective celebration of the positive values of their difference and expressed it through their work. They continued to plot a distinctive course, whether they attempted to share the currents of the mainstream or steered cautiously away from the eddies of newer trends. If *difference* could be viewed as a sign of grace (as it obviously was by the avant-garde) rather than as a racist stigma, then African-American artists were truly and consistently blessed.

Commenting on the absence of nonwhite artists on the evolving postmodern dance scene of the sixties and seventies, Sally Banes notes that Gus Solomons stood virtually alone as an African-American artist who identified with the artistic experimentation of the period. While he was pursuing a degree in architecture at the Massachusetts Institute of Technology, Solomons began studying dance at the Boston Conservatory of Music with Jan Veen, a student of the German expressionist dancer Mary Wigman. He also studied ballet with E. Virginia Williams. Solomons began performing and choreographing in 1960 with the Dance Makers, a modern dance company in Boston. After moving to New York in 1962, he had a performing career that included dancing in the companies of Martha Graham, Pearl Lang, Donald McKayle, Joyce Trisler, and Paul Sanasardo. But, as Don McDonagh points out in his book *The Rise and Fall and Rise of Modern Dance*, the experience that most profoundly influenced the aesthetic development of Solomons was his years with Merce Cunningham's company, from 1965 to 1968.[34]

Though Solomons developed a distinctive choreography that sometimes included dramatic dances such as his 1967 solo *Neon*, which McDonagh described as "a commentary on the restless energy that is symbolized by rock music,"[35] the influence of Cunningham's innovations and other experimental choreographic techniques shaped a major portion of his work. In dances such as *Kinesia #5*, he explored the postmodern concern of developing new relationships with the audience. He requested audience members to organize the random noises that they would normally make so that they would accompany the dance. In *Two Reeler* (1968), Solomons did not appear on stage at all but played recordings of his voice suggesting movements that audience members might execute.[36] His use of chance, games, and other nontraditional methods of creating choreography reflected the avant-garde commitment to redefine what a dance could be. This conceptual approach gave primacy to the consideration of a dance's context, its nonnarrative structure, and the abstract qualities of movement. It was a means of stretching the artist's creative potential and heightening audience members' perceptions.

After founding his own company in 1969, Solomons continued to create work that has been praised for its structural clarity, rigorous logic, and intellectual daring. Not the least of his contributions to the dance world has been his own performance style, which is clearly described by McDonagh: "He cuts through space with a blade-like efficiency and changes directions effortlessly. The pauses in his work emphasize the alertness and grace of his habitual quickness. He has a way of skimming lightly over the performing area, like a dragonfly darting rapidly over the surface of water."[37]

During the same period when Gus Solomons was creating works that reflected postmodern conceptual concerns, another African-American artist, Eleo Pomare, was pursuing his own radical vision of dance. After spending a troubled early childhood in Cartegena, Colombia, and Panama, Pomare arrived in New York at the age of ten. His formative years of dance training at the High School for Performing Arts were a further indication of the ever-changing racial environment that was opening new doors for African Americans who aspired to careers in dance. There were, however, established practices that continued to reflect subtler forms of racial proscription. Pomare later remembered that the curriculum at the high school excluded jazz dance classes, and students were not allowed to choreograph dances that used jazz music.[38]

After graduating from high school, Pomare immersed himself in the heady, creative milieu of the late 1950s New York dance scene. He recounted those years in a 1992 interview with Arthur Theodore Wilson, describing how his artistic horizons began to broaden after the restrictions of his earlier training. He began working on *Blues for the Jungle*, a dance that would eventually become a manifesto for the defiant social consciousness that characterized much of his later work. At the small Eighth Avenue studio where he rehearsed, he could find kindred spirits who were pursuing their own artistic missions. There was Anna Sokolow, who was in the midst of creating *Rooms*, her commentary on the tragedies of urban life choreographed to a plaintive jazz score. Talley Beatty was choreographing his own study of urban life, *The Road of the Phoebe Snow*. During the same period, Donald McKayle was creating *Rainbow 'Round My Shoulders*, and Alvin Ailey was crafting *Revelations*.[39]

Pomare soon received a John Hay Whitney Fellowship that enabled him to study with José Limón, Curtis James, and the German choreographer and theorist Kurt Joos. Pomare did not remember with fondness the years he spent in Europe—1961 to 1964. He later bluntly assessed the period in an acerbic tone that would become one of his trademarks over the years: "I was expelled from the Joos school—they kicked me out. I couldn't take that dogmatic bull. After you've been to Europe for a few years as a black man, your eyes have to come open and, when they do, you have to come back here as fast as you can. That's such a gray place. You realize the difference in esthetics and values between whites and blacks. They are about death with their ancient rituals and we are about life."[40] By the time Pomare returned to America, he was committed to the militant ideas that pervaded African-American inner-city communities where poverty and crime were manifested in expressions of anger, frustration, and hopelessness. Beginning in 1966 with the Watts uprising in Los Angeles, and escalating after the assassination of Martin Luther King Jr. in 1968, urban riots exploded across the nation with predictable regularity and decimated huge swathes of American cities. It was in the late 1960s that Katherine Dunham responded to the current social and political upheaval by establishing a cultural arts center to serve inner-city youths in East St. Louis, Illinois, and Pomare devoted his creative energies to similar social commitments in Harlem. One of the projects that he co-founded in 1967 was Dancemobile, a series of performances by several dance companies that was presented in urban neighborhoods throughout New York City during the summers of social unrest.

Blues for the Jungle premiered in New York in 1966, although an earlier version of the work had been shown in Amsterdam in 1962 when Pomare was touring with a small interracial company in Europe. The dance consisted of six expressionistic vignettes with titles that reflected their often volatile topics—*Slave Auction, Behind Prison Walls, Preaching the Gospel, View from a Tenement Window, Junkie,* and *Riot.* As Talley Beatty had done in his own way several years earlier, Pomare explored the physicalization of high-strung, urban tensions that recoil until they reach a point of explosion. On viewing a restaging of the dance in 1984, the critic Zita Allen commented on the way that *Blues* captured the truth of a particular moment in African-American life. She wrote, "Pomare's piece, 'Blues for the Jungle,' is one of the American dance masterpieces born of this era. From the opening scene of a shackled figure writhing on an auction block to its depiction of contemporary street scenes peopled with bitter, bewigged whores, pimps, bagmen, ladies, 'Blues' is a montage of man's inhumanity to man."[41] Pomare often performed the *Junkie* section of the dance, a powerful evocation of a stumbling, twitching, husk of a man whose life is one long strung-out episode.

Though his biting and confrontational works such as *Blues for the Jungle* have left vivid impressions on viewers, from the beginning of his career Pomare has also explored a wide range of choreographic themes and used a variety of music. In a 1978 review Jennifer Dunning described him as "an apostle of bitterness" and went on to comment that Pomare, in his twenty-year career, had displayed a sensibility that went well beyond the type of work that he was usually associated with. The particular concert she reviewed featured *Fallscape,* an example of his more abstract choreography; a group work, *Serendipity,* choreographed in 1966 to a Handel score; and a "Grahamesque" work, *The Queen's Chamber,* choreographed in 1976 to Bartok music.[42]

One of Pomare's best known works—one that captures his love for passionate subject matter drawn from literary sources—is *Las Desenamoradas.* The work, based on Federico Garcia Lorca's play *The House of Bernarda Alba,* tells the story of a controlling mother's domination of her five daughters. The narrative provides a continuous flow of images of suppressed desires and stifling jealousies that lead to the suicide of one of the daughters. Pomare's theatrical craftsmanship, joined with the relentless drive of the John Coltrane score, propels the dance to its tragic conclusion. The often disturbing beauty of Pomare's distinctive choreographic contributions such as *Las Desenamoradas* and *Blues for the Jungle* is preserved in the repertoire of the Dayton Contemporary Dance Company through the ongoing American Dance Festival project, "The Black Tradition in American Modern Dance."

By the 1970s, though commonalities could often be found in their work, African Americans in modern dance were expressing themselves as never before through different styles and techniques that varied from artist to artist. As in the case of Eleo Pomare, these elements might even vary considerably within the repertoire of a single artist. Another choreographer whose work displayed this range was Rod Rodgers. His aesthetic embraced abstract, nonrepresentational approaches to dance, as well as more literal elements that mirrored the social consciousness of the time. Rodgers's connections to dance were rooted in his childhood experiences. His mother and father were professional dancers who traveled with their three children on what was popularly known as the "chitlin circuit," consisting of "night clubs, theatres, small resorts and dance halls across the United States which featured black talent and catered almost exclusively to the black public."[43] It was a training ground for a host of talented African-American entertainers, most of whom are unrecorded in the annals of American popular culture.

While growing up in Detroit, Rodgers trained with teachers who had studied with Katherine Dunham, Pearl Primus, and Hanya Holm. In addition, viewing a Dunham company performance was one of his first memorable exposures to concert dance. When he arrived in New York in 1963, he continued his exploration of dance techniques and styles with teachers that included Mary Anthony, Erick Hawkins, and Charles Weidman, and he also performed with the Erick Hawkins Dance Company before forming his own company.

One of Rodgers's early statements concerning his company's work sheds light on the different facets of his artistic mission: "The philosophy of the company reflects its director's feelings that black artists must maintain a tradition of being in the forefront of experimentation and innovation while, at the same time, celebrating positive black cultural images."[44] In a 1976 interview, Rodgers noted that his was one of the first African-American companies to be recognized for the non-literal and abstract works in its repertoire. Elaborating on his particular approach to abstraction in dance, he distinguished his work from that of "dry intellectual avant-garde artists" and described his nonliteral work as being "always rooted in sensuous forms and rhythmic musical flow."[45] He went on to comment on the fact that critics refused to give serious consideration to black artists who pursued more experimental work because this was an area that was considered to be the exclusive province of European and white American artists.[46]

Rodgers's choreographic innovations include a number of dances that he categorizes as "rhythm dances." These works often involve the performers playing hand-held instruments or using props to create sound accompaniment. In *Tangents* (1968), for example, the three dancers manipulate yard-long sticks that are used in various ways to enhance and extend the linear designs of the composition. In addition, there are moments when the only sound that can be heard is the swishing of the sticks in the air or the sound they produce when tapped against the floor. Other dances in this genre include *Percussion Suite* (1967) and *Rhythm Ritual* (1973). Among Rodgers's more topical works, a series of dances called *Poets and Peacemakers* was inspired by outstanding African Americans who have contributed to the lives of their people. The works in this series are *Langston Lives* (1981), inspired by the literary works of Langston Hughes; *The Legacy* (1984), in honor of civil rights activist Martin Luther King Jr.; *Against Great Odds* (1986), focusing on the educator and social activist George Washington Carver; *Echoes of Ellington* (1989), celebrating the genius of Duke Ellington; and *Keep on Goin'!* (1990), dedicated to heroic women in black history.

The earliest African-American concert dancers and the growing number of artists who have followed them form a family tree that has established new branches over the decades. As is apparent in the careers of artists such as Solomons, Pomare, and Rodgers, the roots of this tree have been nourished by influences as different as postmodern experimentation and African-American community activism. During the last quarter of the twentieth century, emerging choreographers continued to embrace diverse aesthetics, and they discovered new relationships between contemporary concerns and artistic traditions. In the ongoing spirit of modern dance, new generations bring their own creative vision to the stage by finding subjective expressions that reflect their particular times. Because of evolving aesthetic, social, and political thought, black choreographers have turned to innovative techniques, sensitive subject matter, and controversial themes that earlier artists would not have considered acceptable. Many contemporary choreographers have continued to create art that functions as a positive force in the black community, but in recent decades this direction has been conflated with matters of gender, sexual preference, and a number of other concerns that are not necessarily racial in nature.

In *Dancing Herself,* the dance historian Veta Goler examines some of the newer directions that African-American female choreographers have taken in recent years. She centers her discussion on the role that autobiography plays in the work of three artists who have had distinguished careers over the past three decades—Dianne McIntyre, Jawole Willa Jo Zollar, and Blondell Cummings. These artists often use personal material as a source for their dance theater. In this respect, their work is similar to that of a number of postmodern dancers who, by the late 1970s, had begun using textual material and experimenting with other techniques for incorporating details from their own lives into their choreography. Earlier artists such as Dunham and Primus would have found this approach unthinkable during a time when the details of an artist's life were usually expressed through characters, themes, and narratives that did not have clearly autobiographical connections.

Goler's discussion of the three artists also examines the intimate ways that racial heritage and gender shape their strikingly unique dance theater. Dianne McIntyre, for example, has developed a style of performance and choreography that is steeped in the artist's abiding love and respect for African-American history and culture, a fact that is particularly apparent in the special relationship she has with black musicians and composers. Early in her career, McIntyre began exploring ways that she could facilitate the closest connections between musicians and dancers during her choreographic process, and she experimented with using live musicians in her rehearsals to create an improvisational and collaborative environment. What has resulted in many of her works is a uniquely symbiotic relationship that taps into the Africanist continuum of music and dance. Over the years, McIntyre's collaborations have taken place with an impressive list of avant-garde jazz musicians and composers, including Cecil Taylor, Hamiet Bluiett, Max Roach, Oliver Lake, Gary Bartz, and the artist with whom she has worked most closely since 1984, Olu Dara.[47]

Along with her methods of accessing the deep roots of African-American culture through music, McIntyre—as Goler notes—draws on a number of other sources that give her work a deep appeal for audiences and critics alike. Her most autobiographical work, *Take-Off from a Forced Landing*, uses her mother's early experiences as an airplane pilot as a point of departure and also incorporates material based on the lives of other family members to explore universal human feelings and multiple layers of meaning.[48] In other works such as *Mississippi Talks, Ohio Walks* McIntyre displays her distinctively vibrant way of wedding modern dance with black vernacular dance forms. In this work, the setting is a southern juke joint, and the social dances that are woven into the choreography help delineate characters that convey vital aspects of black life. In summarizing McIntyre's contributions to modern dance, Goler points to the multidimensionality of her work, the fact that she expresses universality through the nuances of African-American cultures, and the ways that she simultaneously embraces and extends black traditions in dance:

> McIntyre's fundamental intention in choreographing is the communication of universal feelings through the specificity of African American culture. African American dance, music, art, and literature are the vehicles through which she expresses the feelings of black people, feelings which are also shared by other peoples. Her specificity-universality dynamic enables her to connect with African Americans and with others. . . . McIntyre herself states that her intention is to present the traditions of black culture in fresh, new forms. Therefore, what she does is different from what some other black choreographers do.[49]

The influence of McIntyre's aesthetic is reflected in the careers of a number of artists who studied at her Harlem studio and performed with her company, Sounds in Motion. Among these is Jawole Willa Jo Zollar, who began her dance training as a child in Kansas City, Missouri, with Joseph Stevenson, a student of Katherine Dunham. Zollar is also connected to Dunham through the similarities in their creative process- es, which base choreography on intense periods of firsthand observa- tion and research. As another prime example of an African-American artist who has absorbed a rich array of influences, Zollar draws on dance material from different branches of the African diaspora, although she is not a trained anthropologist. She has also studied and closely ana- lyzed traditional modern dance and postmodern dance techniques as a way of deciding what is valuable to her work and what is not.

Zollar seamlessly fuses artistic innovation with political activism and social consciousness in her work. Her commitment to this end began in 1984 with her establishment of Urban Bush Women, a dance company composed of African-American women whose lives—both in reality and in their theatrical delineations—reflect the full range of human experiences. In her works, she has often incorporated autobio- graphical material as well as material from the lives of her company members as a way of creating dance dramas that resonate with truth. Goler—citing dances such as *Lipstick* and *Praise House*—points out the importance of Zollar's process of eliciting material from her danc- ers' lives as a source of specific details for her choreography and as a source for the general development of a work.[50] What result are strik- ing theater pieces that draw on a totality of human expression including the wide-ranging movement vocabulary mentioned above, as well as virtuosic use of the human voice. As an important element in most of the performances of Urban Bush Women, vocal material is used in a variety of ways. For example, in *Nyabinghi Dreamtime,* a work based on the Kumina and Rastafarian rituals of Jamaica, vocalization takes the form of spirited singing, chanting, and other sounds of incantation. In these instances the human voice serves deep spiritual purposes. Brenda Dixon Gottschild refers to the importance of verbal power in African diasporan cultures: "[L]anguage (the written and, especially, the spoken work) is conceived as a mobile concept, a shaker and mover, with the power to effect change. Honoring this tradition, Paul Carter Harrison used the Bantu term *Nommo* (which can be roughly trans- lated as 'the power of the word'), for the title of his book on African American drama and its cathartic, catalyzing effect. Words are verbal movement, and the gesture is a physical manifestation of *Nommo*."[51]

In several instances, Zollar uses the voice effectively in extended monologues to sculpt the overall shape of a work, as in *LifeDance III . . . The Empress (Womb Wars)* (1992). The strong content and delivery of these monologues present an uncompromisingly honest portrayal of black women's lives. Zollar's broaching of topics such as incest, rape, and abortion can be unsettling, but her revelations of self-discovery, survival, and triumph bring a sense of artistic and spiritual resolution to her works; and the incandescence of her and her dancers' performances tempers the material in the forge of universality.

This same strength is manifested in the movement vocabulary that Zollar uses, one that refuses to privilege more traditional images of female dancers as delicate beauties, voluptuous seductresses, or even the stony heretics of early modern dance. In dances such as *Shelter*, a work that examines issues of homelessness and themes of ecological disaster, there is a certain fearlessness that burns through dancing that is not afraid to be rough-hewn, discordant, and almost out of control. Such dancing makes the performers' displays of more traditional technical virtuosity all the more striking.

In a passage from her book *Writing Dancing in the Age of Postmodernism*, Sally Banes, in a statement that includes a quote from Zollar, succinctly captures how artistic process, a sense of community, and politics come together in Urban Bush Women's work: "'Improvisation gives the individual a voice,' Zollar asserts. 'It allows for—to put it in political terms—what I call collective individualism.' Zollar's dances have political messages; they speak of women's experience, of black women's experience in particular, as founded in and supported by community. So it seems appropriate to choose a collective political method to create that content."[52]

Both Veta Goler and Sally Banes point out the eclectic background of another African-American choreographer, Blondell Cummings. Banes, in her discussion of the evolution of postmodern dance during the 1980s, mentions Cummings (along with Bill T. Jones, Ishmael Houston-Jones, Ralph Lemon, Bebe Miller, and Fred Holland) as one of the growing number of African-American artists who have gained prominence on the experimental dance scene during the last two decades.[53] These artists, each in his or her own way, have cultivated careers that are impressively eclectic. Cummings, for example, studied with many of the black artists who made earlier inroads on the concert stage—Dunham, Primus, Beatty, and Pomare. She also studied the techniques of white artists such as Martha Graham, Merce Cunningham, and Alwin Nikolais; and she performed in the companies of the postmodern choreographers Yvonne Rainer and Meredith Monk.

African-American artists establishing careers in dance since the 1970s have pursued aesthetics that reflect a variety of relationships to their racially specific cultural heritages. In the choreography of an artist like Ralph Lemon, for example, one can find the rigorous formalism of later postmodern dance combined with a uniquely subliminal form of emotionalism and drama and dreamlike imagery. In a 1991 article in *Dance Magazine* Lemon said that his black experiences were an underlying part of his work, but he had consciously chosen not to bring them to the fore.[54] During the most recent years of his career, his position has changed, reflecting a desire that he has spoken of many times—to always keep his artistry growing and evolving in new directions. It also reflects the central role that the politics of difference has come to play in American artists' lives over the last decade or so.

From his early performance experiences with Nancy Hauser in Minneapolis and Meredith Monk in New York, through the years when he directed his own internationally acclaimed company, Lemon has cultivated his interest in a wide range of artistic disciplines. But when he disbanded his company in 1995, not only did he begin to devote more time to multidisciplinary projects that include writing, photography, and film-making as well as choreography, he also undertook what might be called a period of racial self-discovery. As part of this process, he traveled to West Africa in 1996, and his months of study, research, and reflection resulted in a work that was a radical departure from his previous choreography. In an article in the *New York Times,* the dance historian Ann Daly speaks of some of the artist's underlying conflicts that came to bear on the project. "Through 'Geography,' Mr. Lemon has wrestled with the contradictions between his artistic and personal selves, between his Zen-inflected humanism and his new-found sense of racial difference, and between his passion for dance and his desire to 'include some black in my life.'"[55]

Geography took the form of an experimental movement, sound, and visual landscape inhabited by different members of the African diaspora. These included Lemon himself, six dancers and drummers from Abidjan, Ivory Coast, a Brooklyn-based griot who hailed from Guinea, and a hip-hop/club dancer from Richmond, Virginia. In its vitality and its spirit, the collaboration echoed the work of Katherine Dunham and Pearl Primus, and it also shared commonalities with more contemporary artists such as Dianne McIntyre and Jawole Willa Jo Zollar. For Lemon, *Geography* was both a homecoming and a heartfelt attempt to extend the syncretic processes of his cultural heritage.

Bebe Miller, like Lemon—with whom she has worked on several projects—has not made the ostensible use of racial material a standard part of her choreography over the years. With a background that includes studying with Alwin Nikolais and Murray Louis at a very young age, and later performing throughout America and Europe with the companies of Nina Weiner and Dana Reitz, Miller formed her own company in 1985. She soon began to build a repertoire of work that expressed her love for abstraction and her passion for collaborating with musicians, visual artists, and writers to create stunningly beautiful theater pieces. As she said in a 1995 interview in *Ms. Magazine,* her objective is to create a "mix between the passion and pleasure of plain old dancing and the need to communicate."[56] In the same interview she spoke of the changes that she has seen take place over the years in regard to earlier accusations that her work was not "black" in the conventional ways that some individuals thought it should be:

> As a black American choreographer, I used to feel denied a place on the relevancy scale because my work is not literal. There was a time when people would ask: "Which side of the fence do you stand on? What are you trying to say? Is it what we need to hear?" Now there's been a change in the way questions about black identity are being addressed; people are acknowledging that there's no one identity or experience. And reviewers no longer comment on how I'm different from other black choreographers like Alvin Ailey and Katherine Dunham.[57]

Miller's comments encapsulate the contentious issues of identity that have concerned African-American artists as they have plotted their courses through the mine field of America's racial and artistic politics. As mentioned earlier, this process of negotiation has shaped black artists' relationships to mainstream aesthetics over the years, and in the last few decades it has determined their responses to matters such as the efficacy of adopting postmodern experimentation as a guiding principle in their work. Looking once more at the latter point, it is interesting to note that African-American artists became most actively involved in avant-garde mainstream dance trends beginning in the late 1970s and continuing through the ensuing decades. The earliest years saw an increased number of black choreographers gravitating toward postmodern dance, and these were the same years in which many of the discarded elements from earlier modern dance practices were re-introduced—if in revivified forms—to dance performance. I think that it is not a coincidence that this has been the case.

As individuals who were well aware of the artistic revolt that had been going on for more than a decade, and as performers who were less devoted to historical modern dance traditions than were their prede-cessors, younger black artists, like their white counterparts, had a predilection for change. Yet they were still unwilling to sever the important and revered links to their cultural heritage. In the case of McIntyre, Zollar, and Cummings, for example, there was a love of the organic and spiritual relationship between music and dance, a fasci-nation with storytelling, and an acceptance of emotional expressive-ness as an important part of their art.

We can further understand African-American dance artists' relation-ship to mainstream experimentation over the last three decades if we again look at Sally Banes's historical schema of postmodern dance. She reminds us that the period during which the most severely conceptu-al choreographic innovation took place—approximately 1970 to 1980—was followed by a markedly different time. The new dance that began to appear in the 1980s was characterized by a return to theatrical ele-ments that had been discarded by vanguard choreographers. These elements included expressive costuming, evocative music, a closer relationship between choreography and music, and new approaches to narrative and characterization. These kinds of reconfiguration often resulted in dances that were overall less cryptic and more accessible.[58]

By the early 1980s, as this retrenchment of older values combined with more innovative approaches exerted stronger influence in the concert dance venues, the return to expressiveness, dramatic content, and theatricality became even more pronounced. As Banes puts it, this period saw the emergence of a group of younger artists—both black

and white—"who, themselves impatient with the seemingly puritan-
ical seriousness and dry asceticism of the analytic approach, independently found various means to reinstate theatricality while remain-
ing committed to the avant-garde venue."[59] Many African-American
choreographers could relate to this turn of events. They had always
been committed to the spirit of innovation that is basic to modern art,
but they had never seen the need for the overly zealous dismantling
of older aesthetics that characterized the most radical proponents of
early postmodern dance. Black artists, no doubt, viewed iconoclastic
agendas with a critical eye that came from being historical outsiders.
They were nourished on the mother's milk of valuing and cultivating
alternative perspectives as a survival mechanism. These were individuals who were intermittently suspicious of pursuing the "new" directions of the mainstream, because they were not always so new to them.
However, each individual artist, sensing when the time was ripe, joined
in the mainstream process of artistic assemblage—piecing together
fragments of different traditions—which had always been at the core
of their cultural heritage.

As Brenda Dixon Gottschild writes of Cummings, Zollar, Miller, and
others who have "deconstructed, refashioned, and preserved European
American concert dance aesthetics in their own image,"[60] her words
virtually summarize many of the ideas that have been discussed in this
chapter: "[These artists] are latter-day followers in the African American tradition of wearing many hats and inverting-subverting codes,
descendants of folks who did so long before there were words like
deconstruction or postmodernism. To know the mainstream culture
and play its game, but also to remember and keep one's own—that is
and has always been the task. The flip side of this coin is the fact that
Cummings, Zollar, and others preserve Africanisms in their particular postmodern styles."[61]

In the same discussion, Dixon Gottschild delves deeply into a point
that I only hinted at earlier, the fact that even during the early stages
of postmodern dance—when few if any black artists were involved—
palpably significant influences from African-American culture found
their way into the experimental work. She identifies this situation as
a part of an Africanist aesthetic sensibility that has long been a "subliminal but driving force" in American art and culture.[62] She sees this

reflected in early postmodern choreography that was composed of elements that were radically juxtaposed in ways foreign to European-American aesthetics. She sees it too in postmodern dancers' coolly detached, nonchalant presentation of self, a performance style that reflected the body language of African-American jazz musicians as well as the physical "attitude" of black street life. She finds it in the postmodern penchant for "irony, paradox, and double entendre, rather than the classical European, linear logic of cause, effect, and resolution."[63] In these ways and many others—as I suggested earlier—the "new" was not always so new to African-American dancers and choreographers at various junctures in the evolution of postmodern dance.

Today's African-American choreographers continue to "refashion and deconstruct" mainstream dance aesthetics, in much the same spirit as their forerunners, though the structure, content, and look of their work reveal their own radical differences. Artists such as Bill T. Jones pull together postmodern choreographic techniques with messages that range widely through a vast array of humanistic concerns and highly controversial subject matter. Early in his career, along with his late partner, Arnie Zane, Jones began creating autobiographical and semi-autobiographical works that explored taboo subjects such as homosexual relationships. The encompassing reach of his artistry is revealed in Halifu Osumare's commentary on his 1991 work *Last Supper at Uncle Tom's Cabin/The Promised Land*, an evening-length piece that uses Harriet Beecher Stowe's abolitionist novel as a point of departure: "Indeed, he dramatizes quite clearly the power of the theater to expose and transform—to distill hundreds of years of history into one broad stroke. . . . Jones places the historical American slave system with its inherent contradictions of espousing Christianity within the context of today's issues of sexism, gang violence, disproportionate representation of Black males in prison, the continual recurrence of the Ku Klux Klan, gay bashing, and insensitivity to the AIDS crisis."[64]

In his most controversial work, *Still/Here* (1994), Jones ignited a firestorm of debate over the propriety of using his art to explore one of the most sensitive and painful areas of human existence—terminal illness and death. He gathered his material by conducting what he called "survival workshops" throughout the United States in which participants could speak, interact, and use movement to explore the transformational stages that would lead them closer and closer to their impending deaths. *Still/Here* included video projections that augmented the powerfully emotional images of the performance. For Jones, the work was a part of his continuing meditation on the death of his partner Arnie Zane from AIDS and his own HIV-positive status. *Still/Here*, unlike the earlier *Last Supper at Uncle Tom's Cabin*, had nothing specifically to do with issues of race or ethnicity. I think that it is more than a coincidence, however, that the American choreographer who has forged ahead into controversial territory where no other choreographer has gone before is also an African American.

There are a number of other black artists in addition to Jones who have made an unwavering commitment to breaking new ground with their work. Young choreographers such as Ronald K. Brown delve incisively and fearlessly into America's social, political, and sexual morass. His work mirrors his own astoundingly beautiful performance style, which is built on an approach to movement that pushes physical boundaries as he segues from modern and postmodern dance vocabularies to African dance movements and hip-hop/club dancing. Drawing on many of the same movement sources, David Rousseve makes his unique personal investigations into sensitive subject matter. In vital total theater works such as *Urban Scenes/Creole Dreams*, he uncompromisingly examines his family's mixed-race lineage, the violence of racism, living in the age of AIDS, and other topics that push the boundaries of his art.

Yet another artist who mixes a potently kinetic brew of different dance styles and techniques is Garth Fagan. His 1978 piece *From Before* was a signature statement of a multicultural approach to movement steeped in West Indian and African dance traditions combined with his propulsive and sculptural use of modern dance techniques. On first seeing *From Before,* one is struck by the purity of the Africanist movement that is unfettered by costumes with ethnic associations. There is a formal and pristine quality that shines through the dancers' lithe bodies clad only in glistening unitards. Fagan's later works, such as *Griot New York* (1991), a collaboration with the jazz musician Wynton Marsalis and the sculptor Martin Puryear, continue to expand his aesthetic as he creates works that reflect new visions for black choreographers at the turn of the century.

There are many other artists who deserve to be included here. A discussion of African-American choreographers and dancers who have had a significant impact on the national and international dance scene could go on and on. Again, the omissions in this and previous chapters are further indications of the continuing work needed to document and bring into context the full extent of African-American contributions to theatrical dance. As I mentioned at the outset, I began my research because of an obvious need for information in this area. Fortunately, in the past decade or so, a growing number of scholars—some of whom I have cited here—have taken important steps to create a more inclusive picture of the history of dance in America.

As if to lend credence to the sociological/aesthetic theories of the Harlem Renaissance intelligentsia, African-American artists continue to play a role in American culture that has far more influence than their actual demographic representation might suggest or than some cultural arbiters will admit. But thanks to the strivings of the pioneering men and women who came before, the work of today's black dance artists is receiving ever-increasing acceptance and respect.

The place of African-American art in relationship to mainstream culture will, no doubt, continue to be of concern to artists and scholars of all colors as long as racism—whether subliminal or blatant—plays a central role in American life. Black artists will continue to debate the extent to which they should or should not be expected to include material that foregrounds their racial heritage in their work; they will debate the efficacy of creating art that serves the political and social needs of their people. There is a dimension of artistic creation that can transcend concerns of these kinds, but ultimately it is the artist who must choose the direction he or she will take. Perhaps these paths are not mutually exclusive.

At the beginning of a new millennium, we will, hopefully, continue to realize that African Americans are a diverse group of individuals who have often pursued different directions as they have struggled against the forces that inhibit the free exploration of their human potential. At the same time, in the spirit of their Africanist aesthetic heritage, they have embraced what others might see as the conflict between diversity and unity, just as they have embraced the conflict of so many aspects of their lives.

Notes

Chapter 1: Early Influences on Black Concert Dance

1. Nesta Macdonald, *Diaghilev Observed by Critics in England and the United States, 1911–1929* (New York: Dance Horizons, 1975), p. 132.

2. Nancy Lee Chalfa Ruyter, *Reformers and Visionaries* (New York: Dance Horizons, 1979), p. 13.

3. Ibid.

4. Ibid., p. 20.

5. Ibid., pp. 103–4.

6. Ibid., p. 39.

7. Ibid., p. 66.

8. Ibid., p. 69.

9. Edna Guy, letter to Ruth St. Denis, Jan. 13, 1924, Ruth St. Denis Papers, Dance Collection, New York Public Library at Lincoln Center (hereafter, NYPL), New York.

10. David Levering Lewis, *When Harlem Was in Vogue* (New York: Knopf, 1984), p. 24.

11. Claude McKay, *Selected Poems of Claude McKay* (New York: Bookman Associates, 1953), p. 59.

12. Richard Bardolph, *The Negro Vanguard* (Westport, Conn.: Negro Universities Press, 1959), p. 11.

13. Langston Hughes, "The Negro Artist and the Racial Mountain," *The Nation* 72 (June 23, 1926): 692.

14. Ibid.

15. Lewis, *When Harlem Was in Vogue*, p. 7.

16. James Weldon Johnson, *The Book of American Negro Poetry* (1922; reprint, New York: Harcourt, Brace, 1959), p. 9.

17. Lewis, *When Harlem Was in Vogue*, p. 46.

18. Ibid., p. 48.

19. Ibid., p. 90.

20. Ibid., p. 116.

21. Marshall Stearns and Jean Stearns, *Jazz Dance: The Story of American Vernacular Dance* (New York: Schirmer, 1968), p. 148.

22. Quoted in Fredrick L. Orme, "Negro in the Dance as Katherine Dunham Sees Him," *American Dancer*, Mar. 1938, p. 46.

23. Sterling A. Brown, "Negro Character as Seen by White Authors," in *The Negro Caravan*, ed. Sterling A. Brown, Arthur P. Davis, and Ulysses Lee (1941; reprint, New York: Arno, 1969), p. 180.

24. Ibid.

25. Ibid., p. 198.

26. Ibid., p. 184.

27. Allen Woll, *Dictionary of the Black Theatre* (Westport, Conn.: Greenwood Press, 1983), pp. 1–2.

28. John Martin, "The Dance: A Negro Art," *New York Times*, Feb. 25, 1940, sec. 9, p. 2.

29. Lois Balcom, "The Negro Dances Himself," *Dance Observer*, Dec. 1944, p. 124.

30. John Mason Brown, "'Zunguru' Danced at the Chanin Auditorium," *New York Post*, Apr. 9, 1940, n.p., Dance Collection, NYPL.

31. Brown, "Negro Character," pp. 189–91.

Chapter 2: Hemsley Winfield

1. "Death Claims Hemsley Winfield, Yonkers Resident and Founder of Negro Art Theater," *Herald Statesman* (Yonkers, N.Y.), Jan. 16, 1934, p. 3.

2. "Interesting Items Gleaned from the Age Correspondents—Yonkers, New York," *Age* (New York), Oct. 20, 1928, p. 8.

3. "Death Claims Hemsley Winfield."

4. Christine Phillip, "Yonkers Blacks Recall Hard Times," *Herald Statesman* (Yonkers, N.Y.), Feb. 9, 1932, p. 3.

5. "Hemsley Winfield," *New York Herald Tribune*, Jan. 17, 1934, n.p., Dance Collection, NYPL.

6. Robert E. Gard and Gertrude S. Burley, *Community Theatre* (New York: Duell, Sloan, and Pearce, 1959), p. 8.

7. Ibid.

8. Ibid., p. 9.

9. "Social Progress," *Opportunity*, May 3, 1925, p. 6.

10. W. E. B. Du Bois, "Beside Still Waters," *The Crisis*, May 1931, pp. 168–69.

11. "National Ethiopian Art Theatre School Was Opened in New York City March 17," *Age* (New York), Apr. 5, 1924, p. 1.

12. "Gala Performance for Ethiopian Art Theatre, Jan. 19," *Age* (New York), Jan. 10, 1925, p. 1.

13. William E. Clark, "Ethiopian Art Theatre School in Premier Dance Exhibition and Song Recital on June 19," *Age* (New York), June 28, 1924, p. 3.

14. Helen Deutsch and Stella Hanau, *The Provincetown* (New York: Russell and Russell, 1931), p. 18.

15. "Interesting Items Gleaned from the Age Correspondents—Yonkers, New York," *Age* (New York), July 19, 1924, p. 8.

16. Winfield's name could not be found on the programs for this production that are available at the Billy Rose Theatre Collection, NYPL. In view of the announcement in the New York *Age*, however, it can be assumed that he did appear in the play at some point.

17. "Ethiopian Art School's Students Give Dramatic Offerings to Harlemites," *Age* (New York), Oct. 25, 1924, p. 6.

18. William F. Schuyler, "Theatre," *The Messenger*, Nov. 1924, pp. 342–43.

19. Brochure of the National Ethiopian Art Theatre School, (New York: New York Age Press), n.d., n.p., Gumby Collection, Columbia University.

20. "Interesting Items Gleaned from the Age Correspondents—Yonkers, New York," *Age* (New York), Aug. 22, 1925, p. 8.

21. Bruce Kellner, ed., *The Harlem Renaissance: A Historical Dictionary for the Era* (New York: Methuen, 1984), p. 224.

22. "The Theatre: 'Lulu Belle,'" *The Crisis*, May 1926, p. 34.

23. Hubert H. Harrison, "The Significance of 'Lulu Belle,'" *Opportunity*, July 1926, p. 228.

24. Brooks Atkinson, "The Play," *New York Times*, Feb. 10, 1926, p. 20.

25. Ibid.

26. Doris Abramsom, *Negro Playwrights in the American Theatre* (New York: Columbia University Press, 1969), p. 26.

27. Eric Walrond, introduction to Em Jo Basshe, *Earth* (New York: MaCaulay, 1927), pp. viii–xii.

28. Theophilus Lewis, "The Theatre," *The Messenger*, May 1927, p. 157.

29. James Weldon Johnson, *Black Manhattan* (New York: Atheneum, 1977), p. 175.

30. Lillian G. Genn, "Cellar Drama in New York," unattributed clipping,

Billy Rose Theatre Collection, NYPL.

31. "Triangle Club's Plans," *New York Times,* Apr. 6, 1927, n.p., Billy Rose Theatre Collection, NYPL.

32. "The Drama," *Amsterdam News,* May 18 1927, p. 24.

33. Official program, *1927, Bare Facts,* Billy Rose Theatre Collection, NYPL.

34. Theophilus Lewis, "The Theatre," *The Messenger,* Apr. 1927, p. 121.

35. "Triangle Reopens with a Revival," *Billboard,* Jan.–Mar. 1927, p. 9.

36. "Negro Art Theatre to Give Midnight Performance of 'Salome,'" *Age* (New York), Feb. 18, 1928, p. 6.

37. "Art Theatre's First Offering at Provincetown Playhouse," *Amsterdam News,* July 3, 1929, p. 13.

38. Untitled article, unattributed clipping, *Salome* clipping file, Billy Rose Theatre Collection, NYPL.

39. "Hemsley Winfield Is Great Hit as 'Salome' at the Cherry Lane Theater, N.Y.," *Defender* (Chicago), July 27, 1929, p. 6.

40. Untitled article, unattributed clipping, *Salome* clipping file, Billy Rose Theatre Collection, NYPL.

41. Bruce Kellner, ed., *Keep A'Inchin' Along: Selected Writings of Carl Van Vechten about Black Art and Letters* (Westport, Conn.: Greenwood Press, 1979), p. 8.

42. Randolph Sawyer, interview by Joe Nash, Aug. 26, 1980, New York, audiotape in collection of Joe Nash.

43. Vere E. Johns, "In the Name of Art," *Age* (New York), Jan. 27, 1934, p. 6.

44. Ibid.

45. "An Interview with Bruce Nugent," in *Artists and Influences,* ed. James V. Hatch and Camille Billops (New York: Hatch-Billops Collection, Inc., 1982), p. 99.

46. Samuel L. Leiter, ed., *The Encyclopedia of the New York Stage, 1920–1930* (Westport, Conn.: Greenwood Press, 1985), pp. 395–96.

47. Deutsch and Hanau, *The Provincetown,* pp. 299–302.

48. "Negro Art Players Will Also Remain at the Lincoln Another Week," *Amsterdam News,* Nov. 7, 1928, p. 7.

49. Eulalie Spence, "Negro Art Players in Harlem," *Opportunity,* Dec. 1928, p. 381.

50. Abramsom, *Negro Playwrights in the American Theatre,* p. 33.

51. Ibid., pp. 41–42.

52. Ibid.

53. "When White Is Black," *New York Times,* Feb. 21, 1929, p. 30.

54. Alson Smith, "Other New Plays," *Morning World,* Jan. 22, 1929, n.p., Billy Rose Theatre Collection, NYPL.

55. Richard Lockridge, "Life in 'Harlem'," *New York Sun*, Feb. 21, 1929, n.p., Billy Rose Theatre Collection, NYPL.

56. Marshall Stearns and Jean Stearns, *Jazz Dance: The Story of American Vernacular Dance* (New York: Schirmer, 1968), p. 153.

57. Wallace Thurman, "Harlem's Place in the Sun," *The Dance Magazine*, May 1928, p. 25.

58. Hemsley Winfield, "Speaking o' Harlem," *Amsterdam News*, May 15, 1929, p. 12.

59. Ibid.

60. Jeroline Hemsley, "Wade in De Water," *Amsterdam News*, Mar. 12, 1930, p. 9.

61. "Negro Play Lacks Order," *New York Times*, Sept. 14, 1929, p. 17.

62. "Inez Clough, H. Winfield in New Play," *Defender* (Chicago), Sept. 28, 1929, p. 6.

63. "Art Theater Will Present Eight Plays," *Defender* (Chicago), Oct. 5, 1929, p. 7.

64. "New Negro Art Theatre," *Age* (New York), Feb. 8, 1930, p. 6.

65. W. E. B. Du Bois, *Dusk of Dawn* (New York: Harcourt, Brace, 1940), pp. 272–74.

66. "History of Negro Told in Pageantry," unattributed clipping, Schomburg Center for Research in Black Culture, NYPL (hereafter cited as Schomburg Center).

67. All information about the *De Promis' Lan'* was obtained from the official program, *National Negro Pageant Ass'n Presents De Promis' Lan'* (May 27, 1930), Billy Rose Theatre Collection, NYPL.

68. Edna Guy, "Negro Dance Pioneer!" *Dance Herald*, Mar. 1938, p. 6.

69. John Martin, "Appearance of Tamiris," *New York Times*, Aug. 27, 1933, p. 7.

70. Hemsley Winfield, Miscellaneous Papers, Schomburg Center.

71. Official program, *All Star Benefit Performance for the Colored Citizens' Unemployment and Relief Committee of Yonkers, N.Y., Saunders Trade School, Mar. 6, 1931*, Schomburg Center.

72. Randolph Sawyer, interview by Joe Nash, Aug. 26, 1980, New York, audiotape in collection of Joe Nash.

73. Official program, *First Negro Dance Recital in America*, n.d., Moorland-Spingarn Research Collection, Howard University, Washington, D.C.

74. John Martin, "Dance Recital Given by Negro Artists," *New York Times*, Apr. 30, 1931, p. 27.

75. Ibid.

76. "Along the Color Line," *The Crisis*, Apr. 1927, p. 54.

77. Charles E. Isaacson, "Dance Events Reviewed," *The Dance Magazine,* July 1931, p. 119.

78. Official program, *Negro Dance Recital—Hemsley Winfield* (Roerich Hall, 310 Riverside Drive, Jan. 19, 30, Feb. 6, 1932) Schomburg Center.

79. "Roxy Presents Lincoln Show," unattributed clipping, Schomburg Center.

80. John Martin, "The Dance: A Negro Art Group," *New York Times,* Feb. 14, 1932, sec. 7, p. 11.

81. Ibid.

82. Ibid.

83. Ibid.

84. "Negro Art Theatre to Give 'Gambodi,'" *Amsterdam News,* Apr. 20, 1932, p. 7.

85. "Negro Group Tours," *The Dancers' Club News,* May 28, 1932, p. 10.

86. Official program, *The Friends Amusement Guild Presents a New Negro Art Theatre Dance Production,* n.d., Dance Collection, NYPL.

87. John Martin, "The Dance: A Benefit," *New York Times,* Dec. 11, 1932, sec. 9, p. 4.

88. Official program, *The Dancers' Club Presents a Monster Dance Performance* (Mecca Temple, Dec. 11, 1932), Dance Collection, NYPL.

89. John Martin, "Dancers' Club Stages Successful Benefit," *New York Times,* Dec. 12, 1932, p. 12.

90. "Other Dance News," *New York Herald Tribune,* Dec. 25, 1932, n.p., Music Collection, NYPL.

91. John Martin, "The Dance," *New York Times,* May 13, 1934, sec. 9, p. 1.

92. George Sturm, "Look Back in Anger: The Strange Case of Louis Gruenberg," *Madamna!* 2 (Spring 1981): 13–14.

93. Margaret Just Butcher, *The Negro in American Culture* (New York: Knopf, 1972), p. 85.

94. Olin Downes, "Great Drama for the Lyric Stage," *New York Times,* Oct. 2, 1932, sec. 9, p. 6.

95. Olin Downes, "Gruenberg's 'Jones' in Premiere," *New York Times,* Jan. 1, 1933, n.p., New York Scrapbook, Music Collection, NYPL.

96. Olin Downes, "'Emperor Jones' Triumphs as Opera," *New York Times,* Jan. 8, 1933, p. 26.

97. Paul Rosenfeld, "The Emperor Jones," *New Republic,* n.d., n.p., Dance Collection, NYPL.

98. Downes, "'Emperor Jones' Triumphs as Opera."

99. "O'Neill into Opera," *Time,* Jan. 16, 1933, p. 20.

100. Downes, "'Emperor Jones' Triumphs as Opera."

101. Mary F. Watkins, "With the Dancers," *New York Herald Tribune*, Jan. 15, 1933, n.p., Schomburg Center.

102. "Winfield Players in Active Season," *Amsterdam News*, May 31, 1933, p. 8.

103. "Colored Artists Play Big Part in Workers' Dance in New York," *Washington Tribune*, Oct. 12, 1933, n.p., Schomburg Center.

104. Ibid.

105. "Death Claims Hemsley Winfield."

106. Ibid.

107. "Pneumonia Ends Life of Hemsley Winfield," *Amsterdam News*, Jan. 17, 1934, n.p., Schomburg Center.

108. "Winfield's Group to Continue His Work," *Amsterdam News*, Feb. 7, 1934, p. 8.

Chapter 3: Edna Guy, Randolph Sawyer, and Ollie Burgoyne

1. The Edna Guy letters referred to in this chapter are part of the Ruth St. Denis Papers, Dance Collection, NYPL.

2. Edna Guy, letter to Ruth St. Denis, Oct. 8, 1923.

3. Edna Guy, letter to Ruth St. Denis, Feb. 9, 1924.

4. Ruth St. Denis, *Ruth St. Denis: An Unfinished Life* (New York: Harper, 1939), p. 348.

5. Edna Guy, letters to Ruth St. Denis, July 25, 1923, and May 27, 1924.

6. Edna Guy, letter to Ruth St. Denis, May 27, 1924.

7. Edna Guy, letter to Ruth St. Denis, June 7, 1924.

8. Official brochure, *Denishawn: The Ruth St. Denis and Ted Shawn School of Dancing and Its Related Arts* (ninth season, 1923–24), p. 4, Dance Collection, NYPL.

9. Ibid., p. 15.

10. Edna Guy, letter to Ruth St. Denis, Nov. 7, 1924.

11. Jane Sherman, *The Drama of Denishawn Dance* (Middletown, Conn.: Wesleyan University Press, 1979), p. 4.

12. Ibid.

13. Edna Guy, letter to Ruth St. Denis, undated.

14. Edna Guy, letter to Ruth St. Denis, Feb. 15, 1925.

15. Ibid.

16. Suzanne Shelton, *Divine Dancer* (Garden City, N.Y.: Doubleday, 1981), pp. 215–16.

17. Edna Guy, letter to Ruth St. Denis, Oct. 29, 1928.

18. Shelton, *Divine Dancer*, p. 238.

19. Edna Guy, letter to Ruth St. Denis, undated.

20. Edna Guy, letter to Ruth St. Denis, Dec. 25, 1928.

21. Edna Guy, letter to Ruth St. Denis, Dec. 1, 1929.

22. Edna Guy, letter to Ruth St. Denis, July 7, 1930.

23. Sherman, *Drama of Denishawn Dance,* p. 11.

24. Edna Guy, letter to Ruth St. Denis, undated.

25. Anne Marie Biondo, "Edna Guy McCully Leaves Inspired Legacy," *Fort Worth Star Telegram,* Apr. 29, 1983, sec. C, p. 1.

26. Edna Guy, letter to Ruth St. Denis, undated.

27. Sherman, *Drama of Denishawn Dance,* p. 35.

28. Ibid.

29. Shelton, *Divine Dancer,* p. 233.

30. Guy, "Negro Dance Pioneer!"

31. Ibid.

32. St. Denis, *Unfinished Life,* p. 347.

33. Ibid., p. 348.

34. "Expert Talks on 'Dance as an Art,' *Amsterdam News,* May 31, 1933, n.p., Schomburg Center.

35. "The Callboard," *The Dance Magazine,* Aug. 1931, p. 46.

36. "Salome," *The Dance Magazine,* Dec. 1931, pp. 45–46.

37. Gus Smith, "Theatrical Jottings," *Age* (New York), Apr. 30, 1932, p. 6.

38. Official program, *Washington Conservatory of Music and School of Expression Presents: The Birth of Inspiration* (Roerich Hall, 103d Street and Riverside Drive, May 7, 1932), Moorland-Spingarn Collection, Manuscript Division, Howard University, Washington, D.C.

39. Ralph Taylor, "Edna Guy and Group," *Dance Observer,* May 1934, p. 45.

40. Ibid.

41. *The Proceedings of the First National Dance Congress and Festival* (New York, May 1936), p. 104, Dance Collection, NYPL.

42. John Martin, "The Dance: A Congress," *New York Times,* May 31, 1936, sec. 10, p. 9.

43. Ibid.

44. *Proceedings,* p. 94.

45. "Along the Color Line," *The Crisis,* Apr. 1931, p. 54.

46. All information on the contents of this concert was obtained from the official program, *A Negro Dance Evening* (Theresa L. Kaufmann Auditorium, Lexington Avenue at 92d Street, Mar. 7, 1931), Schomburg Center.

47. J. A. Kaye, "Reviews—Negro Dance Evening," *Dance,* May 1937, pp. 32–33.

48. Ibid., p. 33.

49. Lynne Fauley Emery, *Black Dance in the United States from 1619 to 1970* (Palo Alto, Calif.: National Press Books, 1972), p. 252.

50. Official program, *Rainbow Room Recitals* (Dec. 28, 1937), Schomburg Center.

51. Official program, *Dance Recital—Lincoln School for Nurses* (May 1, 1938), Schomburg Center.

52. Josephine Monica Nicholson, "Three Black Pioneers in American Modern Dance, 1931–1945" (M.A. thesis, George Washington University, Washington, D.C., 1984), p. 24.

53. John Martin, "Dance Notes," *New York Times*, Aug. 28, 1960, n.p., Dance Collection, NYPL.

54. Guy, "Negro Dance Pioneer!"

55. Randolph Sawyer, interview by Joe Nash, New York, Aug. 26, 1980, audiotape in collection of Joe Nash. Unless otherwise noted, all details about Randolph Sawyer's early life and career are taken from this interview.

56. John Martin, "The Dance: A Repertory Movement," *New York Times*, Aug. 30, 1931, sec. 8, p. 4.

57. Ibid.

58. John Martin, "'Zunguru' Offered by a Dance Group," *New York Times*, Aug. 3, 1938, p. 14.

59. Lewis Nichols, "La Belle Hélène," *New York Times*, July 8, 1941, n.p., Dance Collection, NYPL.

60. Lewis Nichols, "Carmen Jones," *New York Times*, Dec. 3, 1943, p. 26.

61. Ibid.

62. Henry T. Sampson, *Blacks in Blackface* (Metuchen, N.J.: Scarecrow Press, 1980), p. 347.

63. Ibid., p. 377.

64. Ibid., p. 347.

65. Unattributed article, Clipping File, Channing-Pollock Theatre Collection, Howard University, Washington, D.C.

66. Ibid.

67. The photograph mentioned can be found in Helen Armstead Johnson's *Black America on Stage* (New York: Graduate Center of the City University of New York, 1982), p. 2.

68. Unattributed article, Clipping File, Channing-Pollock Theatre Collection.

69. Sampson's *Blacks in Blackface* lists Burgoyne's shows but does not include the places where the productions occurred and other important production information.

70. Sampson, *Blacks in Blackface*, p. 485.

71. Lewis Nichols, "Negro Spirituals," *New York Times*, Mar. 2, 1933, p. 21.

72. Doris Humphrey, "Dance, Little Chillun!" *The American Dancer*, July 1933, p. 10.

73. John Martin, "The Dance: A Negro Play," *New York Times*, Mar. 12, 1933, sec. 9, p. 7.

74. Ibid.

75. Ibid.

76. Unattributed article, Clipping File, Channing-Pollock Theatre Collection.

Chapter 4: Charles Williams

1. Robert Francis Engs, *Freedom's First Generation: Black Hampton, Virginia, 1861–1890* (Philadelphia: University of Pennsylvania Press, 1979), p. 142.

2. Ibid., pp. 142–43.

3. Ibid., pp. 143–44.

4. Ibid., pp. 148–49.

5. Kellner, *Harlem Renaissance*, pp. 61–62.

6. Official program, *Folk Lore Concert* (Mendelssohn Hall, New York, Mar. 13, 1908), Hampton University Archives, Huntington Library, Hampton, Va.

7. Official program, *The Fiftieth Anniversary of Emancipation* (Carnegie Hall, New York, Mar. 10, 1913), Hampton University Archives, Huntington Library, Hampton, Va.

8. Official program, *Hampton Afloat and Afield* (1914), Hampton University Archives, Huntington Library, Hampton, Va.

9. Tony Anthony, "C. H. Williams Gains State Honor," *Times Herald* (Newport News, Va.), Mar. 13, 1981, n.p., Hampton University Archives, Huntington Library, Hampton, Va.

10. Ibid.

11. Ibid.

12. Charles H. Williams, "Recreation in the Lives of Young People," *Southern Workman* 46 (Feb. 1917): 96–97.

13. Ibid., p. 98.

14. Ibid., p. 99.

15. Ibid., pp. 98–99.

16. "Hampton Incidents," *Southern Workman* 51 (May 1922): 242.

17. "Social Sidelights on the Denishawn Tour," *Denishawn Magazine*, Spring 1925, n.p., Dance Collection, NYPL.

18. Charles H. Williams, *Cotton Needs Pickin'* (Norfolk, Va.: Guide Publishing Company, 1928), n.p., Dance Collection, NYPL.

19. John Martin, "Dance: The Art of the Negro," *New York Times,* July 7, 1929, n.p., Dance Collection, NYPL.

20. Official transcript, Harvard Summer School, n.d., Charles Williams Collection, Hampton University Archives, Huntington Library, Hampton, Va.

21. Charles Williams, letter to Mr. Nelson Payne, Aug. 1, 1938, Charles Williams Collection, Hampton University Archives, Huntington Library, Hampton, Va.

22. "Expenses, June and July, 1938," Charles Williams Collection, Hampton University Archives, Huntington Library, Hampton, Va.

23. Charles H. Williams, "'Darkest Africa' at 'A Century of Progress,'" *Southern Workman* 62 (Nov. 1933): 430.

24. Ibid., p. 432.

25. Ibid., p. 433.

26. Ibid., p. 436.

27. Edo McCullough, *World's Fair Midways* (New York: Arno Press, 1976), p. 94.

28. "Hampton Incidents," *Southern Workman* 63 (June 1934): 187.

29. Ibid.

30. Walter Terry, *Ted Shawn: Father of American Dance* (New York: Dial Press, 1976), p. 139.

31. Ibid., p. 174.

32. Ted Shawn and Gray Poole, *One Thousand and One Night Stands* (Garden City, N.Y.: Doubleday, 1960), p. 252.

33. Jane Sherman and Barton Mumaw, *Barton Mumaw* (Brooklyn, N.Y.: Dance Horizons, 1986), p. 126.

34. Ibid.

35. "Students Show Possibilities in Negro Dance," *Norfolk Journal and Guide,* Mar. 9, 1935, n.p., Hampton University Archives, Huntington Library, Hampton, Va.

36. Official program, *The Dance: Hampton Institute Creative Dance Group* (Mosque Theatre, Richmond, Va., Mar. 23, 1935), Hampton University Archives, Huntington Library, Hampton, Va.

37. Ibid.

38. "Students Show Possibilities in Negro Dance."

39. "Hampton Dance Event Success Artistically," *Norfolk Journal and Guide,*" Mar. 30, 1935, n.p., Hampton University Archives.

40. "Hampton Pioneers Again," *Daily Press,* Mar. 24, 1935, n.p., Hampton University Archives.

41. "Biographical Sketch of Charlotte Kennedy Moton," manuscript, Hampton University Archives.

42. Charles H. Williams, letter to Mr. L. Harper, Mar. 8, 1937, Charles Williams Collection, Hampton University Archives.

43. Charles H. Williams, letter to Dr. R. E. Diffendorfer, June 2, 1937, Charles Williams Collection, Hampton University Archives.

44. Charles H. Williams, letter to William Kolodney, May 26, 1937, Hampton University Archives.

45. Albertina Vitak, "Dance Events Reviewed," *The American Dancer*, Jan. 1938, p. 22.

46. Walter Terry, "The Hampton Dancers and the Problems of Negro Dance," unattributed, undated article, Hampton University Archives.

47. Lois Balcom was one of several critics who referred to "highjinks," when she commented, "This audience is . . . tickled by Harlem high jinks." See Balcom, "What Chance Has the Negro Dancer?" *Dance Observer*, Nov. 1944.

48. Terry, "The Hampton Dancers and the Problems of Negro Dance."

49. Ibid.

50. Martha Hill, letter to Charles Williams, Nov. 18, 1937, Hampton University Archives.

51. Engs, *Freedom's First Generation*, pp. 145–46.

52. Souvenir program, *Hampton Creative Dance Group* (n.d., n.p.), Hampton University Archives.

53. Ibid.

54. Charles Williams, "The Hampton Institute Creative Dance Group," *The Dance Observer*, Oct. 1937, p. 98.

55. W. R., "Negro Dance," *Boston Evening Transcript*, Mar. 21, 1939, n.p., Hampton University Archives.

56. Walter Terry, "The Dance," *Boston Herald*, Mar. 21, 1939, n.p., Hampton University Archives.

57. Ibid.

58. W. R., "Hampton Creative Dancers," *Boston Evening Transcript*, n.d., n.p., Dance Collection, NYPL.

Chapter 5: Asadata Dafora

1. Robert Goldwater, *Primitivism in Modern Art* (New York: Vintage Books, 1938), p. 67.

2. Ibid., p. 34.

3. Pierre Daix, *Cubists and Cubism* (New York: Rizzoli, 1982), p. 25.

4. Ibid., pp. 32–33.

5. G. S., "La Création du Monde," *Phaidon Book of the Ballet* (Oxford: Phaidon, 1981), p. 196.

6. Kay Boyle, quoted in Jay Bochner, *Blaise Cendrars: Discovery and Recreation* (Toronto: University of Toronto Press, 1978), p. 67.

7. Nathan Irvin Huggins, *Harlem Renaissance* (London: Oxford University Press, 1971), p. 79.

8. Ibid.

9. Ibid., pp. 79–80.

10. Kellner, *Harlem Renaissance,* p. 26.

11. Edward Scobie, *Black Britannia* (Chicago: Johnson Publishing Company, 1972), p. 124.

12. Allen Woll, *Black Musical Theatre* (Baton Rouge: Louisiana State University Press, 1989), p. 36.

13. Ibid., p. 42.

14. Countee Cullen, "Golden Dawn," *Opportunity,* Jan. 1928, p. 21.

15. Butcher, *The Negro in American Culture,* p. 94.

16. "Africans Liked Heat; They Sweat Freely," *New York Evening Post,* July 12, 1934, n.p., Schomburg Center.

17. W. Kline and S. Davis, "Asadata Dafora (Horton)," biographical sketch, Apr. 17, 1980, p. 1, Schomburg Center.

18. Margaret Lloyd, "Dancer from the Gold Coast—Part II," *Christian Science Monitor,* June 9, 1945, p. 5, Dance Collection, NYPL.

19. Margaret Lloyd, "Dancer from the Gold Coast," *Christian Science Monitor,* May 16, 1945, n.p., Dance Collection, NYPL.

20. Kline and Davis, "Asadata Dafora (Horton)," p. 1.

21. Lloyd, "Dancer from the Gold Coast."

22. Official program, *Joint Song Recital* (Mother A.M.E. Zion Church, Jan. 26, 1931), Asadata Dafora (Horton) Papers, Schomburg Center.

23. Chappy Gardner, "African Princess in First American Song Recital at Mother Zion," *Harlem Reporter,* n.d., Schomburg Center.

24. "African Dancers and Singers Appear in Recital in Harlem," *Age* (New York), Oct. 21, 1933, n.p., Schomburg Center.

25. Official program, *All Star Negro Performance* (Town Hall, New York, Nov. 25, 1933), Schomburg Center.

26. "Asadata Dafora," *Kykunkor* (souvenir program), n.p., Schomburg Center.

27. Martha Dreiblatt, "The Story of the Production," *Kykunkor* (souvenir program), n.p., Schomburg Center.

28. Ibid.

29. "The Story of the Dance Opera 'Kykunkor,'" *Kykunkor* (souvenir program), n.p., Schomburg Center.

30. Martin Banham, *African Theatre Today* (New York: Pitman Publishing, 1975), p. 1.

31. "Native African Sketch Given at Saratoga Club," *Age* (New York), Mar. 31, 1934, p. 4.

32. Ibid.

33. "The Story of the Dance Opera 'Kykunkor.'"

34. John Martin, "Native Cast Gives an African 'Opera,'" *New York Times,* May 9, 1934, Schomburg Center.

35. John Mason Brown, "Two on the Aisle," *New York Post,* May 19, 1934, n.p., Schomburg Center.

36. Lincoln Kirstein, "The Dance 'Kykunkor'; Native African Opera," *Nation* 138 (June 13, 1934): 684.

37. Martin, "Native Cast Gives an African 'Opera.'"

38. Ibid.

39. Brown, "Two on the Aisle."

40. Robert Farris Thompson, *Black Gods and Kings* (Los Angeles: University of California Press, 1971), p. 10.

41. John Martin, "The Dance: African Lore," *New York Times,* May 13, 1934, n.p., Dance Collection, NYPL.

42. Ibid.

43. Kirstein, "The Dance 'Kykunkor.'"

44. Ibid.

45. Edwin Denby, "A Glimpse of Real African Dancing," *New York Herald Tribune,* Dec. 21, 1943, n.p., Dance Collection, NYPL.

46. Ibid.

47. Thompson, *Black Gods and Kings,* p. 9.

48. Denby, "A Glimpse of Real African Dancing."

49. Emery, *Black Dance,* p. 251.

50. K. K. Martin, "America's First African Dance Theatre," *Caribe* 7, nos. 1 and 2 (1983): 8.

51. John Houseman, *Run-Through* (New York: Simon and Schuster, 1972), pp. 179–80.

52. Ibid., p. 184.

53. Ibid., pp. 184–85.

54. Barbara Leaming, *Orson Welles* (New York: Viking Penguin, 1983), p. 101.

55. Houseman, *Run-Through,* p. 194.

56. Lewis, *When Harlem Was in Vogue,* p. 167.

57. Leaming, *Orson Welles,* p. 102.

58. Richard France, *The Theatre of Orson Welles* (Cranbury, N.J.: Associated University Presses, 1977), p. 55.

59. Ibid., p. 61.

60. Brooks Atkinson, "The Play," *New York Times,* Apr. 15, 1936, n.p., Schomburg Center.

61. Percy Hammond, "Macbeth," *New York Herald Tribune,* Apr. 16, 1936, n.p., Schomburg Center.

62. Houseman, *Run-Through*, pp. 202–3.

63. Martin, "America's First African Dance Theatre," p. 9.

64. Charles E. Dexter, "'Ha'nt' of Dead Senegalese Plagues African Play Cast," *World Telegram*, Jan. 14, 1937, n.p., Billy Rose Theatre Collection, NYPL.

65. John Martin, "'Bassa Moona' Seen in Harlem Theatre," *New York Times*, Dec. 9, 1936, n.p., Dance Collection, NYPL.

66. John Martin, "The Dance: 'Zunguru,'" *New York Times*, Aug. 7, 1938, n.p., Schomburg Center.

67. Walter Terry, "Dafora's African Group Stages a Dance Drama of Tribal Life," *New York Herald Tribune*, Apr. 9, 1940, n.p., Dance Collection, NYPL.

68. Brown, "'Zunguru' Danced at the Chanin Auditorium."

69. John Martin, "Dance-Opera Given by Dafora Group," *New York Times*, Mar. 21, 1940, n.p., Dance Collection NYPL.

70. John Martin, "The Dance: Africana," *New York Times*, Mar. 24, 1940, n.p., Dance Collection, NYPL.

71. Ibid.

72. Ibid.

73. Ibid.

74. John Martin, "The Dance: Africana," *New York Times*, Dec. 14, 1943, n.p., Dance Collection, NYPL.

75. Ibid.

76. G. W. B., "Asadata Dafora and Company," *Dance Observer*, Jan. 1944, p. 9.

77. John Martin, "African Festival at Carnegie Hall," *New York Times*, Apr. 5, 1945, n.p., Schomburg Center.

78. Irving Kolodin, "African Dancers at Carnegie Hall," *New York Herald Tribune*, n.d., n.p., Schomburg Center.

79. G. W. B., "Asadata Dafora and Company," p. 9.

80. Walter Terry, "The Dance," *New York Herald Tribune*, Apr. 26, 1946, n.p., Dance Collection, NYPL.

Chapter 6: Katherine Dunham

1. Katherine Dunham, "Thesis Turned Broadway," in *Kaiso!: Katherine Dunham, an Anthology of Writings*, ed. VéVé A. Clark and Margaret B. Wilkerson (Berkeley: University of California, Institute for the Study of Social Change, 1978), p. 55.

2. Katherine Dunham, *A Touch of Innocence* (New York: Harcourt, Brace and World, 1959), pp. 32–33.

3. Ibid., p. 195.

4. Ibid., p. 98.

5. Ibid., p. 179.

6. Ibid., p. 187.

7. Ibid., pp. 190–92.

8. Ruth Beckford, *Katherine Dunham* (New York: Marcel Dekker, 1979), pp. 25–26.

9. Terry Harnan, *African Rhythm American Dance: A Biography of Katherine Dunham* (New York: Knopf, 1974), p. 44.

10 Ibid., pp. 46–47.

11. Ann Barzel, "The Untold Story of the Dunham/Turbyfill Alliance," *Dance Magazine*, Dec. 1983, p. 92.

12. Ibid., p. 93.

13. Ibid.

14. Delia O'Hara, "A Lifetime on Edge of Fame," *Chicago Sun-Times*, Mar. 2, 1986, n.p., Newberry Library, Chicago.

15. "The Call Board," *American Dancer*, Oct. 1931, p. 26.

16. Katherine Dunham, "Dunham Technique: Prospectus," in Clark and Wilkerson, *Kaiso!*, p. 36.

17. Barzel, "The Untold Story," p. 92.

18. Official program, *The Negro Dance Group* (Abraham Lincoln Center, Mar. 2 and 4, 1934), Newberry Library, Chicago.

19. Ibid.

20. Flyer, "The Negro Dance Group," 1934, Newberry Library, Chicago.

21. Barzel, "The Untold Story," p. 98.

22. "Chicago Opera Danseuse Offers Ballet Innovation," *New York Herald Tribune*, Dec. 2, 1934, n.p., Dance Collection, NYPL.

23. Edward Moore, "Critic Praises Innovation of Ballet Night," *Chicago Tribune*, n.d., n.p., Dance Collection, NYPL.

24. Lewis, *When Harlem Was in Vogue*, p. 101.

25. Dorathi Bock Pierre, "A Talk with Katherine Dunham," *Educational Dance* 4 (Aug.–Sept. 1941): 7.

26. Robert Redfield, *The Social Uses of Social Science*, vol. 2, ed. Margaret Park Redfield (Chicago: University of Chicago Press, 1963), p. 256.

27. Melville Herskovits, *Myth of the Negro Past* (New York: Harper, 1941), p. 32.

28. Peter Waddington, "Katherine Dunham Raises Primitive Dance Art to New Heights of Sophistication," *Opera and Concert* 13 (June 1948): 13.

29. Beckford, *Dunham*, p. 37.

30. Katherine Dunham, *Dances of Haiti* (Los Angeles: University of California Press, 1983), p. xxiii.

31. Ibid., p. xxiv.

32. Frank L. Hayes, "Haitian Voodoo Dance Thrills Savants of Chicago Schools," *Chicago Daily News,* June 5, 1936, n.p., Newberry Library, Chicago.

33. Edward Barry, "Miss Dunham Is Sensational in Haitian Dances," *Chicago Tribune,* June 4, 1937, n.p., Dance Collection, NYPL.

34. Frederick L. Orme, "Negro in the Dance as Katherine Dunham Sees Him," in Clark and Wilkerson, *Kaiso!,* pp. 59–60.

35. Ibid.

36. Beckford, *Dunham,* pp. 42–43.

37. Katherine Dunham, "The Negro Dance," in Clark and Wilkerson, *Kaiso!,* p. 68.

38. Robert Pollok, "Katherine Dunham," *Chicago Daily Times,* Jan. 28, 1938, n.p., Dance Collection, NYPL.

39. VéVé Clark, "Katherine Dunham's 'Tropical Revue,'" *Caribe* 7, nos. 1 and 2 (1983): 16.

40. Ibid., p. 19.

41. Ibid., p. 16.

42. Kay Dunn [Katherine Dunham], "Sketchbook of a Dancer in La Martinique," *Esquire,* Nov. 1939, p. 26.

43. Ibid.

44. "The Veteran 'Pins and Needles,'" *Playbill,* Sept. 11, 1939, p. 19.

45. All information for the dances included in Dunham's 1940 performance was obtained from the official program, *Katherine Dunham and Dance Group* (Windsor Theatre, Mar. 24, 1940), Dance Collection, NYPL.

46. Walter Terry, "Dunham Dancers," *New York Herald Tribune,* Feb. 19, 1940, n.p., Dance Collection, NYPL.

47. John Martin, "Negro Dance Art Shown in Recital," *New York Times,* Feb. 19, 1940, p. 21.

48. John Martin, "The Dance: A Negro Art," *New York Times,* Feb. 25, 1940, sec. 9, p. 2.

49. Ibid.

50. Ibid.

51. Ibid.

52. VéVé A. Clark, M. Hodson, C. Neiman, and F. Bailey, "Excerpt from the Legend of Maya Deren," in Clark and Wilkerson, *Kaiso!,* p. 36.

53. John Beaufort, "Cabin in the Sky," *Christian Science Monitor,* Nov. 26, 1940, n.p., Dance Collection, NYPL.

54. Kelcey Allen, "Cabin in the Sky," *Women's Wear Daily,* Nov. 28, 1940, n.p., Dance Collection, NYPL.

55. John Martin, "The Dance: Elysian Jazz," *New York Times*, Nov. 10, 1940, n.p., Dance Collection, NYPL.

56. Ibid.

57. "Balanchine Stages a Play," *Dance*, Nov. 1940, p. 10.

58. Ibid.

59. Talley Beatty and Carmencita Romero, interview by author, New York, June 10, 1989.

60. Viola Hegyi Swisher, "Dancers Win Applause at Philharmonic," *Hollywood Citizen News*, Nov. 18, 1941, n.p., Dance Collection, NYPL.

61. F. L., "Dunham Dances at Biltmore," *Los Angeles Examiner*, Nov. 31, 1941, n.p., Dance Collection, NYPL.

62. Clark, "Katherine Dunham's 'Tropical Revue,'" p. 15.

63. Sol Hurok, *S. Hurok Presents: A Memoir of the Dance World* (New York: Heritage House, 1953), p. 59.

64. John Martin, "The Dance: 'Tropical Revue,'" *New York Times*, Sept. 26, 1943, sec. 2, p. 2.

65. Ibid.

66. Edwin Denby, *Looking at the Dance* (New York: Popular Library, 1968), p. 326.

67. Ibid.

68. Ibid.

69. Dunham, "Thesis Turned Broadway," p. 57.

70. In 1980, *Rites de Passage* was filmed for the Public Broadcasting Service's *Dance in America* series. Descriptions of the dance are based upon viewings of that version.

71. Katherine Dunham, "Goombay," in Clark and Wilkerson, *Kaiso!*, p. 91.

72. Elinor Hughes, "The Theater: 'Tropical Revue,'" *Boston Herald*, Jan. 18, 1944, n.p., Dance Collection, NYPL.

73. Elliot Norton, "New Revue Clever and Offensive," *Boston Post*, Jan. 18, 1944, n.p., Dance Collection, NYPL.

74. Margaret Lloyd, *The Borzoi Book of Modern Dance* (1949; reprint, Princeton, N.J.: Dance Horizons, 1987), p. 247.

75. Denby, *Looking at the Dance*, p. 327.

76. James Haskins, *Katherine Dunham* (New York: Coward McCann and Geoghegan, 1982), p. 79.

77. Harnan, *African Rhythm*, pp. 127–28.

78. Ibid.

79. Clark et al., "Excerpt from the Legend of Maya Deren," p. 38.

80. Joyce Aschenbrenner, *Katherine Dunham: Reflections on the Social and Political Contexts of Afro-American Dance*, Dance Research Annual 12 (New York: Congress on Research in Dance, 1981), p. 123.

81. Ibid., pp. 151–54.

82. Ibid., p. 149.

83. Ibid., p. 154.

84. Millicent Hodson, "How She Began Her Beguine," in Clark and Wilkerson, *Kaiso!*, p. 197.

85. Gerald E. Myers, "Ethnic and Modern Dance," in *The Black Tradition in American Modern Dance*, ed. Gerald E. Myers (Durham, N.C.: American Dance Festival, 1988), p. 24.

86. Ibid.

87. Ibid., p. 25.

88. Dunham, "The Negro Dance," p. 73.

89. John Martin, "Dunham Dancers Star in New Revue," *New York Times*, Nov. 8, 1946, p. 29.

90. Ibid.

91. Haskins, *Katherine Dunham*, p. 87.

92. Ibid.

93. Drake quoted in introduction to Aschenbrenner's *Katherine Dunham*, p. xiii.

94. Aschenbrenner, *Katherine Dunham*, p. 12.

Chapter 7: Pearl Primus

1. Lloyd, *Borzoi Book of Modern Dance*, p. 271.

2. Ezra Goodman, "Hard Time Blues," *Dance Magazine*, Apr. 1946, p. 55.

3. Ibid.

4. "Interview with Pearl Primus," *African Carnival* (1961), no other publication information given, Channing-Pollock Theatre Collection, Howard University, Washington, D.C.

5. Lloyd, *Borzoi Book of Modern Dance*, p. 268.

6. Michael Robertson, "Pearl Primus, Ph.D., Returns," *New York Times*, Mar. 18, 1979, p. 34.

7. Ibid.

8. John Martin, "The Dance: Five Artists," *New York Times*, Feb. 21, 1943, sec. 2, p. 5.

9. Ibid.

10. Robertson, "Pearl Primus," p. 34.

11. Lloyd, *Borzoi Book of Modern Dance*, p. 273.

12. John Martin, "The Dance: Laurels—Award No. 2," *New York Times*, Aug. 5, 1943, n.p., Dance Collection, NYPL.

13. Ibid.

14. Ibid.

15. Denby, *Looking at the Dance*, p. 301.

16. Edwin Denby, "The Dance," *New York Herald Tribune*, Jan. 24, 1944, n.p., Dance Collection, NYPL.

17. Lois Balcom, "Valerie Bettis and Pearl Primus," *Dance Observer*, Feb. 1944, p. 15.

18. Jean Ruth Glover, "Pearl Primus: Cross-cultural Pioneer of American Dance" (Master's thesis, American University, 1989), pp. 74–76.

19. Edwin Denby, "The Dance," *New York Herald Tribune*, Oct. 5, 1944, n.p., Dance Collection, NYPL.

20. Ibid.

21. Balcom, "What Chance Has the Negro Dancer?" p. 110.

22. Ibid.

23. Ibid., pp. 110–11.

24. Balcom, "The Negro Dances Himself," pp. 123–24.

25. Earl Conrad, "Pearl Primus Tells Her Faith in Common People," *Defender* (Chicago), Jan. 6, 1945, n.p., Dance Collection, NYPL.

26. John Martin, "The Dance: Current Events," *New York Times*, Dec. 3, 1944, sec. 2, p. 4.

27. Elinor Hughes, "The Dance: Pearl Primus," *Boston Herald*, Jan. 18, 1947, n.p., Dance Collection, NYPL.

28. Emery, *Black Dance*, p. 264.

29. John Martin, "The Dance: Notes," *New York Times*, Aug. 10, 1947, sec. 2, p. 5.

30. Brooks Atkinson, "At the Theatre," *New York Times*, Dec. 7, 1947, n.p., Dance Collection, NYPL.

31. Ibid.

32. "Pearl Primus," *Dance Magazine*, Nov. 1968, p. 56.

33. Walter Terry, "Dance World: Hunting Jungle Rhythm," *New York Herald Tribune*, Jan. 15, 1950, sec. 5, p. 3.

34. Ibid.

35. Ibid.

36. Ibid.

37. "Pearl Primus," *Dance Magazine*, Nov. 1968, p. 48.

38. John Martin, "The Dance: Advices," *New York Times*, June 26, 1949, n.p., Dance Collection, NYPL.

39. Glover, "Pearl Primus," pp. 111–12.

40. Nicole Dekle, "Pearl Primus: Spirit of the People," *Dance Magazine*, Dec. 1990, p. 62.

41. Cyril Beaumont, "Exotic Ballet," *London Times*, Nov. 4, 1951, n.p., Dance Collection, NYPL.

42. "Israel Acclaims Pearl Primus," *Dance News*, Mar. 1952, n.p., Dance Collection, NYPL.

43. John Martin, "The Dance: In Liberia," *New York Times*, July 31, 1960, sec. 2, p. 6.

44. Ibid.

45. Ibid.

46. Pearl Primus, "My Statement," *Caribe* 7, nos. 1 and 2 (1983): 5.

Chapter 8: 1950s–1990s

1. Gerald Myers, "African-Americans and the Modern Dance Aesthetic," in *African American Genius in Modern Dance*, ed. Gerald E. Myers (Durham, N.C.: American Dance Festival, 1993), p. 31.

2. Ibid., p. 30.

3. Ibid., p. 31.

4. Halifu Osumare, "The New Moderns: The Paradox of Eclecticism and Singularity," in *African American Genius in Modern Dance*, p. 26.

5. Ibid.

6. Talley Beatty and Carmencita Romero, interview by author, June 10, 1989, New York.

7. Talley Beatty, in *Speaking of Dance*, dir. Douglas Rosenberg, American Dance Festival, 1993, videocassette.

8. Walter Terry, "Primus, Fonaroff and Others in Non-Balletic Dance Events," *New York Times*, Nov. 17, 1946, n.p., Dance Collection, NYPL.

9. "Talley Beatty and Company," unattributed clipping, Dance Collection, NYPL.

10. Albert Morini, "Tropicana," in *Albert Morini Presents Talley Beatty and His Company in "Tropicana,"* official program (n.d., n.p.), Dance Collection, NYPL.

11. Talley Beatty, quoted in Joe Nash, "Talley Beatty," in *African American Genius in Modern Dance*, p. 13.

12. Morini, "Tropicana."

13. Beatty, quoted in Nash, "Talley Beatty."

14. Mary Burns and William Korff, "The New Dance Group History," in *The New Dance Group Gala Historic Concert, 1930s–1970s* (official program, New York, June 11, 1993), p. 8.

15. Saul Goodman, "Brief Biographies: Donald McKayle," *Dance Magazine*, June 1970, p. 50.

16. Donald McKayle, in *Speaking of Dance*, dir. Douglas Rosenberg, American Dance Festival, 1993, videocassette.

17. Donald McKayle, "The Negro Dancer in Our Time," in *The Dance Has Many Faces*, ed. Walter Sorell (New York: Columbia University Press, 1966), pp. 72–73.

18. John Gruen, "With 'Raisin,' He Rises to the Top," *New York Times*, Nov. 4, 1973, p. 3.

19. Ibid.

20. Walter Terry, "Donald McKayle," *New York Herald Tribune*, Apr. 24, 1962, n.p., Dance Collection, NYPL.

21. Goodman, "Brief Biographies: Donald McKayle."

22. Clive Barnes, "Dance Broadway Style," *New York Times*, Feb. 25, 1966, n.p., Dance Collection, NYPL.

23. Gruen, "With 'Raisin,' He Rises to the Top."

24. Clive Barnes, "What's Opened in the Theater?" *New York Times*, Nov. 4, 1973, n.p., Dance Collection, NYPL.

25. Ibid.

26. Alvin Ailey with A. Peter Bailey, *Revelations* (New York: Birch Lane Press Books, 1994), p. 41.

27. Alvin Ailey, *An Evening with Alvin Ailey*, videotaped interview, dir. Thomas Grimm, Danmarks Radio/ZDF/RM Arts, 1986.

28. Evan Alderson, "Ballet as Ideology: *Giselle*, Act 2," in *Meaning in Motion*, ed. Jane Desmond (Durham, N.C.: Duke University Press, 1997), p. 123.

29. Myers, "African-Americans and the Modern Dance Aesthetic," p. 32.

30. Halifu Osumare, "The Avant Garde, Dance History and Labels," in *Black Choreographers Moving*, ed. Julinda Lewis-Ferguson (Berkeley, Calif.: Expansion Arts Services, 1991), p. 31.

31. Sally Banes, *Terpsichore in Sneakers* (Middletown, Conn.: Wesleyan University Press, 1987), p. xvii.

32. Ibid., p. xxxii.

33. Susan Gubar, *Racechanges* (Oxford: Oxford University Press, 1997), p. xxi.

34. Banes made her observation about Solomons in her *Terpsichore in Sneakers*, p. xxxv. Don McDonagh discussed the Cunningham influence on Solomons on page 101 of *The Rise and Fall and Rise of Modern Dance* (Pennington, N.J.: A Cappella Books, 1990).

35. Ibid., p. 106.

36. Ibid., p. 104.

37. Ibid., p. 106.

38. Arthur Theodore Wilson, "Eleo Pomare: 'Pomare Power!'—Dance Theater Passion," in *African American Genius in Modern Dance*, p. 23.

39. Ibid.

40. Pomare quoted in Thomas A. Johnson, "I Must Be Black and Do Black Things," *New York Times*, Sept. 7, 1969, n.p., Dance Collection, NYPL.

41. Allen quoted in Richard A. Long, *The Black Tradition in Modern Dance* (New York: Rizzoli, 1989), p. 140.

42. Jennifer Dunning, "Dance: Evening of Eleo Pomare," *New York Times*, n.p., Dance Collection, NYPL.

43. Rodgers quoted in Priscilla Chatman, "Making Dance—A Man Sized Job—A Black Dance Artist and His Work," *The Black American*, Oct. 28, 1976, Dance Collection, NYPL.

44. Don McDonagh, *The Complete Guide to Modern Dance* (Garden City, N.J.: Doubleday, 1976), p. 245.

45. Chatman, "Making Dance."

46. Ibid.

47. Veta Goler, "Dancing Herself: Choreography, Autobiography, and Expression of the Black Woman Self in the Work of Dianne McIntyre, Blondell Cummings, and Jawole Willa Jo Zollar" (Ph.D. diss., Emory University, 1994), p. 74.

48. Ibid., pp. 90–91.

49. Ibid., pp. 108–10.

50. Ibid., pp. 159–60.

51. Brenda Dixon Gottschild, *Digging the Africanist Presence in American Performance: Dance and Other Contexts* (Westport, Conn.: Greenwood Press, 1996), p. 11.

52. Sally Banes, *Writing Dancing in the Age of Postmodernism* (Hanover, N.H.: Wesleyan University Press of New England, 1994), p. 343.

53. Banes, *Terpsichore in Sneakers*, p. xxxv.

54. Iris M. Fanger, "Private Man in the Public Arena," *Dance Magazine*, Aug. 1991, p. 42.

55. Ann Daly, "Conversations about Race in the Language of Dance," *New York Times*, Dec. 7, 1997, sec. 1, p. 44.

56. Bebe Miller, "Arts: Body Language," *Ms. Magazine*, Jan.–Feb. 1995, p. 78.

57. Ibid.

58. Banes, *Terpsichore in Sneakers*, pp. xxvii–xxxi.

59. Ibid., p. 308.

60. Dixon Gottschild, *Digging the Africanist Presence*, p. 57.

61. Ibid.

62. Ibid., p. 50.

63. Ibid., pp. 50–51.

64. Osumare, "The New Moderns," p. 29.

Bibliography

Books

Abramsom, Doris. *Negro Playwrights in the American Theatre.* New York: Columbia University Press, 1969.

Ailey, Alvin, with A. Peter Bailey. *Revelations.* New York: Birch Lane Press Books, 1994.

Aptheker, Herbert, ed. *The Negro People in the United States, 1910–1932.* Secaucus, N.J.: Citadel Press, 1973.

Aschenbrenner, Joyce. *Katherine Dunham: Reflections on the Social and Political Contexts of Afro-American Dance.* Dance Research Annual 12. New York: Congress on Research in Dance, 1981.

Banes, Sally. *Terpsichore in Sneakers.* Middletown, Conn.: Wesleyan University Press, 1987.

———. *Writing Dancing in the Age of Postmodernism.* Hanover, N.H.: Wesleyan University Press of New England, 1994.

Banham, Martin. *African Theatre Today.* New York: Pitman Publishing, 1975.

Bardolph, Richard. *The Negro Vanguard.* Westport, Conn.: Negro Universities Press, 1959.

Basshe, Em Jo. *Earth.* New York: MaCaulay, 1927.

Beckford, Ruth. *Katherine Dunham.* New York: Marcel Dekker, 1979.

Bochner, Jay. *Blaise Cendrars: Discovery and Re-creation.* Toronto: University of Toronto Press, 1978.

Bontemps, Arna, ed. *The Harlem Renaissance Remembered.* New York: Dodd, Mead, 1972.

Brown, Sterling A., Arthur P. Davis, and Ulysses Lee, eds. *The Negro Caravan*. 1941. Reprint, New York: Arno Press, 1969.

Butcher, Margaret Just. *The Negro in American Culture*. New York: Knopf, 1972.

Cheney, Sheldon. *The Art Theatre*. New York: Alfred A. Knopf, 1927.

Clark, VéVé A., and Margaret B. Wilkerson, eds. *Kaiso!: Katherine Dunham; an Anthology of Writings*. Berkeley: University of California, Institute for the Study of Social Change, 1978.

Craig, Quita E. *Black Drama of the Federal Theatre Era: Beyond the Formal Horizons*. Amherst: University of Massachusetts Press, 1980.

Daix, Pierre. *Cubist and Cubism*. New York: Rizzoli, 1982.

Denby, Edwin. *Looking at the Dance*. New York: Popular Library, 1968.

Desmond, Jane, ed. *Meaning in Motion*. Durham, N.C.: Duke University Press, 1997.

Deutsch, Helen, and Stella Hanau. *The Provincetown*. New York: Russell and Russell, 1931.

Dunham, Katherine. *Dances of Haiti*. Los Angeles: University of California Press, 1983. This edition is a revision of earlier versions: "Las Danzas de Haiti," *Acta Anthropologica* 2, no. 4 (1947), published in Mexico, in Spanish and English); and *Les Danses de Haiti* (Paris: Fasquel Press, 1957).

———. *Island Possessed*. New York: Doubleday, 1969.

———. *Journey to Accompong*. New York: Henry Holt, Inc., 1946.

———. *A Touch of Innocence*. New York: Harcourt, Brace and World, 1959.

Emery, Lynne Fauley. *Black Dance in The United States from 1619 to 1970*. Palo Alto, Calif.: National Press Books, 1972.

Engs, Robert Francis. *Freedom's First Generation: Black Hampton, Virginia, 1861–1890*. Philadelphia: University of Pennsylvania Press, 1979.

Flanagan, Hallie. *Arena*. New York: Duell, Sloan, and Pearce, 1940.

France, Richard. *The Theatre of Orson Welles*. Cranbury, N.J.: Associated University Presses, 1977.

Gard, Robert E., and Gertrude S. Burley. *Community Theatre*. New York: Duell, Sloan, and Pearce, 1959.

Goldwater, Robert. *Primitivism in Modern Art*. New York: Vintage Books, 1938.

Gottschild, Brenda Dixon. *Digging the Africanist Presence in American Performance: Dance and Other Contexts*. Westport, Conn.: Greenwood Press, 1996.

Grimes, Ronald. *Beginnings in Ritual Studies*. Washington, D.C.: University Press of America, 1982.

Guber, Susan. *Racechanges*. Oxford: Oxford University Press, 1997.

Harnan, Terry. *African Rhythm American Dance: A Biography of Katherine Dunham.* New York: Knopf, 1974.

Haskins, James. *Katherine Dunham.* New York: Coward McCann and Geoghe-gan, 1982.

———. *Black Dance in America: A History through Its People.* New York: Thomas Y. Crowell, 1990.

Hatch, James V., and Camille Billops, eds. *Artists and Influences.* New York: Hatch-Billops Collection, 1981.

Herskovits, Melville. *Myth of the Negro Past.* New York: Harper, 1941.

Houseman, John. *Run-Through.* New York: Simon and Schuster, 1972.

Huggins, Nathan Irvin. *Harlem Renaissance.* London: Oxford University Press, 1971.

Hurok, Sol. *S. Hurok Presents: A Memoir of the Dance World.* New York: Heritage House, 1953.

Isaacs, Edith. *The Negro in the American Theatre.* New York: Theatre Arts, 1947.

Johnson, Helen Armstead. *Black America on Stage.* New York: Graduate Center of the City University of New York, 1982.

Johnson, James Weldon. *Black Manhattan.* New York: Atheneum, 1977.

———. *The Book of American Negro Poetry.* 1922. Reprint, New York: Harcourt, Brace, 1959.

Jowitt, Deborah. *Time and the Dancing Image.* New York: William Morrow, 1988.

Kellner, Bruce, ed. *The Harlem Renaissance: A Historical Dictionary for the Era.* New York: Methuen, 1984.

———. *Keep A-Inchin' Along: Selected Writings of Carl Van Vechten about Black Art and Letters.* Westport, Conn.: Greenwood Press, 1979.

Kirby, John B. *Black Americans in the Roosevelt Era.* Knoxville, Tennessee: The University of Tennessee Press, 1980.

Leaming, Barbara. *Orson Welles.* New York: Viking Penguin, 1983.

Lewis, David Levering. *When Harlem Was in Vogue.* New York: Knopf, 1984.

Lewis-Ferguson, Julinda, ed. *Black Choreographers Moving.* Berkeley, Calif.: Expansion Arts Services, 1991.

Lloyd, Margaret. *The Borzoi Book of Modern Dance.* 1949. Reprint, Princeton, N.J.: Dance Horizons, 1987.

Locke, Alain, ed. *The New Negro.* New York: Atheneum, 1974.

Long, Richard. *The Black Tradition in American Dance.* New York: Rizzoli, 1989.

MacDonald, Nesta. *Diaghilev Observed by Critics in England and the United States, 1911–1929.* New York: Dance Horizons, 1975.

Martin, John Joseph. *America Dancing.* New York: Dance Horizons, 1936.

———. *Ruth Page: An Intimate Biography.* New York: Marcel Dekker, 1977.

Maynard, Olga. *American Modern Dancers.* Boston: Little, Brown, 1965.

McCullough, Edo. *World's Fair Midways.* New York: Arno Press, 1976.

McDonagh, Don. *The Complete Guide to Modern Dance.* Garden City, N.Y.: Doubleday, 1976.

———. *The Rise and Fall and Rise of Modern Dance.* Pennington, N.J.: A Cappella Books, 1990.

Myers, Gerald E., and Stephanie Reinhart. *African American Genius in Modern Dance.* Durham, N.C.: American Dance Festival, 1993.

———. *The Black Tradition in American Modern Dance.* Durham, N.C.: American Dance Festival, 1988.

O'Connor, John, and Lorraine Brown, eds. *Free, Adult, Uncensored: The Living History of the Federal Theatre Project.* Washington, D.C.: New Republic Books, 1978.

Ottley, Roi. *The Negro in New York.* New York: New York Public Library, 1967.

Padgette, Paul. *The Dance Writings of Carl Van Vechten.* New York: Dance Horizons.

Page, Ruth. *Page by Page.* New York: Dance Horizons, 1978.

Redfield, Robert. *The Social Uses of Social Science.* Vol. 2. Chicago: University of Chicago Press, 1963.

Ruyter, Nancy Lee Chalfa. *Reformers and Visionaries.* New York: Dance Horizons, 1979.

Sadie, Stanley, ed. *The New Grove Dictionary of Music and Musicians.* London: Macmillan, 1980.

Sampson, Henry T. *Blacks in Blackface.* Metuchen, N.J.: Scarecrow Press, Inc., 1980.

Schlundt, Christena L. *The Professional Appearances of Ruth St. Denis and Ted Shawn: A Chronology and an Index of Dances, 1906–1932.* New York: New York Public Library, 1962.

———. *The Professional Appearances of Ted Shawn and His Men Dancers: A Chronology and an Index of Dances, 1933 1940.* New York: New York Public Library, 1967.

Scobie, Edward. *Black Britannia.* Chicago: Johnson Publishing Company, 1972.

Seldes, Gilbert. *The Seven Lively Arts.* New York: Sagamore Press, 1924.

Shawn, Ted, and Gray Poole. *One Thousand and One Night Stands.* Garden City, N.Y.: Doubleday, 1960.

Shelton, Suzanne. *Divine Dancer.* Garden City, N.Y.: Doubleday, 1981.

Sherman, Jane, *The Drama of Denishawn Dance.* Middletown, Conn.: Wesleyan University Press, 1979.

Sherman, Jane, and Barton Mumaw. *Barton Mumaw, Dancer.* Brooklyn, N.Y.: Dance Horizons, 1986.

Sorell, Walter, ed. *The Dance Has Many Faces.* New York: Columbia University Press, 1966.

St. Denis, Ruth. *Ruth St. Denis: An Unfinished Life.* New York: Harper, 1939.

Stearns, Marshall, and Jean Stearns. *Jazz Dance: The Story of American Vernacular Dance.* New York: Schirmer Books, 1979.

Terry, Walter. *I Was There.* New York: Audience Arts, a division of Marcel Dekker, Inc., 1978.

———. *Ted Shawn: Father of American Dance.* New York: The Dial Press, 1976.

Thompson, Robert Farris. *Black Gods and Kings.* Los Angeles: University of California, 1971.

Thorpe, Edward. *Black Dance.* Woodstock, N.Y.: Overlook Press, 1990.

Timberlake, Craig. *The Life and Work of David Belasco: The Bishop of Broadway.* New York: Library Publishers, 1954.

Williams, Charles H. *Cotton Needs Pickin'.* Norfolk, Va.: Guide Publishing Company, 1928.

Woll, Allen. *Black Musical Theatre.* Baton Rouge: Louisiana State University Press, 1989.

———. *Dictionary of the Black Theatre.* Westport, Conn.: Greenwood Press, 1983.

Periodicals

"Agnes DeMille." *The American Dancer,* Mar. 1933.

"Along the Color Line." *The Crisis,* Apr. 1927.

"Along the Color Line." *The Crisis,* Apr. 1931.

"Along The Color Line." *The Crisis,* Dec. 1931.

"Balanchine Stages a Play." *Dance,* Nov. 1940.

Balcom, Lois. "The Negro Dances Himself." *Dance Observer,* Dec. 1944.

———. "Valerie Bettis and Pearl Primus." *Dance Observer,* Feb. 1944.

———. "What Chance Has the Negro Dancer?" *Dance Observer,* Nov. 1944.

Barzel, Ann. "The Untold Story of the Dunham/Turbyfill Alliance." *Dance Magazine,* Dec. 1983.

"The Callboard." *The Dance Magazine,* Aug. 1931.

Carmer, Carl. "Run, Little Chillun!: A Critical Review." *Opportunity,* Apr. 1933.

Chatman, Priscilla. "Making Dance—A Man Sized Job—A Black Dance Artist and His Work." *The Black American,* Oct. 28, 1976.

Clark, VéVé. "Katherine Dunham's 'Tropical Revue.'" *Caribe* 7, nos. 1 & 2 (1983).

Cox, Leonore. "Scanning the Dance Highway." *Opportunity*, Aug. 1934.

Dekle, Nicole. "Pearl Primus: Spirit of the People." *Dance Magazine*, Dec. 1990.

Du Bois, W. E. B. "Beside Still Waters." *The Crisis*, May 1931.

Dunn, Kay [Katherine Dunham]. "Sketchbook of a Dancer in La Martinique." *Esquire*, Nov. 1939.

Elias, A. J. "Conversation with Katherine Dunham." *Dance Magazine*, Feb. 1956.

Fanger, Iris M. "Private Man in the Public Arena." *Dance Magazine*, Aug. 1991.

Goodman, Ezra. "Hard Time Blues." *Dance Magazine*, Apr. 1946.

Goodman, Saul. "Brief Biographies: Donald McKayle." *Dance Magazine*, June 1970.

Guy, Edna. "Negro Dance Pioneer!" *Dance Herald*, Mar. 1938.

G. W. B. "Asadata Dafora and Company." *Dance Observer*, Jan. 1944.

"Hampton Incidents." *Southern Workman* 51 (May 1922).

"Hampton Incidents." *Southern Workman* 63 (June 1934).

Harrison, Hubert H. "The Significance of 'Lulu Belle.'" *Opportunity*, July 1926.

Humphrey, Doris. "Dance, Little Chillun!" *The American Dancer*, July 1933.

Isaacson, Charles E. "Dance Events Reviewed." *The Dance Magazine*, July 1931.

"Israel Acclaims Pearl Primus." *Dance News*, Mar. 1952.

Kaye, J. A. "Reviews—Negro Dance Evening." *Dance*, May 1937.

Kirstein, Lincoln. "The Dance 'Kykunkor'; Native African Opera." *Nation* 138 (June 13, 1934).

Lewis, Theophilus. "The Theatre." *The Messenger*, Apr. 1927.

———. "The Theatre." *The Messenger*, May 1927.

Lorant, Michael. "Hampton Institute, Negro's Unique Dancing Academy." *Dancing Times*, Oct. 1938.

Miller, Bebe. "Arts: Body Language." *Ms. Magazine*, Jan.–Feb. 1995.

"Negro Group Tours." *The Dancers' Club News*, May 28, 1932.

"Pearl Primus." *Dance Magazine*, Nov. 1968.

Pierre, Dorathi Bock. "A Talk with Katherine Dunham." *Educational Dance* 4 (Aug.–Sept.).

Primus, Pearl. "Africa." *Dance Magazine*, Mar. 1958.

"Salome." *The Dance Magazine*, Dec. 1931.

Schuyler, William F. "Theatre." *The Messenger*, Nov. 1924.

Smallwood, Bill. "Maudelle, Famous Dancer." *New Vistas*, Dec. 1945.

"Social Progress." *Opportunity*, May 3, 1925.

"Social Sidelights on the Denishawn Tour." *Denishawn Magazine*, Spring 1925.

Spence, Eulalie. "Negro Art Players in Harlem." *Opportunity*, Dec. 1928.

Sturm, George. "Look Back in Anger: The Strange Case of Louis Gruenberg." *Madamna!* 2 (Spring 1981).

Taylor, Ralph. "Edna Guy and Group." *Dance Observer*, May 1934.

"The Theatre: 'Lulu Belle.'" *The Crisis*, May 1926.

Thurman, Wallace. "Harlem's Place in the Sun." *The Dance Magazine*, May 1928.

"Triangle Reopens with a Revival." *Billboard*, Jan.–Mar. 1927.

Waddington, Peter. "Katherine Dunham Raises Primitive Dance Art to New Heights of Sophistication." *Opera and Concert*, June 1948.

Warwick, Florence. "The Dance in the Negro College." *Dance Herald*, Dec. 1937.

Williams, Charles H. "'Darkest Africa' at 'A Century of Progress.'" *Southern Workman* 62 (Nov. 1933).

———. "The Hampton Institute Creative Dance Group." *Dance Observer*, Oct. 1937.

———. "Recreation in the Lives of Young People." *Southern Workman* 46 (Feb. 1917).

Newspaper Articles and Reviews

"African Dancers and Singers Appear in Recital in Harlem." *Age* (New York), Oct. 21, 1933.

"Africans Liked Heat; They Sweat Freely." *New York Evening Post*, July 12, 1934.

"African Witch Doctor Joins Horton Dancers." *Age* (New York), Dec. 2, 1933.

Allen, Kelcey. "Cabin in the Sky." *Women's Wear Daily*, Nov. 28, 1940.

Anderson, John. "The Play: 'Earth.'" *New York Post*, Mar. 10, 1927.

Anthony, Tony. "C. H. Williams Gains State Honor." *Times-Herald* (Newport News, Va.), Mar. 13, 1981.

"Artistic Endeavor of Negro Dance Wins Commendation." *St. Louis Argus*, Feb. 26, 1932.

"Art Theatre's First Offering at Provincetown Playhouse." *Amsterdam News*, July 3, 1929.

"Art Theater Will Present Eight Plays." *Defender* (Chicago), Oct. 5, 1929.

Atkinson, Brooks. "At the Theatre." *New York Times*," Dec. 7, 1947.

———. "The Play." *New York Times*, Feb. 10, 1926.

———. "The Play." *New York Times*, Mar. 10, 1927.

———. "The Play." *New York Times*, Sept. 16, 1931.

———. "The Play." *New York Times*, Apr. 15, 1936.

Barnes, Clive. "Dance Broadway Style." *New York Times*, Feb. 25, 1966.

———. "What's Opened in the Theater?" *New York Times*, Nov. 4, 1973.

Barry, Edward. "Miss Dunham Is Sensational in Haitian Dances." *Chicago Daily Tribune*, June 4, 1937.

Bayard, F. Ennis. "Highly Talented Dance Concert Given by Pearl Primus Group." *Charleston Gazette* (Charleston, S.C.), Nov. 18, 1946.

Beaufort, John. "Cabin in the Sky." *Christian Science Monitor*, Nov. 26, 1940.

Beaumont, Cyril. "Exotic Ballet." *London Times*, Nov. 4, 1951.

"Benefit Performance for Ethiopian Art Theatre to Be a Gala Occasion." *Age* (New York), Jan. 17, 1925.

Berger, Arthur V. "Dance Program by Pearl Primus." *New York Sun*, Oct. 3, 1944.

Biancolli, Louis. "African Dance and Song Has Impact." *World Telegram*, Apr. 26, 1946.

Biondo, Anne Marie. "Edna Guy McCully Leaves Inspired Legacy." *Fort Worth Star Telegram*, Apr. 29, 1983.

Brown, John Mason. "Two on the Aisle." *New York Post*, May 19, 1934.

———. "'Zunguru' Danced at the Chanin Auditorium." *New York Post*, Apr. 9, 1940.

"Cast of Players for Ethiopian Art School Midnight Show, Oct. 15." *Age* (New York), Oct. 4, 1924.

"Chicago Opera Danseuse Offers Ballet Innovation." *New York Herald Tribune*, Dec. 2, 1934.

"C. H. Williams Dies; Headed HI athletics." *Times-Herald* (Newport News, Va.), Nov. 9, 1978.

Clark, William E. "Ethiopian Art Theatre School in Premiere Dance Exhibition and Song Recital on June 19." *Age* (New York), June 28, 1924.

"Colored Artists Play Big Part in Workers' Dance in New York." *Washington Tribune*, Oct. 12, 1933.

Conrad, Earl. "Pearl Primus Tells Her Faith in Common People." *Defender* (Chicago), Jan. 6, 1945.

Daly, Ann. "Conversations about Race in the Language of Dance." *New York Times*, Dec. 7, 1997.

"Dance Group of Hampton to Entertain." *Defender* (Chicago), Mar. 12, 1938.

"Death Claims Hemsley Winfield, Yonkers Resident and Founder of Negro Art Theater." *Herald Statesman* (Yonkers, N.Y.), Jan. 16, 1934.

Denby, Edwin. "The Dance." *New York Herald Tribune*, Jan. 24, 1944.

———. "The Dance." *New York Herald Tribune*, Oct. 5, 1944.

———. "A Glimpse of Real African Dancing." *New York Herald Tribune,* Dec. 21, 1943.

Dexter, Charles E. "'Ha'nt' of Dead Senegalese Plagues African Play Cast." *World Telegram,* Jan. 14, 1937.

———. "Negro Dance Unit Performs an African Dance Drama." *Daily Worker,* Dec. 10, 1936.

Downes, Olin. "'Emperor Jones' Given Again." *New York Times,* n.d. Music Collection, NYPL.

———. "'Emperor Jones' Triumphs as Opera." *New York Times,* Jan. 8, 1933.

———. "Great Drama for the Lyric Stage." *New York Times,* Oct. 2, 1932.

———. "Gruenberg's 'Jones' in Premiere." *New York Times,* Jan. 1, 1933.

"Dunham Dance Group Scores Again." *Los Angeles Times,* Nov. 31, 1949.

"Dunham Dance Group Wins San Francisco Enthusiasm." *Los Angeles Peoples World,* Oct. 14, 1941.

"Dunham Unit Featured in Short Film." *Los Angeles Examiner,* Feb. 24, 1942.

Dunning, Jennifer. "Dance: Evening of Eleo Pomare." *New York Times,* n.d. Dance Collection, NYPL.

Eisenberg, E. "'Kykunkor' Hits the Top." *New York World Telegram,* May 24, 1934.

"'Emperor Jones' Ends Season Here." *New York Times,* Feb. 12, 1933.

"'The Emperor Jones' Scores at Metropolitan." *Amsterdam News,* Jan. 11, 1933.

"Ethiopian Art School's Students Give Dramatic Offerings to Harlemites." *Age* (New York), Oct. 25, 1924.

"Ethiopian Art Students Give Fine Performance." *Age* (New York), May 30, 1925.

"Ethiopian Art Theatre Plays Serious Drama." *Women's Wear Daily,* May 9, 1923.

"Expert Talks on 'Dance as an Art.'" *Amsterdam News,* May 31, 1933.

"First Off-Campus Recital of Student Group Slated for Mosque, March 23." *Norfolk Journal and Guide,* Mar. 9, 1935.

F. L. "Dunham Dances at Biltmore." *Los Angeles Examiner,* Nov. 31, 1941.

Gaffney, Leo. "Tropical Revue May Be Hot, But It's Art." *Boston Daily Record,* Jan. 19, 1944.

"Gala Performance for Ethiopian Art Theatre, Jan. 19." *New York Age,* Jan. 10, 1925.

Gardner, Chappy. "African Princess in First American Song Recital at Mother Zion." *Harlem Reporter,* n.d. Schomburg Center.

"Grace Giles Dancing School Opens." *Age* (New York), Jan. 2, 1929.

Gruen, John. "With 'Raisin,' He Rises to the Top." *New York Times,* Nov. 4, 1973.

"Hall Johnson Show to Open." *Amsterdam News*, Feb. 22, 1933.

Hammond, Percy. "Macbeth." *New York Herald Tribune*, Apr. 16, 1936.

———. "The Theaters: 'Earth.'" *New York Herald Tribune*, Mar. 10, 1927.

"Hampton Creative Dance Group of 30 to Make Southern Tour." *Age* (New York), Nov. 23, 1940.

"Hampton Dance Event Success Artistically." *Norfolk Journal and Guide*, Mar. 30, 1935.

"Hampton Dancers Present Program to Richmond Audience at Mosque." *Hampton Script*, Mar. 30, 1935.

"Hampton Institute Creative Dancers in Finished Revue." *Newport News Daily Press*, Mar. 16, 1938.

"'Harlem' Is Entertaining Melodrama of One Phase of Negro Life in New York City." *Age* (New York), Mar. 23, 1929.

"'Harlem,' Modified by Order of Police, Plays Last Week to Half Empty Chicago House." *Defender* (Chicago), June 22, 1929.

Hayes, Frank L. "Haitian Voodoo Dance Thrills Savants of Chicago Schools." *Chicago Daily News*, June 5, 1936.

"Helmsley [*sic*] Winfield in Benefit for Yonkers' Unemployed Citizens." *Age* (New York), Mar. 7, 1931.

Hemsley, Jeroline. "Wade in De Water." *Amsterdam News*, Mar. 12, 1930.

"Hemsley Winfield." *New York Herald Tribune*, Jan. 17, 1934.

"Hemsley Winfield in New Dance Program." *Amsterdam News*, Sept. 14, 1932.

"Hemsley Winfield Is Great Hit as 'Salome' at Cherry Lane Theater, N.Y." *Defender* (Chicago), July 27, 1929.

Hughes, Elinor. "The Dance: Pearl Primus." *Boston Herald*, Jan. 18, 1947.

———. "The Theater: 'Tropical Revue.'" *Boston Herald*, Jan. 18, 1944.

"Inez Clough, A Review." *Defender* (Chicago), Jan. 12, 1929.

"Inez Clough, H. Winfield in New Play." *Defender* (Chicago), Sept. 28, 1929.

"Inez Clough Joins 'Salome.'" *Amsterdam News*, Aug. 7, 1929.

"Interesting Items Gleaned from the Age Correspondents—Yonkers, New York." *Age* (New York), July 19, 1924.

"Interesting Items Gleaned from the Age Correspondents—Yonkers, New York." *Age* (New York), Aug. 22, 1925.

"Interesting Items Gleaned from the Age Correspondents—Yonkers, New York." *Age* (New York), Oct. 20, 1928.

Johns, Vere E. "In the Name of Art." *Age* (New York), Jan. 27, 1934.

Johnson, Harriett. "Pearl Primus in Broadway Debut; Her Varied Moods Have Power." *New York Post*, Oct. 5, 1944.

Johnson, Thomas A. "I Must Be Black and Do Black Things." *New York Times*, Sept. 7, 1969.

"Katherine Dunham Dances with Group." *New York Post,* Apr. 1, 1940.

Kolodin, Irving. "African Dancers at Carnegie Hall." *New York Herald Tribune,* n.d. Dance Collection, NYPL.

———. "African Dancers Open at Chanin." *New York Sun,* Apr. 9, 1940.

———. "'Black Ritual' Is Danced at Center." *New York Times,* Jan. 23, 1940.

Lewando, Ralph. "Pearl Primus' Dance Recital Wins Acclaim at Settlement." *Pittsburgh Press,* Nov. 14, 1946.

Lloyd, Margaret. "Dancer from the Gold Coast." *Christian Science Monitor,* May 16, 1945.

———. "Dancer from the Gold Coast—Part II." *Christian Science Monitor,* June 9, 1945.

———. "Katherine Dunham's 'Tropical Revue.'" *Christian Science Monitor,* Jan. 18, 1944.

———. "Pearl Primus." *Christian Science Monitor,* Jan. 20, 1947.

Lockridge, Richard. "Life in 'Harlem.'" *New York Sun,* Feb. 21, 1929.

"'Lulu Belle' Not a Negro Play, Although Scenes Are Laid in Harlem." *Age* (New York), Feb. 27, 1926.

Martin, John. "African Festival at Carnegie Hall." *New York Times,* Apr. 5, 1945.

———. "Appearance of Tamiris." *New York Times,* Aug. 27, 1933.

———. "'Bassa Moona' Seen in Harlem Theatre." *New York Times,* Dec. 9, 1936.

———. "Brilliant Dancing by Pearl Primus." *New York Times,* Oct. 5, 1944.

———. "The Dance: Advices." *New York Times,* June 26, 1949.

———. "The Dance: Africana." *New York Times,* Mar. 24, 1940.

———. "The Dance: Africana." *New York Times,* Dec. 14, 1943.

———. "The Dance: African Lore." *New York Times,* May 13, 1934.

———. "Dance: The Art of the Negro." *New York Times,* July 7, 1929.

———. "The Dance: A Benefit." *New York Times,* Dec. 11, 1932.

———. "The Dance: Busy Times." *New York Times,* Dec. 19, 1937.

———. "The Dance: A Congress." *New York Times,* May 31, 1936.

———. "The Dance: Current Events." *New York Times,* Dec. 3, 1944.

———. "The Dance: Dunham." *New York Times,* Nov. 17, 1946.

———. "The Dance: Elysian Jazz." *New York Times,* Nov. 10, 1940.

———. "The Dance: Events Ahead." *New York Times,* Nov. 14, 1937.

———. "The Dance: A Festival." *New York Times,* Nov. 21, 1937.

———. "The Dance: Five Artists." *New York Times,* Feb. 21, 1943.

———. "The Dance: Laurels—Award No. 2." *New York Times,* Aug. 5, 1943.

———. "The Dance: In Liberia." *New York Times,* July 31, 1960.

———. "The Dance: Negro Art." *New York Times,* Nov. 7, 1937.

———. "The Dance: A Negro Art." *New York Times*, Feb. 25, 1940.

———. "The Dance: A Negro Art Group." *New York Times*, Feb. 14, 1932.

———. "The Dance: A Negro Play." *New York Times*, Mar. 12, 1933.

———. "The Dance: Newcomer." *New York Times*, Feb. 27, 1949.

———. "The Dance: Notes." *New York Times*, Aug. 10, 1947.

———. "The Dance: A Repertory Movement." *New York Times*, Aug. 30, 1931.

———. "The Dance: 'Tropical Revue.'" *New York Times*, Sept. 26, 1943.

———. "The Dance: The Week's Program." *New York Times*, Dec. 26, 1937.

———. "The Dance: 'Zunguru.'" *New York Times*, Aug. 7, 1938.

———. "Dance Centre Gives Ballet Premiere." *New York Times*, Dec. 11, 1932.

———. "Dance Centre Gives Prokofieff Ballet." *New York Times*, Mar. 12, 1932.

———. "Dance Centre Scores with 'El Amor Brujo.'" *New York Times*, Dec. 4, 1931.

———. "Dance Centre Wins Acclaim in 'Salome.'" *New York Times*, Apr. 20, 1933.

———. "Dance Notes." *New York Times*, Aug. 28, 1960.

———. "Dance-Opera Given by Dafora Group." *New York Times*, Mar. 21, 1940.

———. "Dance Recital Given by Negro Artists." *New York Times*, Apr. 30, 1931.

———. "Dancers' Club Stages Successful Benefit." *New York Times*, Dec. 12, 1932.

———. "Dunham Dancers Star in New Revue." *New York Times*, Nov. 8, 1946.

———. "Hadassah Dances in Program Here; Joins Josephine Premice and Pearl Primus in 'India-Haiti-Africa' at Times Hall." *New York Times*, Jan. 12, 1945.

———. "Native Cast Gives an African 'Opera.'" *New York Times*, May 9, 1934.

———. "Negro Dance Art Shown in Recital." *New York Times*, Feb. 19, 1940.

———. "'Petrushka' [sic] Given By Dance Centre." *New York Times*, Jan. 28, 1933.

———. "Swing 'Cabin in the Sky.'" *New York Times*, Nov. 10, 1940.

———. "'Zunguru' Offered by a Dance Group." *New York Times*, Aug. 3, 1938.

Moore, Edward. "Critic Praises Innovation of Ballet Night." *Chicago Tribune*, n.d. Dance Collection, NYPL.

"Mrs. Downs to Present the Negro Art Theatre Players at the Lincoln." *Age* (New York), Nov. 3, 1928.

"Mrs. Wolter Appeals for Ethiopian Art Theatre." *Age* (New York), May 16, 1925.

"National Ethiopian Art Theatre Benefit Recital Is Interesting." *Amsterdam News*, Dec. 13, 1924.

"National Ethiopian Art Theatre School Holds an Enthusiastic Meeting." *Age* (New York), July 19, 1924.

"National Ethiopian Art Theatre School Was Opened in New York City March 17." *Age* (New York), Apr. 5, 1924.

"Native African Sketch Given at Saratoga Club." *Age* (New York), Mar. 31, 1934.

"Negro Art Players Will Also Remain at the Lincoln Another Week." *Amsterdam News,* Nov. 7, 1928.

"Negro Art Theatre Announces Its 4th Season." *Amsterdam News,* Mar. 20, 1929.

"Negro Art Theatre to Give Children's Plays." *Age* (New York), Nov. 12, 1927.

"Negro Art Theatre to Give 'Gambodi.'" *Amsterdam News,* Apr. 20, 1932.

"Negro Art Theatre to Give Midnight Performance of 'Salome.'" *Age* (New York), Feb. 18, 1928.

"Negro Art Theatre to Give Performances at Abyssinian Baptist Church." *Age* (New York), June 10, 1933.

"Negro Art Theatre to Give Wilde's 'Salome.'" *Age* (New York), Dec. 17, 1927.

"Negro Art Theatre Locates in Harlem." *Age* (New York), Sept. 3, 1927.

"Negro Art Theatre to Present Dance Recital in Chanin Bldg." *Age* (New York), Apr. 18, 1931.

"Negro Art Theatre in Rehearsal for Another Play." *Amsterdam News,* Aug. 14, 1929.

"Negro Art Theatre to Repeat Children's Play." *Age* (New York), Nov. 19, 1927.

"Negro Ballet for 'Jones.'" *New York Times,* Jan. 7, 1933.

"Negro Dance: Hampton Institute Group in Program." *Boston Evening Transcript,* Mar. 21, 1939.

"Negro Play Lacks Order." *New York Times,* Sept. 14, 1929.

"New Negro Art Theatre." *Age* (New York), Feb. 8, 1930.

"New Negro Art Theatre Plans Active Season." *Amsterdam News,* Nov. 20, 1929.

Nichols, Lewis. "Carmen Jones." *New York Times,* Dec. 3, 1943.

———. "La Belle Hélène." *New York Times,* July 8, 1941.

———. "Negro Spirituals." *New York Times,* Mar. 2, 1933.

———. "Show Boat." *New York Times,* Jan. 7, 1946.

Norton, Elliot. "New Revue Clever and Offensive." *Boston Post,* Jan. 18, 1944.

O'Hara, Delia. "A Lifetime on Edge of Fame." *Chicago Sun-Times,* Mar. 2, 1986

Oliver, W. E. "Dunham's Concert Brilliant." *Los Angeles Herald and Express,* Nov. 13, 1941.

"Ollie Burgoyne in White Cast." *Defender* (Chicago), Mar. 23, 1929.

"Other Dance News." *New York Herald Tribune,* Dec. 25, 1932.

"Pay Battle Closes New York 'Harlem.'" *Defender* (Chicago), May 18, 1929.

"Pearl Primus and Her Dancing Group Are Well Received." *Durham Morning Herald* (Durham, N.C.), Nov. 16, 1946.

"Pearl Primus' Dance Schedule." *New York Times*, Sept. 28, 1944.
"Pearl Primus to Direct Arts Center in Liberia." *New York Times*, Oct. 25, 1959.
"Pearl Primus at Lee Festival." *Springfield, Mass. News*, Aug. 8, 1947.
"Pearl Primus Tells Her Faith in Common People." *Defender* (Chicago), Jan. 6, 1945.
Phillip, Christine. "Yonkers' Blacks Recall Hard Times." *Herald Statesman* (Yonkers, N.Y.), Feb. 9, 1982.
"Pneumonia Ends Life of Hemsley Winfield." *Amsterdam News*, Jan. 17, 1934.
Pollok, Robert. "Katherine Dunham." *Chicago Daily Times*, Jan. 28, 1938.
"De Promis' Lan' a Negro Pageant." *New York Times*, May 28, 1930.
Rapp, William Jourdan, and Wallace Thurman. "Detouring 'Harlem' to Times Square." *New York Times*, Apr. 27, 1929.
"Roberts and His Dance Group to World's Fair." *Norfolk Journal and Guide*, Mar. 4, 1939.
Robertson, Edythe. "N.Y. Audience Acclaims Creative Dance Group from Hampton Institute." *Age* (New York), Mar. 25, 1939.
Robertson, Michael. "Pearl Primus, Ph.D., Returns." *New York Times*, Mar. 18, 1979.
"Sekondi Players to Open Season at 135th Street Library on September 22." *Age* (New York), Sept. 17, 1927.
"The Sekondi Players of Yonkers Present a Comedy Sketch at the Red Cross Exercises." *Age* (New York), July 10, 1926.
Smith, Alson. "Other New Plays." *Morning World*, Jan. 22, 1929.
Smith, Gus. "Theatrical Jottings." *Age* (New York), Apr. 30, 1932.
"Students Show Possibilities in Negro Dance." *Norfolk Journal and Guide*, Mar. 9, 1935.
Swisher, Viola Hegyi. "Dancers Win Applause at Philharmonic." *Hollywood Citizen News*, Nov. 18, 1941.
Terry, Walter. "The Classicism of Afro-Oriental Dances Defended and Described." *New York Herald Tribune*, Aug. 4, 1946.
———. "Dafora's African Group Stages a Dance Drama of Tribal Life." *New York Herald Tribune*, Apr. 9, 1940.
———. "The Dance." *Boston Herald*, Mar. 21, 1939.
———. "The Dance." *New York Herald Tribune*, Apr. 26, 1946.
———. "Dance World: Hunting Jungle Rhythm." *New York Herald Tribune*, Jan. 15, 1950.
———. "Donald McKayle." *New York Herald Tribune*, Apr. 24, 1962.
———. "Dunham Dancers." *New York Herald Tribune*, Feb. 19, 1940.
———. "The Negro Dances." *New York Herald Tribune*, Apr. 28, 1940.

———. "Primus, Fonaroff and Others in Non-Balletic Dance Events." *New York Times,* Nov. 17, 1946.

———. "Reflections on Bond Between African, Western Dance Forms." *New York Herald Tribune,* Nov. 2, 1947.

"They Are 'Wading in De Water' at the Cherry Lane." *Amsterdam News,* Sept. 18, 1929.

"Up from the Black Belt of Manhattan, 'Harlem.'" *Boston Transcript,* Oct. 8, 1929.

"'Wade in de Water' Opens in Greenwich Village." *Amsterdam News,* Sept. 18, 1929.

Wallace, Kevin. "Anthropology, Rhythm Mix in Dunham Dances." *San Francisco Examiner,* Aug. 2, 1942.

Watkins, Mary F. "With the Dancers." *New York Herald Tribune,* Jan. 15, 1933.

Wershba, Joseph. "The Gift of Healing Is Not Always a Medical Matter: Pearl Primus." *New York Post,* Aug. 9, 1960.

"When White Is Black." *New York Times,* Feb. 21, 1929.

Williams, Charles H. "Cultural Development of Dance as an Art Form Is Interestingly Traced." *Norfolk Journal and Guide,* Mar. 16, 1935.

Winfield, Hemsley. "Speaking o' Harlem." *Amsterdam News,* May 15, 1929.

"Winfield in Dance Program Sunday." *Amsterdam News,* Oct. 11, 1933.

"Winfield in Dance Recital Here Sunday." *Amsterdam News,* Aug. 30, 1933.

"Winfield Dead at 27; 'Emperor Jones' Dancer." *New York Herald Tribune,* Jan. 16, 1934.

"Winfield Discovers a New Baritone Singer." *Age* (New York), Apr. 30, 1927.

"Winfield Memorial Service." *Age* (New York), Feb. 10, 1934.

"Winfield Players in Active Season." *Amsterdam News,* May 31, 1933.

"Winfield's Group to Continue His Work." *Amsterdam News,* Feb. 7, 1934.

"Winfield Will Present Ballet." *Amsterdam News,* July 19, 1933.

Wood, Mabel Travis. "Dramatization of Negro History." *Amsterdam News,* July 4, 1923.

"Yonkers' Players Won Favor with Rural Play." *Age* (New York), Mar. 21, 1925.

Letters

Guy, Edna. Letters to Ruth St. Denis, 1923–30, Ruth St. Denis Papers, Dance Collection, New York Public Library at Lincoln Center, New York.

Hill, Martha. Letter to Charles Williams, Nov. 18, 1937, Hampton University Archives.

Williams, Charles H. Letter to Mr. L. Harper, Mar. 8, 1937, Charles Williams Collection, Hampton University Archives.

———. Letter to William Kolodney, May 26, 1937, Charles Williams Collection, Hampton University Archives.

———. Letter to Dr. R. E. Diffendorfer, June 2, 1937, Charles Williams Collection, Hampton University Archives.

———. Letter to Mr. Nelson Payne, Aug. 1, 1938, Charles Williams Collection, Hampton University Archives.

Interviews

Bates, Add. Interview by James Hatch. New York, 1974. Hatch-Billops Collection, New York.

Beatty, Talley, and Carmencita Romero. Interview by the author. New York, June 10, 1989.

Dunham, Katherine. Interview by the author. Port-au-Prince and Kyona Beach, Haiti, 1987.

Nash, Joe. Interview by the author. New York, 1989.

Sawyer, Randolph. Interview by Joe Nash. New York, Aug. 26, 1980. Audiotape, Collection of Joe Nash.

Dissertations and Theses

Belcher, Fannin Saffore, Jr. "The Place of the Negro in the Evolution of American Theatre, 1767 to 1940." Ph.D. diss., Yale University, 1945.

Craig, Quita E. "For What Shall It Profit a Man: A Re-Evaluation of Black Drama of the Federal Theatre Era." Master's thesis, George Mason University.

Glover, Jean Ruth. "Pearl Primus: Cross-cultural Pioneer of American Dance." Master's thesis, American University, 1989.

Goler, Veta. "Dancing Herself: Choreography, Autobiography, and Expression of the Black Woman Self in the Work of Dianne McIntyre, Blondell Cummings, and Jawole Willa Jo Zollar." Ph.D diss., Emory University, 1994.

Lally, Kathleen Ann. "A History of the Federal Dance Theatre of the Works Progress Administration, 1935–1939." Ph.D. diss., Texas Women's University, 1978.

Monroe, John Gilbert. "A Record of the Black Theatre in New York City, 1920–29." Ph.D. diss., University of Texas, Austin, 1980.

Nicholson, Josephine Monica. "Three Black Pioneers in American Modern Dance 1931–1945." Master's thesis, George Washington University, 1984.

Nisbett, Robert Franklin. "Louis Gruenberg: His Life and Work." Ph.D. diss., Ohio State University, 1979.

Programs and Playbills

All Star Benefit Performance for the Colored Citizens' Unemployment and Relief Committee of Yonkers, N.Y., Saunders Trade School, Mar. 6, 1931. Official program. Schomburg Center, NYPL.

All Star Negro Performance. Program. Town Hall, New York, Nov. 25, 1933. Schomburg Center.

The American Common, World's Fair of 1940 in New York, African Program. Program. Oct. 6, 1940. Schomburg Center, NYPL.

El Amor Brujo. Program. The Dance Center, n.d. Dance Collection, NYPL.

"Bamboche." *Playbill.* 54th Street Theatre, Oct. 22, 1962. Billy Rose Theatre Collection, NYPL.

Bassa Moona. Program. Lafayette Theatre, n.d. Library of Congress Federal Theatre Project Collection, George Mason University Library, Fairfax, Va.

"La Belle Hélène." *Playbill.* Westport Country Playhouse, week beginning July 7, 1941. Schomburg Center, NYPL.

"Cabin in the Sky." *Playbill.* Martin Beck Theatre, beginning Sunday, Feb. 23, 1941. Billy Rose Theatre Collection, NYPL.

"Carib Song." *Playbill.* Adelphi Theatre, beginning Thursday, Sept. 27, 1945. Dance Collection, NYPL.

"Carmen Jones." *Playbill.* Broadway Theatre, week beginning Sunday, Feb. 6, 1944. Billy Rose Theatre Collection, NYPL.

Chauve Souris. Souvenir program, n.d. Billy Rose Theatre Collection, NYPL.

The Dance: Hampton Institute Creative Dance Group. Program. Mosque Theatre, Richmond, Va., Mar. 23, 1935. Hampton University Archives.

Dance Recital—Lincoln School for Nurses. Program. May 1, 1938. Schomburg Center, NYPL.

The Dancers' Club Presents a Monster Dance Performance. Program. Mecca Temple, Dec. 11, 1932. Dance Collection, NYPL.

Earth. Program. New Playwrights Theatre, n.d. Billy Rose Theatre Collection.

The Emperor Jones. Program. Ridgeway Theatre, White Plains, N.Y., week of June 19, 1939. Schomburg Center, NYPL.

The Fiftieth Anniversary of Emancipation. Program. Carnegie Hall, New York, Mar. 10, 1913. Hampton University Archives.

The First Annual Convention of American Dance Association, May 14, 15, 16, 1937. Program. New School for Social Research. Hampton University Archives.

First Negro Dance Recital in America. Program, n.d. Moorland-Spingarn Research Collection, Howard University.

Folk Lore Concert. Program. Mendelssohn Hall, New York, Mar. 13, 1908. Hampton University Archives.

The Friends Amusement Guild Presents a New Negro Art Theatre Dance Production. Program, n.d. Dance Collection, NYPL.

Hampton Afloat and Afield, 1914. Program. Hampton University Archives.

The Hampton Institute Creative Dance Group. Program. Goodhart Hall, Bryn Mawr College, Nov. 9, 1937. Hampton University Archives.

The Hampton Institute Creative Dance Group. Program. Theresa L. Kaufmann Auditorium, New York, Nov. 14, 1937. Hampton University Archives.

The Hampton Institute Creative Dance Group. Program. Ogden Hall, Mar. 14, 1939. Hampton University Archives.

Hampton Institute Creative Dance Group. Souvenir program, n.d. Hampton University Archives.

Harlem. Program. Shubert-Apollo Theatre, n.d. Billy Rose Theatre Collection, NYPL.

Katherine Dunham and Dance Group. Program. Windsor Theatre, Mar. 24, 1941. Dance Collection, NYPL.

Katherine Dunham and Her Dance Company. Program. Biltmore Theatre, Los Angeles, Oct. 30–Nov. 1, 1941. Dance Collection, NYPL.

Katherine Dunham and Her Company in a Tropical Revue. Program. Martin Beck Theatre, 1943. Dance Collection, NYPL.

Katherine Dunham in Tropical Revue. Program. Opera House, San Francisco, Apr. 19, 20, 21, 22, 1945. Dance Collection, NYPL.

Kathleen Kirkwood Presents the New Negro Art Theatre in "The Triangle Blues." Program. Triangle Theatre, Aug. 14, 1928. Gumby Collection, Columbia University.

Kykunkor. Program. Chanin Playhouse, n.d. Billy Rose Theatre Collection, NYPL.

Kykunkor. Program. Saratoga Club, New York, Mar. 24, 1934. Schomburg Center, NYPL.

Kykunkor. Program. Unity Theatre, May 5–20, 1934. Billy Rose Theatre Collection, NYPL.

Kykunkor. Souvenir program, n.d. Schomburg Center, NYPL.

"Lulu Belle." *Playbill.* Belasco Theatre, Oct. 11, 1926. Channing-Pollock Theatre Collection, Howard University.

National Negro Pageant Ass'n Presents De Promis' Lan'. Program. May 27, 1930. Billy Rose Theatre Collection, NYPL.

A Negro Dance Evening. Program. Theresa L. Kaufmann Auditorium, Lexington Avenue at 92d Street, Mar. 7, 1931. Schomburg Center, NYPL.

The Negro Dance Group. Program and flyer. Abraham Lincoln Center, Mar. 2, 4, 1934. Newberry Library.

Negro Dance Recital—Hemsley Winfield. Program. Roerich Hall, 310 Riverside Drive, Jan. 19, Jan. 30, Feb. 6, 1932. Schomburg Center, NYPL.

The New Negro Art Theatre Presents Hemsley Winfield as Salome. Program. Cherry Lane Theatre, n.d. Gumby Collection, Columbia University.
1927, Bare Facts. Program, n.d. Billy Rose Theatre Collection, NYPL.
Pearl Primus. Souvenir program, n.d. Dance Collection, NYPL.
Pearl Primus in a Dance Recital. Program. Hunter College Auditorium, June 1, 1944. Dance Collection, NYPL.
The Proceedings of the First National Dance Congress and Festival. Program and proceedings. New York, May 1936. Dance Collection, NYPL.
De Promis' Lan'. Program. Carnegie Hall, May 27, 1930. Billy Rose Theatre Collection, NYPL.
Provincetown Playhouse Presents "Him." Program. Provincetown Playhouse, n.d. Billy Rose Theatre Collection.
Rainbow Room Recitals. Program. Dec. 28, 1937. Schomburg Center, NYPL.
"Run, Little Chillun!" Playbill. Harris Theatre, Chicago, beginning Monday eve., Oct. 29, 1934. Dance Collection, NYPL.
"Run, Little Chillun!" Playbill. Lyric Theatre, beginning Monday evening, Mar. 27, 1933. Billy Rose Theatre Collection, NYPL.
Special All-Ballet Program, Chicago Grand Opera Co. Program. Nov. 30, 1934. Program. Dance Collection, NYPL.
Ted Shawn and His Men Dancers. Program. Ogden Hall, Apr. 20, 1935. Hampton University Archives.
Ted Shawn and His Men Dancers, 1934–35. Souvenir program. Dance Collection, NYPL.
"The Veteran 'Pins and Needles.'" Playbill, September 11, 1939. Billy Rose Theatre Collection, NYPL.
Washington Conservatory of Music and School of Expression Presents: The Birth of Inspiration. Program (Edna Guy). Roerich Hall, 103d Street and Riverside Drive, May 7, 1932. Moorland-Spingarn Collection, Howard University.

Miscellaneous

"Appearances of the Hampton Institute Creative Dance Group since 1934." Touring schedule. Hampton University Archives.
Denishawn: The Ruth St. Denis and Ted Shawn School of Dancing and Its Related Arts. Brochure, ninth season, 1923–24. Dance Collection, New York Public Library.
"Expenses, June and July, 1938." Financial records of Charles Williams. Charles Williams Collection, Hampton University Archives.
"Hampton Institute Blazing New Trail in Creative Dance Expression for Negro." Press release, n.d. Hampton University Archives.

Harvard Summer School. Official transcript of Charles Williams, n.d. Charles Williams Collection, Hampton University Archives.

"Hemsley Winfield, World's Greatest Negro Dancer and His Concert Dance Group." Flyer. Roerich Hall, Jan. 19. Schomburg Center, New York Public Library.

"Joint Song Recital." Flyer. Mother A.M.E. Zion Church, New York, Jan. 26, 1931. Schomburg Center, New York Public Library.

Kline, W., and S. Davis. "Asadata Dafora (Horton)." Biographical sketch, Apr. 17, 1980. Schomburg Center, New York Public Library.

"Let Freedom Ring." Flyer. Roxy Theatre, n.d. Schomburg Center, New York Public Library.

National Ethiopian Art Theatre School. New York: New York Age Press, n.d. Brochure. Gumby Collection, Columbia University.

"A Tale of Old Africa." Flyer. Carnegie Hall, Apr. 25 and 26, 1945. Schomburg Center, New York Public Library.

Winfield, Hemsley. Miscellaneous Papers. Schomburg Center, New York Public Library.

Index

JOHN O. PERPENER III is an associate professor in the Department of Dance at the University of Illinois at Urbana-Champaign, where he teaches dance history. He has been a performer, choreographer, and teacher of dance technique.

University of Illinois Press
1325 South Oak Street
Champaign, IL 61820-6903
www.press.uillinois.edu

Printed by Printforce, United Kingdom